KU-335-926

'This book is a great achievement. It is beautifully written. It renders complex experiences and scientific detail in an accessible but precise style . . . Many positive qualities shine through in the experience recounted, not least honesty, humility and humour. Most of all perhaps what shines from this book is the wisdom of the author. In an era of "evidence-based practice", it is refreshing to be reminded of the power of "wisdom-led" practice – wisdom derived from intuition and reflection on experience and knowledge . . . What is very exciting about this book is how Kate gives voice to the lived reality of the minutiae of caring for troubled youngsters . . . There are some very profound insights about the nature or stance of caring for children very deeply troubled with themes of loss and intimacy.' Robbie Gilligan, Professor of Social Work and Social Policy and Director of the Children's Research Centre, Trinity College, Dublin, *Adoption & Fostering*

'. . . beautifully written, combining clarity of analysis with an articulate prose style that is often lyrical, sometimes witty . . . this is a powerful book that speaks eloquently of the contribution that foster carers can make in providing a therapeutic environment in which children can heal and flourish; a contribution that is too often undervalued and unsupported. [Cairns] provides an account of the core principles of therapeutic fostering that could be invaluable for foster carers and adoptive parents, to people who are involved in supporting or training them, and to anybody working with children in foster care.' Anna Fairclough, Lecturer in Social Work, Goldsmiths College, University of London, *Child and Family Social Work*

'A superb book . . . Kate Cairns writes with great understanding and wisdom. Her experiences and her vision provide a brilliant and inspirational guide for anyone working with or fostering unhappy, damaged children.' Pru, five star review, Amazon.co.uk

'For anyone who has an interest in learning more about attachment theory this is an excellent read.' J.A. Lipscombe, five star review, Amazon.co.uk

'Absolutely marvellous book! Recommend to any reader interested in a career in fostering, social work etc. Good reference for child development and therapeutic intervention with a real life perspective.' Andrea Southall, five star review, Amazon.co.uk

About *Fostering attachments*

'It's not often that you can say 'this is a truly inspirational book'. However, this is one of those books . . . it is filled with insights about the needs of children in alternative care and the families who care for them. It is highly recommended for both carers and professionals in this field – and indeed anyone else who wants to be inspired!' Dr Cas O'Neill, Research Fellow, School of Social Work, University of Melbourne, *Children Australia*

'Although the book tells of an admirable achievement, no hint of self-satisfaction is apparent and the writing contains flashes of wry humour . . .' Alan Rushton, Institute of Psychiatry, London, *Child and Adolescent Mental Health*

Attachment, trauma and resilience

Therapeutic caring for children

Kate Cairns and Brian Cairns

coramBAAF
ADOPTION & FOSTERING ACADEMY

Published by
CoramBAAF
41 Brunswick Square
London WC1N 1AZ
www.corambaaf.org.uk

Originally published by BAFF
Reprinted 2002, 2004, 2006, 2007, 2008, 2010
This edition © Kate Cairns and Brian Cairns 2016
Reprinted by CorumBAAF in 2019

British Library Cataloguing in Publication Data
A catalogue record for this book is available
from the British Library

ISBN 978 1 910039 35 9

Designed by Helen Joubert Designs
Typeset by Avon DataSet Ltd, Bidford on Avon
Printed in Great Britain by TJ International

Contents

PART III PROMOTING TRANSPERSONAL RESILIENCE
Brian Cairns

The authors

Kate Cairns is a social worker and teacher. Her long career has included working for BAAF as a trainer consultant, and gathering a group of associates from many disciplines to establish a training company, KCA Training, working across children's services to share transformative knowledge about attachment, trauma and resilience – www.kca.training.

Brian Cairns started his professional life as a teacher, then became a social worker, and a teacher of social workers. He now enjoys the variety of pursuing a range of interests and activities, including serving as a Tribunal and Panel member within his own areas of specialist knowledge of mental health, social care and foster care.

Preface

In 1975 our two person household expanded to become a much larger family unit, and throughout most of the next 25 years we were part of a family group of a dozen or so people. We offered permanence to the children who joined us to become part of this family group; nearly all of them were children for whom adoption was not an option at the time, and we did not adopt any of them. We could say that they adopted us, however, for all but one remain in contact, and most are in regular and frequent contact with us. By the time the youngest had grown up, the family consisted of 15 people in addition to the two of us. Three of those were born to us, and 12 had joined us at various stages of their childhood, ranging in age from 4 to 15 at the time of joining the family.

Our house for most of that time was provided by a charitable trust, and the trustees also acted as the responsible authority for our registration as a children's home. We aimed to provide the benefits of group care, whilst retaining the family atmosphere and support of a foster family, and the security and permanence of adoption. We worked hard to ensure that we were seen as a family in the local community, and related as a foster family to schools and health professionals. All the children retained or recovered contact with members of their birth families. We learned many lessons over the years, and made many mistakes. In keeping with the practice of the time, we failed to recognise the powerful dynamics of persistent abuse and rejection, and of racism and oppression. Our family group was constructed on the basis of a balance of age and gender, with risk assessment in relation to the impact of prior experience not yet something we had in our awareness, and it was multi-cultural and multi-ethnic. For all the care, attention and love that we could provide, we did some harm in our ignorance. We now strongly advocate placements matched so far as possible for recovery needs, ethnicity, culture and "race", in which children can unfold into a sense of their own heritage, worth and dignity in an unforced and natural way.

One of the earliest discoveries we made in living with children who had lived through great harm in their early life was that "common sense" would not be enough to see us through. We started to read and learn as much as we could about ideas from the wider world that might help us make sense of what we were learning from the children. Some of these great organising ideas are presented here. Others have been assimilated, and then expanded by more recent research and theory, so that we can make even more sense in retrospect than we could at the time (if we had known then what we know now, we might have made fewer mistakes). References are provided so that you can go through the literature yourself if you wish. We have included in the references both the concepts and ideas that first excited and informed us, and some examples of the immensely exciting more recent research that is opening up whole new vistas of possibility in promoting the recovery of children who have been harmed by their early experiences. We hope that we have faithfully represented the theories and research of others; any errors are ours and not theirs, and we are grateful to them for their wisdom and insight.

This book is not intended to be a manual. It does not tell you how to do it. Instead it provides a story to illustrate the experience of family life with children who have lived through overwhelming stress, and an account of the ideas drawn from theory and research that helped us to make sense of this experience. It also includes suggestions for families and agencies about what we can do to promote recovery and resilience in children who have survived such adversity. These ideas are just that, and should never be treated as blueprints, but rather as prompts to your own creative thinking about the needs of the children entrusted to you.

It is particularly important to recognise that living with traumatised children evokes strong feelings and powerful dynamics. Every family is at risk of becoming dangerously disordered when living with such disorder. It is vital that good supervision and support are available to families providing therapeutic parenting. Such supervision should be emotionally responsive enough to carry the family through the many turbulent experiences that will assail them, and professionally informed enough to be able to discern the points at which the family is slipping towards the powerful vortex of disorder that follows traumatic stress. We hope this book will therefore be useful to such supervisors, and their supervisors, as well as to families.

The children here presented are composite. All the separate elements of the events described actually happened, but to different children at different times across the whole 25 years. Those concerned have seen and read the book, and have been enthusiastic that it should be available to others. We all hope that it will be useful to new generations of children separated from their families, and the adults and children of the new families that care for them.

A note about this book

This book is structured in three parts. The first two comprise the text of the first edition of *Attachment, Trauma and Resilience*, by Kate Cairns, whilst the third is an account of practical parenting strategies first published in the book *Fostering Attachments*, by Brian Cairns.

Both of these books deal with our experience of fostering children over a 25-year period, but present different perspectives on this shared experience. Kate's writing focuses on trauma and brain injury, and the theoretical and research basis behind our fostering, and how this can be used to help children recover, whilst Brian's work is more intensely practical, exploring day-to-day approaches and important aspects of interaction with children which can help to promote their resilience and encourage healing.

Together, this work forms a holistic whole. We are sure that you will find this beneficial, and that it enhances the usefulness and importance of this seminal work.

Kate and Brian Cairns

Part I

Making love
A story of creation and destruction

Kate Cairns

1 In the beginning

This is a story; it tells the truth, but it is not a factual account. All the events and conversations recorded here took place. The children, however, are composite and not intended to represent individual children in our care. Those concerned have seen and approved what has been written. Shane, Kelly and Tina show aspects of life for, and with, children who have unmet attachment needs and disrupted attachments. Jay and Kelly illustrate the experience of living with complex post-traumatic stress disorder. Tina provides an image of living with the grief of losing a parent. Rachel, David and Tim represent aspects of the experience of birth children in the caring family. As for the ending, we have never yet lost a child entrusted to us to suicide, but this has not always been for want of trying on the part of those children and young people who wrestle so bravely with the giants of pain and despair.

This is the imaginary true story of seven days in the life of a foster family. Let it be dedicated to all the children who must live apart from their original families. The courage, grace and dignity with which they face their situation is their gift to us all; never forgetting that, without the tolerance, strength and wisdom of the homegrown members of the families who care for them, there would be no homes to offer.

These are the strong emotions. Desire. Rage. Fear. How they change us, these three, from toe tip to crown. Adrenaline rushing, nerves tingling, senses focused . . . we are, truly, never the same again, the patterns of our brains forever altered by the power which moves us.

And what do we desire? The objects of our attachment. Buddhists know. If you want to stop changing, stop wanting. No easy task, however, even if we choose to make it our life work. For we are born with it, this longing for attachment. That little morsel of humanity knows nothing else but 'want'. Not 'I want', too soon for that, just 'want'.

And if that wanting is frustrated? Why then, little one, rage. New heart pumping new blood to new muscles, thrash, flail, shout it out, small scrap of almost person. Stretch those new lungs and scream. Tell the world 'Me. I'm here. Listen to me. I want . . .' Becoming a person already. Needing others, another at least, beginning to know dependency and trust. Making relationships.

Later, not much later, for we are clever creatures, after rage comes fear and the beginning of imagination. What if I am abandoned? I am dependent, I am vulnerable, I can be hurt, I am afraid. This, too, imprinted in the brain forever. And if it is not imagination, if it is real and true, then terror rules. No terror will ever surpass the terror of the abandoned child. All later fear an image only of this first and primal fear, the annihilation of the utterly dependent.

Then comes grief. Not an emotion, this, but a complex state of being in response to loss. Still an agent of change, though, the next experience on the way to personhood. Beyond fear, there is the reality of loss, and not one of us can live a life without it. Beginnings lead to endings, lives lead to deaths. How will the growing person build this knowledge into their being in the world?

The truly human emotions begin here. Solitude, compassion and the inner peace and joy of a self-aware tranquillity. Desire and rage and fear engage the primal nervous system of the brain stem, filling us with instant energy, priming our muscles for immediate action, providing a build up of inner force which resolves explosively. By contrast, solitude and compassion and tranquillity build energy which is sustainable and which resolves cathartically in an "oceanic" experience of connectedness and well-being.

Beyond grief, then, if all goes well, is solitude. Alone but not lonely in a supportive universe, we can explore the full height and breadth and depth of our personhood. If, that is, our universe has supported us. If all has indeed gone well for us. If we have taken desire and rage and fear and grief in our stride and into our being, and have grown strong and flexible and resilient, then we will not be scared to be alone.

After solitude, compassion. Alone we come into the world, and at the end we go to our graves alone. When we know this in our hearts, we can reach out to others. Equal in our mortality, we can at this point grow into our full humanity as we learn to share the sorrows and the excitements which shake the lives of our companions.

And, at the deep heart's core, tranquillity. A human has been created. In a world of chance and change, love has been made.

2 Attachment

Affective attunement

Set down this. A long journey we had of it, to come to this birth. Nine months and more, you being in no hurry to emerge from your warm sanctuary. I the impatient one, longing for our first meeting, rejoicing already in your otherness. And a meeting it was indeed. You opened your eyes in an unfocused gaze of milky desire, and I was caught forever in a bond of love like no other I had known.

> I can remember ten heads of home. I know their names. I remember my mother, and my gran, and my auntie, and three foster parents, and my mum's friend Gus whose real name was Caesar but they took me away from him.

For children who suffer disorders of attachment, nothing, absolutely nothing, is easy or straightforward. Today breakfast has come and gone and he has not appeared. Yesterday, our day of rest, he arrived in our room at 5 a.m. with mugs of coffee. 'I wanted to do something for you. Aren't you pleased?'

Struggling to sit up in bed, I remember when we used to sleep naked, limb against limb, the friendliness of it. Those days ended with fostering, which could be sponsored by the makers of flannelette nighties. Struggling, too, to find a calm voice, knowing he truly means well, has no access to the same basic understanding of others that most of us happily take for granted. 'It's a good thought, but we still need to sleep, Shane. You go back to bed, and we'll have a drink together later.'

Slam. Crash. Coffee and mugs meet wall and carpet. A meeting which will lead to a permanent relationship if I don't get up and do something about it. And I have to get him to help me, get him to stay connected and take responsibility for what he has done. At five o'clock in the morning. Please can I have an easier job in my next lifetime?

Wrestling bears or breaking rocks come to mind.

This morning is a not-getting-up day, however. It is also a visit-from-my-social-worker and a finding-out-my-mum-still-doesn't-want-to-see-me day. Perhaps these things are connected. Tim offers to go and wake Shane. I think his usual method, as regularly applied to older brother David, of six ice cubes down the back of the neck, while effective, might not be quite what Shane needs today.

Stern compassion seems to be closer to the mark. 'Shane!' I yell from the bottom of the stairs, 'I've made your sandwiches, ironed your shirt, and if you're not up and about in five minutes there'll be consequences!' I'm good on consequences. Sounds horrible, means nothing, and judged properly is nearly always effective. My father, a headmaster, used to threaten that there would be 'blood on the moon', but I take after the less violent side of the family.

Brian puts his arms round me. 'Do I need to shout at him?' 'No, I think that will have done the trick,' I say, listening to the morning litany of swearwords moving towards the bathroom. 'Then I'll take the dog for a walk,' he says, matching the actions to the words as she enthusiastically endorses the idea.

On a morning like this, it would not do to leave Shane and the dog in the same space. He will fall over her, drop scalding tea on her, "accidentally" tread on her, in any case she will end up hurt and he will protest vigorously, and for all I know accurately, innocence of any intention to do harm.

Tim, aged two: 'Where are you going?'

'Out for a meal.'

'If I scream and scream when you go out the gate, will you turn round and come back?'

'No. And if I hear that's what you did, I'll be cross about it.'

'Oh. Can I have a little scream now?'

'Of course.'

'A . . . a . . . h!'

'Is that all right now, Tim?'

'Yes. Will you come and kiss me goodnight when you come back?'

'Yes I will.'

David, ringing home at lunch time, 'There's been some sort of fight in the school yard. I think you might need to ring school and sort something out.' 'Do you know what it's about?' 'I think Shane might be in some sort of trouble.' Tactful, this one. Not about to drop anyone in anything they haven't stirred up for themselves.

I ring Janice, the school secretary, a regular contact this, after all these years. She won't make mountains out of molehills, I know I can trust her judgement. 'I'm glad you've rung, Kate. The head of year was wondering whether to bring you in or deal with it himself. I think he'd like you to come in and see him.'

We meet in a classroom, the form tutor, the head of year and Shane gathered around a table at the front of the room as I arrive. Shane is wearing his blank defiance look. Uh oh. This does not bode well. The story is that Shane has stolen a pencil case belonging to another boy. The boy demanded it back. Shane denied all knowledge of the theft, the pencil case and anything else relevant or irrelevant to the matter under discussion. A fight ensued.

Once the form tutor became involved, he asked Shane to turn out the contents of his bag. There the missing pencil case was found. Shane, however, was adamant that the pencil case was his, and that he had stolen nothing. Since the pencil case had the name of the other boy inside it, as well as a dozen pens with his initials and a calculator with his name stamped on it, Shane's story sounds a little thin. Except that he is so convincingly certain that this pencil case belongs to him, and so evidently bewildered that anyone doubts his word.

Thank goodness David rang me. The school staff, to their great credit, are patiently continuing to exercise reason and rationality with Shane. I know that they could do this forever and it would take them no further. I pick up the pencil case, and look at Shane until I am sure he is making eye contact with me. 'Shane, this pencil case belongs to . . .' quick check inside to get my facts right '. . . Daniel. It is blue. Your pencil case is red. Where is your red pencil case, Shane?' 'I think it's on my dressing table.' 'Right. You can put it in your bag tonight and make sure you have it for tomorrow. Now we'll give this one back to Daniel and you can say sorry. Then perhaps Mr Johnson will lend you a pen for today.'

I look at the teachers. They look surprised, but seem prepared to go along with this solution. The "fight" was really a scuffle, and no one has been hurt. Shane gives the pencil case back to Daniel, and apologises so pleasantly that I should think I am the only one who knows he still has no real idea of what he's done.

Rachel, aged six: *My friend Tessa's mum and dad have split up and she has got to choose who to live with. If you ever did that I would go and live with Granny and I wouldn't ever come and see either of you ever again.*

Shane arrives home cheerful. 'Have you had a good day?' I ask, interested. 'Yeah, great. We watched a video in English.' He looks back at me with a face innocent of all guile. He genuinely has construed this as a good day, and that is how he will remember it. We have some work to do on this, I make a mental note, but not right now.

His social worker is due to arrive at any moment. I suggest we put the kettle on to make tea and biscuits for him, and Shane takes up the task with enthusiasm. He likes seeing his social worker. This is one of his most successful and comfortable relationships. He is central to it, and is clearly the focus of care and concern within it, yet it remains occasional and therefore superficial and, most importantly for Shane, it is a relationship in which his actions do not have evident consequences. I am grateful for this on his behalf. Grateful, too, that here we have a local authority still able to provide some service to the children it looks after.

After they have gone off to the burger bar, or pizza palace, or wherever else is serving its turn as a social work office, the rest of us gather for the evening meal. These occasional breaks allow us to have meals together without the continual jolting reminders of the painful gaps in Shane's understanding of the most basic things about the ways human beings relate to one another. He is intelligent, and sensitive, and loving. And at some very early stage of his development he missed out on vital and fundamental learning.

Day by day he makes us aware of the basic relational skills which otherwise we would take entirely for granted. Non-verbal signals and simple relational sensitivities are nearly all missing for him. Trust is missing. Fun and playfulness are missing. Curiosity and interest in the world around him are missing.

In place of all these he is left with a massive defensive egocentricity, and a divided self which simply cannot take responsibility or make plans since the left hand has no idea what the right hand has done, is doing, or may be going to do. Yet with strangers he appears open and friendly and trusting. His beautiful spaniel eyes gaze adoringly at anyone who might let him call them his friend. We, who love him, are afraid for him.

Now he arrives bouncing and spluttering with excitement. He has, by agreement, gone on from his meeting with his social worker to play in the park. There he has met up with a friend. Wants to go back to his friend's house. Wants us to lend his friend a bicycle to make the journey easier. 'Who is your friend, Shane?' 'Oh, he lives up the other side of the estate. He's in my class at school.' 'What's his name?' He looks at me blankly. 'I forgot to ask him. Oy!' he shouts towards the front door, 'What's your name? The old dear wants to know!'

'Shane,' I begin, thinking I ought at least to try, 'friends are people we know well. People we like and trust. Not just . . .' I give up. This is a time for decision not explanation. 'No,' I say, 'the answer's no. But you can bring him in and introduce him to me, and he can stay here for a while if you like.' Happy enough with this, he brings in a bedraggled waif, and proudly introduces him, having checked his name afresh in the hallway. I give them both drinks and biscuits, and Brian takes them off for a game of snooker.

Bedtime brings tantrums. The social worker had brought news of fresh rejections, as we knew he would. Now, at last, in the peace and quiet of the ending of the day, the message sinks in. 'Come on, Shane, time you were thinking of bed,' I suggest. 'You shut your face,' he explodes, 'leave me alone. You're not my mum. I hate you. Just leave me alone.' Brian steps in, his deep quiet voice almost always effective in this situation. 'That's enough, Shane. Go to your room. We'll talk about it later if you want to.' Shane stamps upstairs, slams one door, two doors, turns on his radio at full volume. We wait, look at one another, wait a little longer. Sigh thankfully as the music is turned down. Now Brian will go and see if Shane wants to talk. 'Remember to make sure he packs his pencil case in his bag,' I say, as I wander off to find my own quiet corner of the household.

Tim, aged six, asked by his teacher to complete a written sentence beginning 'I am good at . . .' writes in a bold hand 'I am good at BEING ME.'

Rage

I carried you screaming, face red and twisted with rage, back arched, legs kicking, arms flailing, and laid you on the settee, placed cushions on the floor in case you fell, and waited. Much later, still wracked with the occasional sob, you came and climbed on my knee. 'I wanted an ice cream and you wouldn't let me have one.' 'That's right.' 'And then I wanted to kill you.' 'Yes.' Snuggling closer, 'Are you all right, Mum?' 'Yes. I'm fine.' Long pause. 'Can I have an ice cream now?' 'No. But you can have a drink if you'd like one.' Silence so long I think you might have fallen asleep. 'Can I have a drink, please?'

'It was my job to look after the babies. But I got really tired and fell asleep. When he came back my dad dragged me out of bed and belted me, buckle end. After that he said I was useless, so he just lent me to his friends when they wanted me.' 'How old were you then?' 'Five, I think. Maybe six.'

We have a meeting today. Kelly has left us. 'Run away,' her social worker says. 'Run to . . .' seems more the shape of it to me. Kelly, now at the local children's home, agrees with me. When they asked her, 'So what went wrong at your foster home, then?' 'Nothing,' says Kelly, 'I just wanted to go home to mum.'

That 'nothing' of course does not take account of the tantrum we had to deal with, although I am still smarting from the bruises indicating the difference between two and 13 when it comes to managing major outbursts of rage.

The meeting is to be held in the conference room, a grand title for a tatty office with a big table in the middle. Everyone seems to be there when we arrive: social worker, senior social worker, father, stepmother, and the two of us. Everyone? 'Where's Kelly?' I ask. In the outer office looking after the latest batch of babies, her social worker explains. I protest. Rather angrily, the social worker opens the door and shouts out, 'Kelly! Do you want to come in here and join the meeting, or stay there and look after your brothers?' 'I'll stay out here.' The social worker looks at me as though she has won a point, though I'm not quite sure what it might be.

We carry on with the meeting. I describe the difficulties Kelly seems to experience around contact with home. How often following telephone calls from home we have incidents of violence or self-harm. How last week just such an incident occurred after Kelly had a telephone call telling her that her brother was in hospital after falling from a swing. How she has described vivid memories of bruises in her own early childhood being frequently explained as the results of accidents; that falling off swings was a particularly common explanation given in these circumstances.

Dad has picked up just one word from my report. 'Violence?' he says 'What violence? My daughter's not violent.' I pull down my roll neck jumper a little to show the now fading bruises on my neck and shoulders. He studies these with the eyes of a connoisseur. 'Well, that's not violence,' he pronounces, 'that's just hitting people.'

Kelly has made a statement to her social worker. She has said she feels confused and upset. That she wants to live with us, but that she also wants to look after her brothers and sister. However, since her return to her home area has simply left her living in a children's home, and no one has any intention of letting her go back to live with her family, she would like to come back and live with us. She also said that she was sorry for getting in such a temper and lashing out at me.

We have a statement from all the family saying that we want to have Kelly back, but that we would like the social services department to take more active responsibility for ensuring that Kelly's brothers and sister stay safe, so that she can leave that burden behind her. The senior social worker assures us that they are fully aware of their responsibilities, and doing everything possible within the resources available to them.

The decision is made that Kelly will return to us and with us. This is happy news. Less hopeful is the fact that absolutely nothing else in the situation looks like changing, except that some assurances have been given.

David, introduced to his new baby brother Tim, seems interested, even pleased. Later I hear him toddling to the bathroom and go to help him manage the mysteries of buttons and elastic. Instead, I find him attempting to flush his teddy bear down the toilet. As the manoeuvre fails, he drags the sodden creature out by its ear and holds it aloft. 'This is Tim,' he announces cheerfully.

In the car on the way home Kelly maintains an endless flow of meaningless chatter. Eye contact produces a sweet and dazzling smile. She is evidently as happy as a child can be. I run through a mental checklist – tablets locked up; knives locked away; chemicals all safely stored. I think we have it all covered.

Arriving in time for the evening meal, Kelly is delighted to see everyone again. She might have been away a year instead of a week, so excited and pleased is she to be home. Throughout the meal she chatters on about friends in school, the latest gossip, television programmes she has seen and those she has missed. The others take the barrage good-naturedly, pleased to have her back, while reminding themselves of the need to put earplugs on their next shopping list.

Later the whole group get drawn into their own idiosyncratic version of hide and seek, and the evening passes cheerfully till supper time. Now suddenly Kelly is pale and quiet, sipping milk and nibbling at biscuits which the others are consuming with gusto. I look across at Brian, note that he too has registered the change, is on the alert. 'I'm going to get ready for bed. 'Night,' she says, and disappears.

Within seconds we hear the sound of heavy dragging, followed by a crash. Both of us run for the stairs. Her door is closed, and blocked by some piece of furniture dragged across it. We can hear her sobbing, but she makes no response to me as I call her name. Brian fetches David and Rachel. Sometimes Kelly will respond to Rachel when she has gone beyond hearing the rest of us. 'Come on, Kelly, it's me, Rachel. Open the door, love.' 'I can't, Rae, I've had it. I can't do any more.' Then suddenly, shouting, 'I hate him, Rae, I fucking hate him. I wish he'd killed me when he had the chance.'

Together we force the door open enough for Rachel and me to squeeze in. You can lock away the drugs and the knives, but light bulbs shatter into sharp and cruel edges. Her hands and arms are bleeding profusely. Rachel pulls the chest of drawers away from the door, David arrives with a clean towel, Brian takes a pillow and a duvet to the car, and we set off for the casualty unit 15 miles away.

I hold her in my arms all the way there. She shivers and occasionally sobs, but has finally gone beyond words. In the hospital they remove remaining fragments of glass, and dress her wounds. We point out that this is self-inflicted and that we believe that Kelly is still very angry and upset. Is there any possibility of a referral for psychiatric assessment, we ask. With the resources available, injuries like this, which do not constitute attempted suicide, do not merit automatic referral. We are offered the option of going to our GP and asking for a referral to the waiting list, currently standing at about nine months. We try to picture what Kelly might be doing in nine months' time.

At home, all of us by now very sleepy, we help her up to bed. I lean over and kiss her forehead. 'Good night, sweetheart, remember we all love you.' From somewhere she summons a cheeky grin, 'Just as well really, innit? 'Night.'

In my dreams, I retaliate. Smash. Batter to a pulp. Ferocious violence pours through me. I wake refreshed and relaxed, grateful for the versatility of the human mind.

'I did hate you, Mum.'

'Yes.'

'I wanted to kill you.'

'Yes, you did.'

'And now I love you.'

'I know. I love you too. Sleep well.'

3 Trauma

Fear

Rachel, aged three: 'Time for bed.' 'But the fox might eat me.' 'Which fox?' 'The one in my room.' We search the room together, trusting small hand gripping mine. Under the bed, in the cupboard, behind the curtains. 'I think he's not here. You can go to bed now.' Three-year-old's bedtime rituals complete, I give a goodnight kiss. 'Sleep well. Sweet dreams.' 'Night, Mum. Leave the light on.'

Jay: 'When I was five, my dad used to belt me every day. And I was, like, really violent at school. So they sent me away to a boarding school. I was six then. At that place, if I shouted out in the night, I was dragged out of bed and put in a little room called the snug. Just a stone floor and nothing to do. Once there was snow outside, and I was left there from half past five in the morning until breakfast time.'

Begin, as I must, with the scream in the dark. One terrified cry: 'no . . . o . . . o!' Threads of fear from the nightmare reach out through the house, chilling me in my warm bed. I grope for the clock; just after three, not the worst night we've had. Wait now, five minutes, ten minutes; then the coughing starts. Five minutes more and a tap at the door.

I go out to the landing. He is 15 years old, taller than me by a full head, all bones and adolescent angles, shy placatory smile warding off peril. 'Sorry to wake you. I can't sleep. This cough is terrible. Can you give me something for it?' The smile is belied by the eyes – dear God, who left you with terrors like this? – it hurts me to look at his eyes. I put an arm around him, 'It's all right, I don't sleep much, you go back to bed and I'll bring you a warm drink.'

When I arrive with the drink, he is huddled under the covers in a foetal position, shivering. The room smells of fresh cigarette smoke, the window wide open and letting in a gale.

Closing the window, 'I thought perhaps you'd had a bad dream?' 'No. I never dream. It's just this cough that woke me.' 'Do you think you'll sleep now?' 'Mm.' 'Well, I'll be awake for a while. Come and find me if you need me.'

Back in my warm, safe bed, Brian snuggles up to me. 'One of Jay's nightmares?' 'Yes.' 'Will you wait till he's settled?' 'Yes, I'll read for a while.' As dawn breaks, I know we've had an easier night than some, and drift off to sleep.

By seven, the others are tucking into breakfast, relishing the one time of day they know they can share untroubled. 'Bad night?' – this from Rachel, over her shoulder, bleached blonde hair skimming her cereal as she does a quick check, registers baggy eyes and dragging feet. 'Aren't they all?'

'Let him sleep,' she says, 'give us some peace. I'll drop him at school on my way to work.' 'Can I have a lift too?' this from Tim, a few months younger than Jay, vulnerable I know, but what can I do? 'If you don't want your bike at school.' I watch him thinking, weighing the issues, even a simple lift becomes complicated.

'No, I'll ride.' And he reaches over, punches David on the arm, 'Check my maths for me?' Gentle David looks up from his otherworld, slaps his little brother – tall as he is and twice as wide – on the back of the head. 'Bring it to my room. We'll have a look at it.' They amble amiably away. Rachel hugs me. 'You take Jay a drink, and I'll get one for Dad.'

I knock on the door and go in. In sleep I can see his face clearly, his features relaxed, his expression peaceful. Waking, tension distorts and bunches the lines of his face, his eyes never free from terror or rage. I lean over and touch him gently on the shoulder, waking him softly, 'Jay, a drink for you.' Anything sharper and he will spring into life as a soldier under fire will wake to a sound. He opens his eyes and smiles, 'Mum! Thanks.' I'm not his mum, but in the half-sleep it's close enough, and all the comfort he'll have.

Now there's no rest till he's ready for school. He is as needy as a baby, as dependent as an infant, as touchy as a toddler. 'Where's my . . . ?' 'Who's got . . . ?' 'Somebody's taken my . . . !' The others go to earth, waiting for the morning storm to pass. At last Rachel shoos him out the door, and David and Tim emerge, still arguing differential equations, to make their own less frazzled way to school.

A quick coffee with Brian, and I'm at the telephone for my morning call, so routine by now I could put it on tape, responses and all. We need help with this child. Promises were made to us, all of them broken, that we should have full support, everything we needed to make the placement work.

There was a time in our work when such promises meant something, when we safely took into our home and our hearts children whose battered lives and wounded spirits could find comfort and healing in a peaceful environment. But those days have gone, now the same needs stretch us to the limit and beyond, as those who once supported us have had their own work redefined. Once we could share the burden, which then became no burden; now priorities have changed, services reduced, and we are left dangerously exposed as the objects of attachment for seriously wounded children.

'She's in a meeting at the moment. I'll ask her to ring you.' 'Tell her it's urgent.' (Tell her I'm falling apart. Tell her we're desperate. TELL HER TO READ MY LETTERS!) 'She'll ring you within an hour.' I say thank you nicely, the way I was taught, but know I won't be holding my breath for the phone call. Promises butter no parsnips; speaking of which, there are things to be doing.

A few tasks on, and the telephone rings. A miracle? No, the school head of year. Jay has attacked a boy during the games lesson, and needs to be picked up. Ever since his last suicide attempt, when the psychiatrist said he was too traumatised for psychotherapy to be anything but dangerous, Jay has been accepted at school on the basis of a special arrangement whereby if things get too tough he can come home at any time.

At school, Jay is with the nurse. This attack, unlike others, was actually minor. Friends saw Jay start to "flip" and held him back from doing any great damage. But he is sitting huddled in the chair, shaking uncontrollably and hot to the touch. 'I'm sorry! I'm sorry! I didn't mean to!' Then he looks up, searches my face, 'I wanted to kill him. I really wanted to kill him. What's wrong with me?' I can't answer that, certainly not now, not here. The school staff have been wonderful; he is so able, so eager to learn and do well, they have made space for him, and, so far, he has not been excluded. Let's not push our luck. I soothe him, thank them, and take him home.

Five minutes in the car, and the verbal torrent starts. My driving, my looks, my age, my relationship with Brian, my tastes, my friends, all are targets for the stream of jibes. I stonewall, focus my attention on the person behind the words, stay peaceable. As we get into the house, I stop him, turn him to face me, 'You're pushing me, Jay. Why are you doing that?' 'It's fun. Winding the staff up – it's what I'm good at.' 'So what happens then?' 'They send you away. Send you to your room. Tell you to get out of the Unit.' 'Do you want me to send you away?' 'NO!'

I look at him and smile. He grins, laughs, grabs me in a bear hug. 'You're too little to hug properly.' 'Perhaps you're too big. You should have been with us sooner. Lots of child-hugs on offer here.' He moves away from me, looks at me full in the face, 'I got lost on the way.' Ain't *that* the truth.

Peaceful now, we make cakes for tea. Yet still he is anxious, scanning my face and body language constantly for signs of displeasure, checking his progress with the simple tasks, belittling his own abilities. Then the mood changes, tension begins to build. I glance at the clock; the others will soon be home, more people to relate to, more mistakes to make.

I leave him clearing up and go to water the hanging baskets, knowing he will follow. As he comes round the side of the house, I spray him with water. Our game. He runs, and I chase him. He laughs, shouts, grabs me and wrestles the spray from me. Now he chases, I run. He catches me and sprays me. 'Right,' I say, 'we're quits now.' His face sets, he whisks the top from the spray and empties a stream of water over my head, drenching me. Then he steps back, trembling, begging me with his eyes not to be angry. 'Did I win?' 'Yes, Jay, you won.' 'Is that all right? You're not angry?' 'It's fine, Jay. It's a game. Now why don't you go and see if you can win against the computer?' He runs off happily, and I go and change my clothes.

Back in the kitchen, Tim arrives home and I ask, 'Good day?' 'So so. Where's Jay?' Always the first question. 'Playing on the computer.' He can relax now, slumped down, long legs stretched out, munching fresh cakes and chatting about school, the casting for the school play, what to take as an audition piece. David arrives, both boys love to be on stage, wander off together to rehearse.

Rachel and Brian arrive together as the meal is ready. Both look the question they will not ask in case the news is bad. I tell them about the attack in school, no injuries this time, Jay calmed down by an afternoon at home. Rachel goes to fetch the boys, David lost in a book, Tim and Jay now playing together on the computer.

For once the meal goes calmly, no tantrums, no upsets. We enjoy each other's company. During washing up, though, Jay begins to niggle at Tim, punching, pinching, flicking with the tea towel. Tim takes it for a while, then goes off to watch television. I listen, but it sounds as though things have settled; leaving the household to its own devices, I curl up in an armchair with coffee and a crossword puzzle.

Brian, angrily, 'That boy is nothing but a walking bloody penis!' We stare at one another, appalled. The way we learn what we already knew. 'I just meant he's so arrogant, so cocky, you know?' I do know, exactly. What, specifically, provoked this, though? Half an hour of non-stop baiting of Tim, who at last has gone to his room, too angry to talk to anyone. 'Do something, Kate, talk to Jay. Get him to back off.' Brian shakes his head, bewildered, used to taking an equal part but here frustrated and held at a distance by Jay's evident and intractable fear of all men.

I sigh, and go to look for Jay. Finding him in the living room, staring into space, I say I need to talk to him. He glares at me. I start in on how he's been pushing at Tim again, making his life unbearable, about how we need to respect one another, and give one another breathing space. Suddenly he shouts, 'I don't understand! What do you want? I don't know what you want from me! Do you want a fucking blow job or what?'

I'm speechless. Then he looks at me, sees me at last. 'You've gone red. What is it? What's the matter?' 'I'm embarrassed and angry,' I say, as calmly as I can. 'I'm embarrassed because you've crossed that line we've talked about before. You can talk to me about anything, including sex, but you may not talk to me as though I was your age, or anything other than I am. I am an adult who is responsible for you and who cares for you, and I take that responsibility seriously. I will not abuse you and nor will anyone here. Do you understand me?' Face hidden in a cushion, voice thick with tears. 'Yes.'

'I'm angry because I've been trying to talk to you about not hurting other people, and you are not listening to me. You have been pushing Tim beyond the limit, and you have to stop. Are you listening to me now?' 'Yes. I know it's wrong. I'm sorry.' Then suddenly, bursting out, 'It's just, Tim's like me, you know, I feel close to him, I feel I have the right.' 'So you feel close to Tim, he reminds you of yourself, so you feel it is all right to treat him as you've been treated?' 'A bit. Yes.'

Now the cushion comes down from the face. He acknowledges that he does not have the right to make Tim a victim, and does not truly want to do so. We discuss strategies for his coping. Using the punchbag. Going for a bike ride. Going to his room. I know he means it, know too that the problem for him is in recognising his own actions, coming to terms with his own moods and the feelings which drive him.

'Can I go to Youth Club?' 'Of course.' 'I don't think I . . . My foot hurts, can I have a lift?' I smile at him. 'It wasn't too painful for football earlier. What's the real problem?' 'You know.' 'Say it, Jay. It's nothing to be ashamed of.' 'I get scared. You know. Walking on my own.' 'Then I'll give you a lift. Go and get ready.'

At half-past-nine I pick him up from the Club. Park at the other side of the car park to see him walk across. Pretty steady on his feet. Test the air as he gets into the car; cannabis, I think, no sign of anything stronger tonight. A few days ago it was petrol ('Hey, I've discovered the meaning of life. It's something to do with . . .', puzzled,

'. . . roundabouts?') Before that it was speed, acid, sometimes ecstasy, sometimes alcohol. Brian says, 'Where does he get the money?' – another remark that leaves us staring at each other, speechless.

At home, he gets ready for bed, comes down in his dressing gown, limping. 'My foot really does hurt.' 'What's wrong with it?' 'I think it's . . . what do you call it . . . an ingrowing toenail. Will you look at it for me?' I go with him to the bathroom. The toe has been hacked and chopped about, is oozing blood and pus. 'What happened here?' 'I was trying to stop it from hurting.' I wash it gently and put on a dressing, then send him off to bed. 'Come up and say goodnight?' 'Of course, if you like.'

Downstairs, Brian has opened a bottle of wine for us to share with Rachel. David and Tim wander down to watch the news with us and share a quiet half hour. This night unusually peaceful. No police on the doorstep. No sitting up waiting for the worst effects of substance abuse to pass. No storms and tantrums, leaving windows and doors to repair. Just a little time to relax and draw breath before we see what nightmares the new night may bring.

But first, a promise to keep. I tap on the door. He is sitting in bed, sticking football stickers in a scrapbook. His music is on, but not too loud. It really is an unusually peaceful night. I kiss him on the forehead.

'Good night, sweetheart. Remember we all love you.'

'I know. Thanks. I love you too. Leave the light on.'

Grief

When the guinea pig died, we put her gently in a shoe box and covered her with flowers. We chose a spot in the garden under a rose bush, and dug a hole for her grave. She was laid to rest there, and we remembered what joy she had brought us in her long (for a guinea pig) life of gentleness and affection, her funny little ways, and how she helped to bring up Charlie the duckling when his mother was taken by the fox. We put a heavy stone over the grave, for we wanted her to return to the elements in her own sweet time. The fox should not have her.

I remember a baby boy. My mum bathed him and the water was too hot and he cried and cried. Then he stopped crying, and he was still, and my mum put him in the airing cupboard. After that I got taken away.

When my mum died, I was in a foster home. Two people came to see me, and they talked at me for about half an hour. I didn't know what they were on about. Then one of them said, 'I'm sorry, but your mum's dead.' And the other one said, 'Do you want to go to the funeral?' I said 'No, thank you,' and they went away.

At the age of eight, Tim became ill. Viral meningitis as a complication of mumps. Soaring fever and obviously excruciating pain. Rushed to hospital for tests, the good news being that it was viral and not life-threatening, the bad news that it must run its painful course, with no help for it but some relief of pain and endless patient sitting by the bedside providing soothing washes, and sips of fluid to prevent Tim dehydrating.

We brought him home and put him to bed, and everyone did their bit of being sympathetic and moving around as quietly as usually boisterous children can remember to be. They offered games and toys which Tim was too ill to use or appreciate, made him cards and picked flowers for his room.

Then suddenly, as happens with children, Tim was better. One minute lying still and silent, utterly drained of energy and life, the next sitting up demanding chicken and chips, lemonade, and why can't I go out on my bike *right now*?

Now we were the ones who were drained, eight days and nights of constant attendance, no break and no relief, and suddenly all the household back to normal. We sat back with glazed eyes, and watched it all going on around us. And that, of course, was just the moment for the beloved old guinea pig to turn up her toes.

'She's not moving around much,' says Tina, her carer-in-chief, 'do you think she might have mumps like Tim?' 'I think she's got old age,

Tina. Just be gentle with her and try to make sure she's comfortable.'

She watched as tirelessly as we had tended Tim. Sought out the tenderest tips of dandelion, provided extra sweet hay for bedding, touched and stroked as gently as a loving mother with her new-born babe. But nature had to take its course. At last not moving much became not moving at all, and even Tina had to accept her dear pet had gone.

We asked her what she wanted to do now and followed her requests, helped her to say goodbye. Afterwards, she cried a little, then carried on her life as though nothing had happened. No comments, no discussion, no issues arising, not even any change of mood or pace. Well, fine, we thought, after all it was only a guinea pig.

A few days later, though, the situation changed. This was not just a little clouding over, this was huge, billowing, storm-bearing, cumulonimbus monsters blotting out the sky. 'Come and play in the garden, Tina.' 'Don't want to.' 'Then come and play cards.' 'Don't want to.' 'What about just watching telly?' 'Don't want to, all *right*?'

Then, suddenly, she is biting herself. Drawing blood from her hands and arms. Clawing at her face until she looks as though a cat has savaged her. I run to her and pull her to me, sit her on my knee on the settee, cradling her to me and holding her hands. She stiffens, every muscle tense, and starts to scream. It is ear-splitting, this scream, the cry of every abandoned baby in the world gathered together and echoing off the walls of our living room.

I check that I am not gripping her too tightly. In fact my grasp is very light, in reality not holding her at all. Yet it is clearly symbolic, for if I let go she instantly returns to clawing at her face and biting her hands and arms. And the screaming goes on. And on.

If you have never experienced this, and I hope for your sake you have not, you will not be able to grasp fully the horror of it, however true the colours in the picture I paint for you. The scream is deafening, ear-splitting, that much must be obvious. But it is an experience involving more than one of the senses. I can feel it in my belly, this scream. My nerve endings vibrate with it.

The tension in her body makes it seem that if I let her go she will leap from my lap and run and run for miles before she drops exhausted. Yet in fact, if I let go my slight hold of her, she stays firmly in place, tearing at her own flesh as though she would flay herself alive.

Minutes pass. Half an hour. Someone brings me a drink. I transfer her two hands to my one, and gratefully drink it, her screaming making my throat feel dry and sore. She makes no response to this. Allows me to hold her safe with just one hand while I refresh myself. But will not herself eat or drink or rest or relax, will not, for more than the moment or two it takes occasionally to draw breath, cease from this awful scream.

After an hour, I lift her to her feet, walk with her to the bottom of the garden. She goes with me unprotesting, still intent on her one task of screaming her protest to the universe. Leaning on the fence, looking out over the valley, we give the rest of the household a break from the endless, unremitting sound. The neighbours will have to put up with it, I know the others have to have a chance to hear something else, talk to one another, get themselves to bed in peace.

Brian comes to tell us that supper has been and gone, and the others have all gone to bed. Still utterly passive but for the extreme tenseness of her muscles and the now hoarse but still unending screaming, Tina allows herself to be led back into the house, sits again on my knee, and carries on the process, whatever it is.

Suddenly, from nowhere, there is an ending. Every muscle relaxes, she curls against me, tears pour down her face. 'I want my mum,' she whispers, 'I just want my mum.'

David's best friend is dying. Sixteen years old, so much living to do, and no time left to do it in. At last, David is the only companion he wants. Visiting every day, bearing the pain of it, learning so much so soon. Arriving home from visiting late one evening he says, 'I think he's going to be all right, Mum.' I am troubled. 'David. Love. No-one can do any more for him, you know.' 'Oh, I don't mean he's going to get better. I just mean he's going to be all right. He's on a journey, you see, and he's moving on it faster than the rest of us. But I think he knows what it's about now. I think he's going to be all right.'

4 Resilience

Solitude

Arriving for the evening meal, four years old, carrying a huge book under your arm like a city executive with his briefcase. 'Where have you been? I've been looking for you for ages.' 'In the caravan. I've been practising being on my own.'

> When they went out in the evening to the pub, my dad used to lock me in the bedroom and tie up the door with rope so I couldn't get out. All they left was a bucket in the corner. I used to draw on the walls with shit. Nothing else to do.

All good things, they say, must come to an end. In our household, washing machines do it with monotonous regularity. This last one consigned in disgrace to the garage, awaiting collection to go to the tip. The new one installed in its place in splendid, and no doubt short-lived, modernity.

I am making bread while putting the new machine through its paces. Bread dough is the one thing readily available to me that I know genuinely and palpably benefits from being treated roughly. Taking out all the frustrations of the week on this simple, wonderfully tactile mixture, I am convinced that this will be, by God, the best bread ever.

As I set the dough to prove, I notice for the first time what has been evident in the background for some time, sounds of activity in the garage. Brian, I think, doing something vaguely mechanical with car or lawnmower. The other good thing about making bread is that there are stretches of time when the yeast is doing all the work, but I can still convince myself that I am busy. I pick up the paper and sit down to read.

Brian wanders in from the living room for a cup of tea, makes one for both of us. I try to think what it is about this which is strangely disconcerting. I know what it is – what's going on in the garage?

The garage, in this least mechanical of households, has become a workshop. All over the floor are little heaps and piles of things. In the middle, covered in grease and oil and utterly absorbed, is Shane. What was a washing machine has become treasure trove. At first sight the heaps seem random, but in fact there is clearly a sort of order and rationality informing this dismantling. Casing is stacked separately from coils, circuit boards and wires separately from hoses and valves.

Shane looks up, his face transformed with a smile of pure joy. 'Look,' he says, 'look what I've found. This is for you, this bit. It's a fruit bowl.' He picks out what was once the glass door of the machine. He's right. It has a sort of beauty and an undoubted utility. It will sit on our table for years. Shane's gift to us all.

'And look at this,' he stutters, words tumbling over one another in his excitement, 'this is a magnet, see. It's huge, really strong. And see how this coil goes round it. It's lovely, that, like bright copper. Is it copper, do you think?' I agree with him that it is copper, and that copper is indeed very beautiful. I explain in simple terms my rudimentary understanding of the working of electric motors. He is spellbound, caught up in the magic of the way the universe works.

'Can I have this magnet? Please? For my own?' I say that of course he can have it. That he can have any parts of the old machine he wants to keep. But that magnets are very powerful, that he must be very careful about where he keeps it, and what he puts near it. His eyes widen with awe. That something so simple and plain could carry such power. That he can be trusted with it.

I leave him to the delights of his self-imposed task, and go back to put the bread in the oven, and share a quiet cup of tea with Brian. And where are the others, this peaceable day? Brian has done the rounds of the house, has it clear in his mind that this is one of those occasions when each one is happily occupied.

Kelly is busy with her "family". For weeks now she has been taking over and transforming the old caravan into a home for the family of old dolls and battered teddies she has found and rescued from all the corners of the house where they have been abandoned in the course of other people's childhoods. Day by day she acts out the story of her life, the life she has lived and all the alternative lives she wishes she might have lived. Once, in the days when service provision of this sort was routine, we would have been able to find her a play therapist, to help her make sense of the stories in her head. But those services have long since disappeared in this area for anyone over five. Now she must just do the best she can. These are not things she wants to share with us, this family now being too important to her in its own right and function to risk mixing it up with other images of families in her head.

So she devotes herself with utter absorption to her work of discovery and perhaps of healing. Sometimes we wonder what is going on in this home within our home, but we know it is a very private place, and we do not intrude. Sometimes the raised voices coming from the caravan, alternative versions of the one voice we all know so well, make us wonder if we should not be setting in motion doll protection proceedings. But it is clear from her demeanour when she emerges from these sessions, that at some level these stories all have happy endings for her. How we wish her own life more truly reflected the optimism of her life of fantasy.

I remember a day when you were little more than infants, when we took the three of you to the seaside. Released from the confines of the car after the long journey, you scattered. Three individuals, setting off in three directions, to three self-appointed tasks. Such perseverance you showed, and at the end of it, when we gathered you together for our picnic meal, how clearly you had each learned a little more about yourselves. Rachel arrived with a bucket full of beauty. Every shape and colour of shell the beach could provide, a cascade of loveliness to pour out on the sand at our feet. David, then in his sorting and naming phase, had played the part of a beachcomber. Stones, flint and limestone and crystal, driftwood, and once sharp glass worn pebble smooth by the sea. Tim, the baby, trudged back purposefully from who knows what far flung region of the beach, dragging what must have been the longest piece of bladder wrack ever laid claim to by a determined two-year-old.

Tina, fundamentally more at ease with animals than with people, has taken to breeding rabbits. At least, as she explains, 'They do the breeding, really. I just put them together and let them get on with it.' Which they do with evident enthusiasm and success. She has a good eye for stock and genetic line. Her rabbits sell well and fetch a good price, though only after she has checked thoroughly and convinced herself her babies are going to good homes. 'I will not have my rabbits breeding babies for the pot,' she declares with staunch determination. No soft touch, Tina. No illusions that the world is a gentle place, really, full of people who will avoid harming the vulnerable and defenceless. She knows differently.

Today is a day of concentrated solitary work for her. Every part of this work she has created for herself she performs with stolid pleasure. The rabbits live in the conservatory, as indeed her old guinea pig had done in its day, in an environment as closely modelled as Tina can make it to a natural world for them. A huge trough of earth provides burrowing ground, while another, shallower tray grows grass and alfalfa and any other tasty morsels she can import. Logs and stones make jumping and playing spaces, and provide shelter on hot and sunny days. There are cages full of straw and sweet hay for sleeping in, but these are usually left open, unless one of the animals is sick, or for some other reason needs isolating for a while. Generally Tina finds that the creatures are quite orderly in their own environment, and messing out need only involve one or other limited area of the space. Sometimes, though, like today, she will do a grand clean through, knowing that tying down animals who normally occupy a larger area to a more confined habitat may increase the risk of infection.

In school, Tina is regarded as barely educable in the mainstream, with a concentration span that teachers feel has passed in the blink of an eye, so hard it can be to engage her attention. Yet here she has researched and studied. She keeps meticulous records of her animals and their offspring. She has identified one ready market in local institutions which run pets' corners, primary schools and adventure playgrounds, and is often consulted by caretakers about the needs of their small furry charges. The local vet, more used to the ailments of cows and horses, has taken pleasure in developing some expertise in the medical needs of rabbits, and somehow Tina has never had reason to discover that veterinary surgeons charge hefty fees for the use of their time. And when one does have to come to the end of its span, the vet is as gentle with Tina as with any devoted owner of a pedigree hound similarly confronting the harshness of nature.

If Tina is in with her rabbits, then for a while at least, all will be well with the world.

What of Jay? How does he fill his hours of solitude? Here is a mystery indeed. This child of chaos and offspring of disorder has discovered music. The school has a brass band, every student invited to join. 'I'll do that,' says Jay, 'I'll play a cornet.' Not at first, he didn't, at least not by any definition of playing that we could imagine. The sounds generated by that combination of boy and brass were excruciating. 'You see,' he said despairingly, 'I told you I was useless.'

Yet somehow he persevered. Hour after hour of solitary musical disaster. Then finally, and rather suddenly, music began to appear. Then what a world opened up. Not just the sounds he was beginning to be able to make, but 'Listen,' he would say, running into the kitchen and grabbing my hand, dragging me into the living room, 'come and listen to this!' A tape is playing, he goes and stops it, winds it back to a point on the tape counter, 'This is by someone called Bach,' he announces, full of the joy of discovery, 'now listen to this bit.' And he plays the bit of tape he has selected, listening with rapt attention. 'There. Hear it? That's another trumpet joining in with the first one. Can you hear it? And listen, it plays almost the same tune, see, but just not quite. Isn't that clever? Just that little change there? Beautiful.'

The trumpet has become his instrument. More versatile than the cornet, he can now play not only in a brass band but also in an orchestra and consort, and has travelled to various parts of the country to share in concerts and musical events. We found him a bursary, a special fund for gifted children ('Gifted? Me?'), and bought him a trumpet of his own.

If today is to be a day of solitary delights, I have no doubt what Jay will be doing with his time.

Compassion

'I'm glad we grew up with fostering,' you said, years later. 'The most dangerous thing in the world is one-sidedness. With fostering, you have to know there's always more than one side to everything. You have to be able to see other people's points of view. To feel how it might be to be standing in someone else's shoes.'

I know you love me. I know I've got more in my life than I ever thought I could have, everything I ever dreamed of. But it's not enough. It's just not enough.

We wake to an unearthly wail. A vixen? Surely they are already in cub. Running feet on the stairs, and Tina bounds into the room without so much as a knock. She whose experiences leave her painfully wary of adults, bedrooms, adults in bedrooms, and anything which might have anything to do with the sexuality of any creature larger than a rabbit. This must be an emergency.

The rabbits are the cause of it. 'Come. Please. Come now. There's something wrong. Something terrible.' She is so distressed I begin to be flustered myself, fumble over pulling on trainers and a sweatshirt.

Arriving in the conservatory, I can see the cause of her distress. Through the spring and summer she often lets her rabbits take advantage of the fresh sweet grass by putting them out in runs in various parts of the garden. They must, I think, have had some contact with wild rabbits. Now they are clearly ill, eyes glazed, breathing shallow; I fear the worst.

With an arm around her shaking shoulders, I guide her into the house, persuade her to sit down and eat some breakfast, promise we will ring the vet at the first opportunity. He, true to form, calls in on his way to the surgery, is clearly devastated by the scene which meets his eyes. He confirms what I had feared. 'Myxomatosis,' he pronounces, 'it's hitting the wild population again at the moment. They must have picked it up from their cousins in the garden.' Tina knows about rabbits, believes that this is the death sentence he has just

31

announced, is clearly bewildered, and frightened, as he reaches into the bag he has brought with him.

'Right,' he says, 'we'll need an isolation hutch for each rabbit affected. Here's a supply of syringes, cotton wool, saline solution, and glucose. Bathe the eyes of the affected rabbits every hour, and force a few drops of glucose solution down their throats.'

I take him to one side. 'This is hopeless, isn't it? Please don't raise false hopes for Tina. It wouldn't be fair.' 'I wouldn't do that. I know her too well. Myx is not the absolute killer it used to be, a proportion of domestic rabbits can survive if they get the right attention. Just let her know that it's doubtful but not impossible.'

We gather in the kitchen to check that the plans for the day are clear. Kelly wanders down for breakfast, is immediately and evidently touched by the anxiety in Tina's eyes. 'What's up, Teen? Boyfriend eloped with Madonna, has he?' Hearing the facts, she rolls up her sleeves. 'Right. Come on then. I'll start scrubbing out hutches, you go down the farm and get some fresh hay, it's softer than straw.' Tina relaxes just a fraction. 'Thanks, Kelly. It'll be a long job, though.' 'So what. I'm used to bad nights. Me and Florence Nightingale both, never did need any sleep really.'

The two of them take shifts, turn and turn about, for as long as it takes. And Tina is right, it is a long job. But not one rabbit dies. The vet is astonished at the outcome, the total success. 'Never, never let your rabbits escape,' he warns, 'set that degree of immunity loose in the wild and you'll have half the farmers in the county gunning for you!'

Shane is expecting a visit from his mother. That deserves saying twice, such excitement it has produced. Shane is expecting a visit from his mother. Perhaps "expecting" is putting it too strongly. He has had a letter from his social worker, and a telephone call from his mum; the date has been set, has been written into his diary, and inscribed in huge capitals on the family wall calendar. But we know he has not got as far as expecting it to happen, is maintaining hope in the face of long and bitter experience.

Now he gets up and eats breakfast in stony faced silence. Or rather, tries to eat breakfast, ends up drinking half a glass of milk and pushing some toast around a plate for a while. 'Right,' he says suddenly, with determination, 'I'm off to catch the bus.' He will travel the 15 miles to our nearest city to meet his mum. This is his choice. He is not exactly ashamed of her, in fact he loves her with a passionate commitment. But her mental health problems make her behaviour unpredictable, and he prefers to meet her away from his immediate environment.

Two hours later the telephone rings. I answer it. 'Oh, Shane, I'm so sorry. Are you sure? Yes, that sounds pretty definite . . . No, give me your number, I'll ring you back.'

Jay is passing through the hall, stops and looks at me enquiringly. 'It's Shane. His mum hasn't turned up.' 'Is he going to wait for her?' 'No, he's rung her lodgings. The landlord says she's just too drunk to make it to the meeting.' I know Jay and Shane often exchange stories of parents with problems of alcohol dependence, know that Shane will want Jay's support more than he will care about Jay knowing the situation.

'Wait there,' says Jay, running upstairs, 'Oy, you lot, Rachel, where are you?' Three minutes later, Rachel, David, Tim and Jay are gathered in the hall. 'Right,' Jay is forceful, organising, determined to do some-thing about the situation, 'You ring Shane back and tell him to stay where he is. Rae's going to give us a lift in, she's going shopping and us lot are going to take him to the match. If he's got to feel gutted, a good shout should be the best medicine.'

They set off together. Rachel blonde, fine boned but broad should-ered, able to carry the weight of it, and three jostling adolescents, loud and loutish is all the world will see, on their way to shout themselves hoarse at the match.

Love makes itself in the strangest disguises.

Tranquillity

I love these summer days in the garden. Everything is so peaceful and calm. The world just seems a good place to be.

If I could really feel at peace inside myself, just once, I could believe perhaps I might be going to be all right.

Summer Sundays we live outdoors unless it rains. This late summer sunny day an extra, a bonus, a gift for us to enjoy before the darker days of autumn set in.

The tennis season has been and gone with the winning, or losing, depending on your allegiances, of Wimbledon. But cricket still has all to play for. The old Labrador serves her turn as a fielder, skilful enough for all her advanced years to be of interest to the England test selectors, we think, except that she never seems quite sure to whom the ball should be returned. On second thoughts, perhaps she really is good enough to go for selection.

First we cut the grass. Mowers and shears, lawn rakes and loppers. Taking it in turns to work and to flop down gratefully on the cool grass, keeping the jugs of iced lemonade under the shade of the trees topped up for anyone to help themselves.

The latest batch of baby rabbits, old enough now to be leaving home, are out in a run in the corner. Word has gone out that they are ready, we will have a steady trickle of visitors today coming to choose their new pets. Other visitors will arrive as well. Friends of the children know that Sundays like this one are open house, that food on these days is free and easy, that there will always be games and activities to join and share.

Twenty-seven French schoolchildren arrived once with their English hosts, bringing their own picnic lunches, spending the afternoon learning the secrets of rounders and French (Really? French?) cricket.

That was the exception, however. Most Sundays, a gentle flow of peaceful activity, sometimes individual, sometimes shared, marks the passing of the hours. Hairdressing is one recent experiment, I notice. Hours of mutual grooming, daring forays with scissors and clippers. I remember how we thought we were bold getting to work with the Amami and the rollers on a Friday night. Now hair is truly a medium of self-expression for boys and girls both, and not at all shy about sitting on the grass with a towel round the shoulders trying an apparently endless range of styles from the interesting to the frankly outrageous. Somehow they put it all back to something approaching my definition of normality at the end, as I breathe a sigh of relief thinking of the conservatism of schools and teachers and shopkeepers and, heaven help us, policemen and potential employers.

A water fight is being set up. I escape to the kitchen to prepare trays of food. Cooling watermelons and salads, home-made bread, cold meat and cheese, crisps and nuts. We carry them out and set them on tables. Hairstyles glamorous and outrageous are now uniformly transformed into the new wet and shaggy look, obviously set to take the world of youth culture by storm.

I shout to draw attention to the food, and the ravening hordes descend as the locusts once descended on the grain fields of Egypt. A new competition has developed, a watermelon-seed-spitting contest. We are, I learned long since, a household doomed to coarseness and vulgarity. As I notice that Brian is hotly arguing that, if not the winner, he has at least come an honourable second in the contest, I can see that it is just as well I have no aspirations to greater gentility.

Once replete, the gathering settles into quietness. Some wander off to be alone with their reflections. Others sit or lie companionably propped against one another, quietly reading, or playing cards, or simply snoozing in the sun. Some customers arrive for rabbits, are provided with boxes and bedding for their new pets, and strict instructions on the tender loving care such vulnerable babies need to survive and thrive.

Gradually the garden empties as people wander off to take the dog for a walk, keep dates with boyfriends or girlfriends, prepare home-work for the week ahead. Brian and I sit for a little longer reading the Sunday papers, relaxing as we also prepare ourselves for the new week. We know these times of peace and tranquillity are vital for all of us, providing rest and refreshment, helping us all to grow in strength and resilience, know too that for some of our children none of this can be enough.

Childhood creates persons. We have seen it, the unfolding, the wonder of it. But whatever creates, can also destroy. Children are tough and resilient. The children we have brought into our family to grow up alongside those born to us, children we have cared for and grown to love as we love our own, these children are strong and brave. Amazingly strong, and more courageous than any child should have to be, more hurt than any human should have to bear. Children can be injured with wounds beyond healing. And when the community ceases to understand or to care, when services are reduced and facilities are withdrawn, then even the healing which might have been possible may be taken away.

The hospital ward is hot and stuffy, but I think that nothing will ever warm the ice in my bones. The fingers in mine are equally cold, and limp, and unresponsive, only the faintest curving to the shape of my hand indicating that we are still attached.

Brian stands behind me, his arms cradling me lightly. Otherwise, I think I would collapse, would simply lose all my strength, could not stand up, could not bear it.

Suddenly the grip tightens on my hand, the eyes open and gaze into mine. 'I'm dying, aren't I?' 'Yes.' 'I'm sorry.' 'So am I.' This time we came too late. This time too much harm has been done.

'All my life I waited for the good time to come. Now it's here. This is the best time of my life. And I just want to die.' 'I know.' I know that for you being loved is like coming into the warm after suffering frostbite. I know that no amount of good experience now can compensate for the harm added to hurt added to injury which made up your earlier life. I know that healing itself if it happened would involve you in pain beyond my imagining. I know that there are worse things than dying.

The fragile grip eases. Then you touch me again, open your eyes again, a long direct gaze. 'Say goodnight?'

I lean over, kiss the pale, cold forehead. 'Good night, sweetheart. We love you very much.' 'I know. Thanks. I love you too.'

Years later, we are all glad you overcame the odds and failed to die. Your strong young body survived the drugs that should have killed you, and your courageous spirit recovered enough hope to go on living with the pain. As the years pass life becomes less sharply painful, fear and grief are less often overwhelming. Your living becomes less of an ordeal and more of an adventure. You teach us the meaning of resilience.

Part II

Making sense
Theory, research and practice

Kate Cairns

5 About feelings

On the map of the soul's journey there are no short cuts
George Steiner (1961, p. 335)

Themes of shared humanity

There are certain themes in human experience which recur often
enough in art and literature and everyday life for us to be able to
consider them universal. If we think of our own lives or those of
people close to us, we can recall experiences of love, joy, grief, despair,
tenderness and anger. These themes are reflected in art and music,
literature and drama. They cross boundaries of time and space and
culture; they are discovered in records of the anguish and ecstasy of
great saints and mystics, and in the intrigues and jealousies of the
humblest soap opera. Our fluctuating moods and feelings mark out
rhythms and processes in our lives which form the ground of our
shared humanity.

We may think of emotional experience as being rather like music.
The notes, which can be isolated and named, may sound singly or may
blend together to produce harmony or discord. The music may use
many notes or few, may be complex or simple. The musicians have
available the whole range of notes which can be produced from their
particular musical instruments, although they may not know what
those notes are or how to play them. Every note can be recognised and
echoed by other instruments, each with its own unique timbre
and inflection.

Or we could envisage a network of every possible human feeling
forming a matrix within which our feelings flow. A useful image might
be that of the television screen as a fixed network on which a recognisable pattern is produced by the movement of an electron beam
continually picking out and activating different points on the screen.
Similarly our feelings change; peacefulness is succeeded by rage, grief

is transformed by joy, as now one and now another point on the network becomes dominant.

In considering the experiences which form our personalities and continue to change us across our life span, it is important to remember that these experiences began at the beginning of our life. In much that is written about children it would appear that these great themes of human life are either absent or qualitatively different in childhood. 'It is, of course, our sense that children are essentially different, other, that underlies the way we regulate their lives. This sense is central to the official psychology of childhood' (Salmon, 1985, p. 30).

Such an assumption contradicts my experience as a child and my experience with children. I can remember in my own childhood emotional processes every bit as real and passionate as those of adult life, which carried meanings simpler but no less profound than those discovered later. Observing and listening to other children through the years has convinced me that this is true for others as well as myself. Violet Oaklander confirms this from her own experience: 'I remember that when I was a child I had wonderings and feelings that came from a place so deep inside me that I know I never could have put them in words if I had wanted to' (Oaklander, 1978, p. 320). Or, as Phillida Salmon concludes: 'Though their situation may be different, children do seem, *as persons*, to be very much like their elders' (Salmon, 1985, p. 33).

The search for common ground

Many years of my life have been spent caring for other people's children, or working with those who look after children. Our children often come to us neatly tagged like house plants with instructions for care: 'Needs firm handling and clear boundaries.' What does this mean? How does it relate to the stubborn, foul-mouthed individual who tells us exactly where we can put our firm handling? Or this one: 'Needs a warm, loving environment.' Is that a description of the sodden, steamy bed they present us with each morning? It surely cannot have been written by anyone who has ever tried putting an arm around this child and been met with ear-piercing screams and bites and kicks.

Advice has traditionally come in one of two main wrappings, however various the tape it was tied with. There is the range of approaches which are based on psychoanalytic theory. These may explain, for instance, that we should not be surprised that young Bradley cut up all his clothes and shoved them down the toilet, or that little Kylie invited all the boys in her class behind the bicycle shed; they behave in these disturbed ways because events in their past have been so disturbing. We recognise the truth of this, and may, in time, cease to be surprised. But what are we to do? Our own life stories are so different; even when there are similarities, the striking thing will be the unique dimensions of the suffering experienced by each individual. Searching our own life history is likely to give us little clue how to respond at a day-to-day level to the destructive or sexual behaviour, no obvious hope for Bradley or Kylie.

The behaviourists seem to offer more positive guidance for us, suggesting that, through various systems of rewards and punishments, undesirable behaviour may be extinguished and desirable behaviour substituted for it. There are problems with these approaches. Although cognitive behavioural techniques in different guises can be helpful to people whose behaviour is out of control, results can be unpredictably inconsistent, and attempts to replicate success in one setting can fail in a different environment. A more significant difficulty is the violence which such approaches can do to the roots of the personality. We can usually feel that Bradley and Kylie are truly responding to events and situations in ways which make some sort of sense in the context of their unique life stories; if we set out to change the behaviour we are in danger of destroying the meaning which that behaviour holds.

We can unite with the children in our care neither through a common history nor through shared behaviour. Even those closest to us are unique in the exact unfolding of their own life stories, and each individual expresses the unique meaning for them of their relation to the world through their behaviour. Yet if we cannot find unity with the children entrusted to us, our separateness makes it impossible to care for them. Loving others implies moving towards them in community of spirit, seeking unity in our diversity, finding a common ground on which to build a living relationship.

Starting with feelings

I have found it more serviceable to begin from a rather different base in seeking this common ground. I recognise that when I am challenged to consider something which I have done, or a particular pattern in my behaviour, my first recourse is to my feelings. As I try to understand and explain my behaviour I generally begin by exploring what I felt at the time. I know that if I feel sad or happy, angry or tender, fearful or confident, these feelings will affect the things I choose to do and the way I do them. Once I have located and described my feelings, I may go further and look for the roots of my anger or insecurity or whatever in some other chapter of my story, so as to change feelings in the present through a healing of hurts in the past. Or I may instruct myself in the art of not taking things out on others, acknowledging and accepting the feelings but choosing to change my response to those feelings. Either way I am able to alter my unacceptable behaviour without doing violence to my inner life.

It is clear to me that others, adults and children alike, are able to undertake a similar discipline, and that such a shared discipline releases all of us into our full stature as unique individuals capable of making and acting upon moral choices. To recognise and honour the reality of the inner experience, as well as the external phenomena of events and behaviour, is a courtesy which we usually claim for ourselves but often fail to extend to others.

Feelings are not the roots of our behaviour. These are found in a complex interplay between our genetic inheritance, temperament, environmental influences, early experience, later learning, and the conditions in which we currently find ourselves; we shall explore all these later. But feelings are part of the ground of our behaviour, a part which we hold in common and which we can therefore take as the basis of our unity, a meeting place where we can recognise the landmarks because we have been there before. I remember a comic parody of a psychiatrist saying something like: 'Which of us can honestly say we have never set fire to a great public building? I know I have.' The parody works because it contains a grain of truth, not just about psychiatrists, but also about all our relationships. If we are ever to offer comfort, strength, hope and healing to one another, we do need to find something in common. Yet our genetic inheritance, personal histories and learned patterns of behaviour are all quite different. The common ground we do have is our shared experience of anger or despair or loneliness or curiosity. Feelings are our starting point.

One word of caution at this point. Emotional experience, like Oscar Wilde's truth, is rarely pure and never simple. There is a risk that in directing our attention towards the feelings of others we may come to believe that we understand them. There is no intention in this exercise to analyse, or explain, or even sufficiently describe the inner world of the children in our care. This remains private, and will, fortunately, resist any disrespectful attempts to make it otherwise. We are, more appropriately and humbly, looking for a little common ground on which to stand, a little 'insight into and stern compassion with the state of being' of others (Tustin, 1981, p. 178). This insight and unsentimental compassion can form the basis for a loving and perhaps a healing relationship.

The process of relationship thus begins with what we know and what we have learned about ourselves and others. We set this alongside our observations of the behaviour of the other and our understanding of what we have learned of their story. We can then begin to make guesses about which element of the repertoire of human emotional experience is predominant in this person at this time.

As we test this out, in our actions and words, things begin to happen. We find that we are reaching towards the other, whatever their age or status, from those who are newly born to those who are on the threshold of dying, where they are, not in some set pattern of relationship, but in a real interchange between individuals. People usually respond to this, feeling not only that they have had their feelings recognised and acknowledged, but also that they have been recognised as persons with dignity and value. Even when our guesses are wildly wrong, and they often are, our children may respond at this level. Indeed we may elicit their kindly sympathy: 'They may be stupid but at least they try.'

Self-assertive and self-transcending emotions

Writing about human creativity, Arthur Koestler usefully described emotional states as either self-assertive or self-transcending (Koestler, 1964). Self-assertive emotions are the primitive, active emotions such as fear or rage. They involve gross physiological changes and a dissociation of reasoning from feeling. Individuals experiencing emotions of this type are usually aware of themselves as discrete organisms, separate from other individuals. Self-assertive emotions tend to involve an accumulation of energy which is resolved by explosion.

Self-transcending emotions are also described by Koestler as participatory emotions, which are more likely to occur in, or induce, awareness of being part of a greater whole; compassion, awe and joy are examples of such emotions. They are more passive emotional states involving physiologically the more subdued parasympathetic reactions. There is no clear dissociation between thought and feeling in such experiences. The kind of energy changes involved tend to be resolved by catharsis: '. . . an inward unfolding of a kind of "oceanic feeling", and its slow ebbing away' (Koestler, 1964, p. 88).

This concept of emotion as involving changes of energy is helpful. Energy may be either creative or destructive. It may of course be both at once, or it may be impossible for us to discern the difference. But let us hold fast to simplicity. Energy may be creative or it may be destructive. Every emotional state has the potential to be creative or destructive, to add to or diminish the person experiencing the emotion.

Hurt people, including many of the children with whom I have lived and worked, usually experience emotions in the destructive mode. By approaching people through their feelings we can offer a route to change which does not insist that the person eradicate or deny their experience, but which offers the possibility of transforming that experience into a creative, life-giving force. We can say, for example, with or without words: 'I think you feel angry. It's all right to feel angry. Sometimes I feel very angry. Now – what are you going to do with all that energy?' Or, as Violet Oaklander describes working with a deeply unhappy girl: 'We talked about her loneliness for a while, and then I told her something about my own loneliness.' (Oaklander, 1978, p. 9). People can be torn apart by the destructive force of emotional experience; they can be locked up in a private world of confusion and isolation; they can be driven to despair and suicide. Yet the same energy, turned to creativity, can generate healing and growth.

Seven emotional states serve as examples. These reflect the development of human beings from undifferentiated unity through separation towards community. Three of these – desire, rage, and fear – may be described as self-assertive emotions. They are active emotional states involving gross physiological change and having a tendency to resolve explosively. They originate in the primitive limbic brain and are part of the innate biological systems of affect described by Silvan Tomkins (Demos, 1995).

Grief is a compound emotion, and has elements which are self-assertive and elements which are self-transcending. The other three – solitude, compassion and tranquillity – are passive, cathartic and participatory so may be considered as self-transcending emotions. Each of these has a claim to be universal in human experience, may be creative or destructive in its impact on the individual, and has the capacity to change us and to change the world.

These seven emotions are considered in Part II. The seven examples of emotional development will be grouped in three sections, as we think of the three key sets of experiences in childhood: the formative experiences of attachment, the transformative experiences of trauma and loss, and the affirmative experiences of building resilience.

The section on attachment looks at the ways in which the most basic dependence on others for survival develops into relationships which produce attuned, responsive individuals able to live as part of the human community, able to regulate their own needs and impulses, and able to engage in reciprocal relationships and manage anger.

The next section sets out the effects of life changes which come about through the disintegration of established patterns. Trauma is a common experience and the loss of those we love, or of significant structures of daily life, is universal; at any stage of life these are transformative experiences which disrupt the fabric of our lives and change us, sometimes radically. In childhood such transformations are particularly significant in their impact on the still developing personality.

The third and final section examines the affirmative experiences of building resilience, exploring the personal, social and spiritual developments through which children discover their unique place in the world and the gifts they bring to it.

6 Attachment: formative experience

In fair desire thine earth-born joy renew.
Robert Bridges

The depth and dream of my desire,
The bitter paths wherein I stray –
Thou knowest Who hast made the fire,
Thou knowest Who hast made the clay.
Rudyard Kipling

Feeling good, being good: affective attunement and reintegrative shame

This chapter examines the experience of stress arousal and desire in infancy, the processes of attachment that result from such arousal, and the implications of attachment for human development. Desire and arousal in this context do not relate to adult concepts of sexuality, which are a later development in our human experience. Desire and arousal here relate to the universal experience of needing being translated into wanting and, through resolution of this stress, into satisfaction. The second section provides a description of the behaviours and patterns which indicate secure attachment in babies, infants and older children, and those that suggest unmet attachment needs. Finally, the third section proposes activities and interventions which we can provide to promote and enrich secure attachment and to compensate for the harm caused by unmet needs and promote recovery from impairment.

What happens?: thinking about attachment

Born to be sociable: babies in their social setting

Human babies are born defenceless, vulnerable and utterly dependent on the community that receives them. Fortunately, if all goes well, the receiving community will be disposed to nurture the child. For it is clear that the whole community, consisting of the family, its supporting network and the wider society which contains them all, is enriched and strengthened by the new life this birth brings.

Research and robust theory drawn together during the later years of the twentieth century demonstrate that this containment of the developing person is not, as was once thought, a process of the social structure providing as it were a safe space within which the individual develops along genetically determined lines. It is not even a process of genetically determined individual development in parallel with socially mediated learning, as later versions of child development theory might suggest. This old nature or nurture debate around child development, while not resolved, has become largely irrelevant in the face of more recent understanding of the processes of human growth and change.

We now know that from the moment of birth, indeed it may be argued from the moment of conception, the growing individual is in a complex interaction with the environment. Through this process of mutual attunement and adaptation, each changes the other forever. We humans are not separate from our environment, we are inextricably a part of that which we learn to consider as separated other.

Throughout the latter half of the last century, John Bowlby and his followers were creating an astonishingly rich theory of attachment and the significance of the making and breaking of affectional bonds. Bowlby and many others who worked on his theories subjected his ideas to the test of thorough and painstaking research, finding great consistency across many different human groups; differences of ethnicity or culture within the current extensive research show that attachment behaviour is a universal human phenomenon, with some variations in the distribution of different patterns of attachment, but with the majority of children across cultures and classes (around 55–60 per cent) showing secure attachment (Howe, 2011, p. 51).

Revolutionary as this thinking was, research in neurophysiology and the new understanding of the human brain which emerged later in the century have led to important additional insights. In particular, it is now clear that the brain of the developing infant is more radically shaped and structured by the quality of the interactions between the infant and the environment than we have previously thought. Children whose environment is hostile or lacking in nurture end up thinking with a very different brain. In the United States, Allan Schore (1994, 2003), Louis Cozolino (2013) and Daniel Siegel (2012) have impressively brought together this emerging neuroscientific evidence to build understanding of the impact of childhood experience on brain development. Further, the extensive work of Bruce Perry points to example after example of research evidence on the structure and function of the brain. Vivid illustrations are provided showing the differences between the brains of people of all ages who have experienced childhood trauma and those who have grown in a more secure and nurturing, or less traumatic, environment.[1] In the UK, David Howe, David Shemmings, Stephen Joseph and Sean Cameron, among many others, have produced key texts enabling practice to develop alongside knowledge and understanding.

Every one of us has been present at the birth of a baby, for here we all are. One of the difficulties in grasping attachment theory and issues of infant trauma is that we touch areas of our own deep and hidden experience. Each of us has our own attachment history, experiences from the time before we could speak and create narrative memory, experiences that have set the shape and structure of the very processes by which we are able to think about anything else. When people speak to me about looking after babies they often talk in terms of "common sense". I ask them to consider the phrase: 'common sense is what you learned before you were two.'

Once this profound limitation is clear to us, we become considerably more patient with the difficulty we all have in thinking about our own early history. This leads to the difficulty we have in thinking accurately about the inner life of a baby, and the effects the baby has as an agent of change in the world. We have also lived through several generations of alienating analyses of the human condition. For all the

---

1   See the website www.ChildTrauma.org for a full list of information and resources.

gems of truth they contain, they have nevertheless made it hard to deal with one another with the tenderness and loving respect we need in order to learn and change. And we do need to learn and change.

Those writers who most helpfully lead us through the complexity of research are making it clear that learning and changing are possible. All those cited have an interest in, and many actively practice, therapeutic interventions based on this understanding of how our minds, our brains and our social relationships interact to enable us to continue to develop and change, moving beyond set patterns of thought and feeling and behaviour to find new ways of being. As we reflect on the development of young humans, it is important to recognise that it is the adaptability of adult humans that will enable the next generations to grow to their own adulthood with greatest resilience and least harm. Our own ability to learn and change is central to the well-being of our young.

In the beginning: brain development and attachment from conception to the end of the first year

In the beginning, for the developing foetus, the world is without form and void, but it does not stay that way for long. Brain cells begin to develop within the first few weeks of pregnancy, and by 24 weeks the final number of brain cells is reached. By about 30 weeks the neurons have migrated to the location in the brain for which they are fitted, and the process of differentiation whereby these cells take on their specific functions continues from then until the end of the first year after birth. Along with the development of brain cells, the foetus begins to experience its environment and becomes actively responsive to environmental stimuli from about two months gestation. All the senses develop before birth, and a foetus without sensory impairment will show responsiveness to touch, taste, hearing and vision (Karr-Morse and Wiley, 2013, Chapter 3).

Injury to the developing foetus will have an impact on this new brain and body. Such injuries may be caused by any toxic substance able to cross the placental barrier. Drugs, alcohol, nicotine, some toxins produced by illness, prenatal malnutrition and possibly the toxic effects of traumatic stress in the mother may all interrupt and damage the rapid proliferation of cells in the new brain (Karr-Morse and Wiley, 2013). Thus babies may be born already injured, or depleted in their resilience to the stresses and strains of life. They may also suffer injury during the birth, and again these may include significant injuries to the forming brain.

Once the baby is born the real work of brain building begins. This little scrap of humanity is, as we have said, utterly dependent for her very survival on the goodwill of those who nurture her. If she is in fact he, then the vulnerability is at least as great, and may be even greater; certainly it will be likely to manifest itself later in different ways depending on the gender of the child, of which more later. Yet right from birth the baby does show behaviours which actively contribute to her own survival. When placed under stress such as hunger, discomfort or fear, the baby produces distinctive activity which serves to draw the attention of a caregiver. We call this activity attachment behaviour.

Broadly speaking, there are three types of attachment behaviours. Babies can do things which make the adults around them want to interact with the baby in order to get them to stop it; this has been called aversive behaviour. It would include such behaviours as crying, screaming, breath-holding, and anything the baby can invent or discover which draws a response from the one who holds the key to life itself, the primary caregiver. The infant soon discovers that there are other types of behaviour which can produce an even more agreeable response from the caregiver. These are behaviours in the baby which have been described as *attractive*, and they include smiling, making eye contact, vocalising, laughing, and other mutual delights which the baby will explore with the encouragement of a suitably engaged and doting carer. Finally, the baby becomes increasingly able to produce active behaviours such as moving towards the caregiver in order to grab the needed attention and achieve the desired relief of stress (Howe, 2011).

Like everything associated with infant attachment, these types of behaviour are very persistent, and it is noticeable that even in adulthood, people who did not find attractive behaviours rewarding, people whose caregivers did not respond to infant charm, are likely to resort to aversive behaviours under stress. They do things which make those around them act to get them to stop it. Others, fortunate enough to have had more responsive caregivers, are likely to take a more active or interactive approach to the relief of stress.

Growing points: four stages of brain development

The baby's brain is now organising itself at an astonishing rate. This organisation begins from the foundations, the brainstem, which forms the substratum which will determine the possibilities open to later levels of brain structure, the midbrain, the limbic brain and the cortex. It is clear that, once the basic number of brain cells has been set by halfway through the pregnancy, the brain is then organised and shaped by the formation of connections within those cells. This organisation, building the brain from the foundations upwards, is "use-dependent" (Perry, 2000). The number, nature and location of the connections made are determined by the interaction between the baby and the environment.

Attachment behaviours are the key to this early infant brain development. Stress is toxic to the brain, causing profound changes in brain structure and function in the interests of survival. When the baby attempts to engage the caregiver through attachment behaviour, the urgent desire is for the carer to enable the baby to modulate and recover from the stress which has provoked the behaviour. Babies with available and responsive caregivers enter into a relationship in which each attunes to the other and together they experience relief of stress. Both baby and carer will go through a cycle of stress arousal, stress modulation and the pleasurable experience which follows the soothing of stress. Most babies (55–70 per cent) are fortunate enough to have such a relationship with their caregiver (Howe, 2011).

Under these conditions, babies' brains develop optimally given the particular genetic and temperamental inheritance they each have at their disposal. Such infants will be producing connections between neurons at a phenomenal pace. In a sample of brain tissue the size of the head of a pin, there are 124 million connections at 28 weeks gestation (Karr-Morse and Wiley, 2013). At birth this has risen to 253 million, and by eight months the same size tissue sample shows 572 million connections. This is many more than the child will eventually need, and shows the brain in the first eight months of life producing the maximum capacity for versatility and adaptability in the growing child.

Infants whose caregivers do not respond appropriately to their attachment behaviour present a very different picture. On the one hand, the lack of interactive stimulation leads to a lack of production of some brain connections and a "pruning" of connections already overproduced and not being used. There is thus a quantitative difference between the brains of securely and insecurely attached children. Securely attached children develop bigger brains.

On the other hand, the failure to modulate stress arousal leads to the nature and location of those connections which are made being different. Confronted with persistent unresolved stress, the infant brain forms characteristic use-dependent structures, of either hyper-arousal or defensive dissociation; hyperaroused infants show perpetual signs of distress and irritability, while dissociated infants show none despite being in a physiological state of high arousal.

Several factors affect this primary adaptive response to threat. Gender has a part to play; dissociative responses are more common in girls, hyperarousal more common in boys. Dissociation is also more common in younger children; it is more common as a result of traumas which involve pain or torture; and it more often occurs in situations of helplessness or inescapability. Hyperarousal more often follows trauma involving older children; it also more frequently occurs after traumas in which the child is either a witness or alter-natively is an active participant rather than a helpless victim (Perry, 1999). This complexity naturally means that many children use a combination of these responses to survive, although sometimes we do see a very clear example of one or the other having proved adaptive for a particular child. Thus there is also a qualitative difference between the brains of securely and insecurely attached children.

Insecurely attached children really do think with a different brain.

At least four key periods, or growing points, have been identified in this building of the brain (Perry, 2000). Throughout gestation and the first year of life, and particularly in the period up to eight months after birth, the brainstem is forming. The organisation of this underlying brain structure is critical to the healthy development of the rest of the brain and the functioning of the entire human organism. The sequential development of the brain means that later brain structures cannot form in a normal manner if the brainstem structure is depleted or injured. The primary functions of the brainstem are to regulate physiological states, including stress arousal, sleep and fear. It should be remembered that many leading clinicians, including Bruce Perry, consider that injuries and developmental deficiencies at this stage of brain development are permanent and irreversible. Later therapeutic work will need to be directed towards enabling the child to live with the impairment comfortably and productively, for the damage cannot be repaired (Perry, 2000).

During the first and second years of life the midbrain is developing. During this stage of human development the many sensory stimuli received by the body begin to be integrated into recognisable patterns and the growing body begins to be able to regulate motor activity. This is also the time when these integrated patterns of experience and purposeful movements are closely linked to social experience, so that we see the beginning of an affiliative approach to the world. The infant is born dependent and therefore sociable, and this sociability can now be expressed through purposeful activity.

From years one to four the limbic system forms. This part of the brain will allow for the regulation of complex emotional states, the development of social language and the interpretation of social information. During this time we see the full development of attachment and empathy, and the ability to express these through activity and narrative. By the end of the third year the brain will already have reached 90 per cent of adult size.

During years two to six the cortex develops. Here is the grey matter which we think of as so typical of the human brain. It allows abstract thought of all sorts, and the integration of all experience into a stream of consciousness. The functioning of this part of the brain will determine many of the attributes which will define the growing personality: creativity, abstract reasoning, humour, mathematical ability, verbal competence, artistic flair, musical ability, aesthetic appreciation, and the ability to integrate all these into social relationships.

Family matters: the part adults play in infant attachment

The first effective empirical procedure for testing the theory of attachment being developed by John Bowlby was the "strange situation" experiment devised by Mary Ainsworth. Since attachment behaviour is produced by babies and infants in response to stress, this procedure involves exposing infants to minor stress and recording their responses. The key to the success of this procedure was the production of an ethically acceptable stress situation which was entirely and reliably repeatable and therefore valid as a tool for comparing the responses of different infants. The elements of the test situation which produce the stress are: a room which is a new environment to the child; the presence of a stranger; the temporary absence of the primary attachment figure.

These basic elements were combined into an effective procedure which allowed Ainsworth, and many others since, to draw a clear picture of the range of behaviours infants in the age range one year to 18 months produce in response to stress. She became aware of three distinct and different patterns in these behaviours, which she classified as secure attachment, insecure avoidant attachment and insecure anxious ambivalent attachment (Howe, 2011, Chapter 4). Main and Solomon (ibid, pp. 47–48) later added a fourth distinct type of response which they called disorganised attachment.

It was clearly now possible to analyse and classify the behaviour of the young children in this situation of stress and anxiety. Yet at the heart of attachment theory was the understanding that the infant is not developing in a vacuum. It became a matter of urgent importance to try to discover what part the adults were playing in the development of the patterns of attachment behaviour. Main and Goldwyn (Howe,

2011, p. 57ff) developed the Adult Attachment Interview to enable accurate comparison between the accounts different people give of their childhood. They demonstrated that it was possible to discern four distinct patterns or styles of narrative in response to this structured interview.

Researchers were then able to carry out the Adult Attachment Interview with parents-to-be before the birth of their child, and to compare the results in due course with the behaviour of those children at one year to 18 months in the "strange situation" research procedure. The results have been an overwhelming vindication of attachment theory. A clear correlation has been discovered between the attachment style of the caregiver and the attachment pattern of the infant.

Such studies have shown that adults invited in a structured way to provide a narrative about their childhood do so in a characteristic fashion which allows a classification into four groups, or four different attachment styles. The researchers describe these as secure and autonomous, dismissing, preoccupied, and unresolved. Whilst there are obviously factors which add complexity, broadly speaking, infants develop an attachment pattern at one year which is closely linked to the attachment style of their main caregiver or caregivers. If the attachment style of the main caregivers is very different, the infant may develop a different attachment pattern towards each of the carers. These patterns are essentially the mechanisms whereby the infant meets the needs of the caregiver in order to try to ensure that the caregiver will in turn meet the intense dependency needs of the infant.

The majority of people (usually 55–70 per cent) show a secure and autonomous style of attachment. They produce a coherent, emotionally congruent narrative, which gives a clear sense that they have processed and dealt with the issues of their childhood. This seems to be true whatever the quality of their childhood experience. As adults they are in touch with those issues but not actively engaged with them. Such parents, all other things being equal, have infants who develop secure attachment patterns. These are babies who are cared for by adults who are emotionally available and responsive without being interfering or overwhelming. The baby can safely trust that in a stress situation the adult will be able and willing to protect and comfort the child, and to provide soothing so that the stress response diminishes and is replaced by pleasurable sensations. The pleasure derived from such soothing is mutual in an attuned attachment relationship; the carer as well as the child show physiological evidence of a pleasure response (Hughes, 1997, p. 11ff).

About one in five of the population produces a dismissing style of Attachment Interview. They provide a narrative which is thin and sparse and lacks any congruent feelings. Indeed they are actively dismissive of the importance of feelings or of the importance of childhood at all for themselves as an adult. They perceive a discontinuity between childhood and adulthood, and claim to be independent of and unaffected by the events of their childhood, whatever the quality of those events. These parents have children who develop an insecure and avoidant attachment pattern. Such babies do not make any demands upon adults to soothe their stress, but instead avoid displaying the distress this causes them. Physiologically they are children suffering stress, but their behaviour gives no sign of it.

About one in ten people shows a preoccupied style of Attachment Interview. They have not moved on from the events of their childhood, whatever the quality of those events, but instead provide a rambling incoherent account in which the emotions they express are still clearly those of the original events. They do not appear to have processed and resolved the experiences of their own childhood, often remain dependent on the good opinion of their own parents, and are preoccupied with their own unmet childhood needs. Such parents cannot reliably be available to their infants, although when they are responsive the response is likely to be warm and soothing. For the infant, however, this inconsistency is destructive. Trust that the adult will provide the necessary soothing for the stress response becomes contaminated with frustration and rage as a result of those times when the adult is present but unavailable. The attachment pattern developed by infants in this situation is described as insecure and ambivalent or insecure and resistant. Again, like avoidant infants, they have developed a strategy for managing their primary carers which does not lead to adequate regulation of stress arousal. They have adapted to the inability of their carers to respond to the full range of their attachment needs. They can survive, their carers do respond, but the price of that survival is high. Unregulated stress injures the growing brain.

Finally, there is a group of people who are suffering some measure of post-traumatic disorder as a result of their childhood experience. The traumas from which this disorder arises may be very different, but the result for their own infants is the same. Post-traumatic disorders leave people in a permanent state of inner terror, which becomes their normality. This terror is, however, transmissible to the infants who are invariably very sensitive to the emotional state of the carers on whom their lives depend. Babies born to parents suffering unresolved trauma from their own childhood (adults who show an unresolved attachment style) are confronted with an insoluble dilemma – they experience overwhelming fear in the presence of the very person on whom their continued existence depends.

Such infants cannot develop any attachment strategy at all. They may try out aspects of all the other attachment patterns, or they may give up and freeze completely, but always their response to stress is inappropriate and bizarre. They cannot distinguish between one adult and another, or if they do so it is not a meaningful distinction. They cannot plan their behaviour. They cannot play. They cannot develop trust, or curiosity, or empathy, or social behaviour. Instead they are likely to develop strange, stereotyped behaviours which may be self-stimulating, such as head banging, or biting, or masturbating, or may be self-soothing such as rocking, or sucking, or stroking. Babies who are more fearful in the presence of their carers than in their absence are in urgent need of help from the rest of the community.

Patterns persisting over time: common sense is what we learn before we are two

Our inborn desire for attachment creates the deepest structures of our lives. From conception through till the end of the first year of life we are developing the capacity to regulate our own internal states, our reactions to stress, our patterns of sleep and wakefulness, and our responses to physical soothing. Patterns laid down at this stage in our lives are likely to be highly persistent, and our lifelong tendency will be to react to stress by way of the response systems which were adaptive in infancy. Our most primitive discoveries about survival are imprinted in our brains and bodies and are deeply resistant to change.

Throughout the second year of life, as the midbrain forms, we are learning to integrate all the mass of sensory information our environment presents to us, to develop control over our muscles and to relate to other people. At this stage repetitiveness is our delight. Not only is the world full of patterns, we discover, but also we can change it. And how we practise. Concert pianists and sportsmen and women at the top of their form cannot begin to equal the sheer persistence and energy infants devote to practising their developing skills.

From years one to four the limbic system develops. Now we are building on the foundations laid in the brainstem to regulate our emotional life and to establish complex interactive communication based on the full flowering of our capacity for attachment and empathy. We discover that words are also patterns, and have meaning, and, astonishingly, can change the world. We discover that human beings live in a matrix of communication, nearly all of which is non-verbal, and we build patterns of interaction which again will be persistent throughout our lives, and deeply resistant to change. We also begin to discover that we live in a wider environment to which we can relate as separate individual beings, and not just through the medium of our attachment figures, and that we can have an effect on that environment.

These foundations will be well established before the thinking cortex really begins to be organised, and the shape it takes will be largely dependent on the infrastructure already built. From years two to six this immensely complex integrative and cognitive structure will be forming. Now we become capable of abstract thought, of cognition and meta-cognition, of learning and learning how to learn (Bateson, 2000). If all goes well, this cortical development will be taking place after a foundation of secure attachment has been laid, for only then will we be able to develop our full human capacity for integrating our physical, emotional, intellectual, social and spiritual development into a graceful and harmonious dynamic structure which will become the unique and infinitely valuable entity – a human personality.

And if all does not go well, what then? Personality is not a given from birth: we grow as persons as our brains grow, and as brains can be damaged, depleted or injured, so can the developing personality be harmed. Fortunately all is not lost. People (and brains) are constantly changing and developing. All our lives we recover from harm, and discover and develop new resilience in the process (Joseph, 2011), and what cannot be repaired can be helped. At no time in our lives are we immune from harm or from help; we can never get away from our vulnerability as humans, but neither are we ever beyond reach of healing. The next section describes the behaviours and patterns we can observe in securely attached babies, infants and older children, and in somewhat more detail the behaviours and patterns we can observe in those surviving unmet attachment needs. The final section proposes activities and interventions that can enrich the developing brain and provide healing for those already impaired.

What do we observe?: life with the child

Securely attached children
Babies
Attunement is the key to attachment in babies; the mutual and reciprocal relationship between the caregiver and the baby through which each learns about the other and becomes changed themselves (Hughes, 1997, Chapter 2). A baby does not enter the world as a blank slate, waiting simply for the world to make its mark on this emptiness. Every child born arrives with their own pre-birth history, their own unique experience of birth itself, and their own individual genetic predisposition and temperament.

Babies may be born placid or irritable, sleepy or wide awake, shy or outgoing; they are unique individuals from the moment of their arrival. It is for this reason that a parent may have two children and be able to attune to one and not to the other, producing a very different attachment outcome within one family group. We can therefore assess the quality of attachment and the progress of development in babies not primarily by the nature of the child's individual behaviour, but by observing the baby in relationship with the primary caregivers.

Whatever their temperament, babies in an attuned relationship show their distress when they feel it, and respond to the caregiver who responds to them. If physically healthy and unimpaired, they will show firm muscle tone without rigidity, and will respond with pleasure to touch and rhythm. If there is no sensory impairment, they show an early preference for the human face and the human voice, and will track to sight or sound; this tracking soon shows signs of distinguishing between the main caregivers and other people.

Securely attached babies move easily from aversive to attractive attachment behaviours; they smile, gurgle and coo and vocalise both actively and responsively with the carer. They show playfulness and curiosity and are generally interested in the world around them. Although it may take some time, babies with attuned caregivers usually establish a settled pattern of feeding and sleeping. They also begin early to make active attempts to interact with and reach out to the caregiver when needed. They will show sensory preferences, rejecting tastes or smells they find offensive.

Babies who are securely attached are therefore developing a richly endowed and complex brainstem within the limitations of their unique inheritance and temperament. The critical brainstem functions of regulating arousal are being created both through being provided with appropriate stimulus by the caregiver, and through receiving an appropriate response from the caregiver to the baby's attachment behaviours when the baby is disturbed by stress. These babies are growing powerful, responsive, flexible and resilient brains which will provide a strong foundation for all later development.

Infants and toddlers
Young children enjoying the benefits of secure attachment live in a world of endless interest, delight and frustration. As I write this, my toddler grandson takes a tumble, thinks about crying, decides he is not much hurt, gets to his feet and tries the same manoeuvre this time

with more care and new skill, and, having succeeded, catches my eye and produces a huge grin of shared delight in his discovery. At this age muscles are for using, limits are for testing, relationships are for exploring, games and songs and simple stories are for repeating (ad nauseam for adults), and accidents and minor stresses are for surviving.

This is also the stage at which securely attached children begin to discover the function of shame in their lives. Silvan Tomkin (Demos, 1995) suggests that there are nine innate affects – the secure child will have experienced most of these in the first year of life. Interest, joy, surprise, rage, fear, distress, disgust (the affect relating to things that taste bad) and dissmell (relating to things that smell bad) are all common experiences in the early months. The remaining affect, however, is unique in that it is only generated as a result of interaction between persons (Kaufman, 1992); it is the affect of shame. Affect precedes feeling or emotion; it is the experience common to all humans which is the physiological precursor to the vast subtlety of human emotional life.

Shame is an affect which is uncomfortable, and most infants seek to minimise it. It therefore functions as the affect which provides for that part of the attachment cycle which enables the infant, still unable to think logically or experience the full range of limbic system emotional functioning, to develop impulse control and therefore to stay safer. This has clear survival value. The increasingly active infant does something which could lead to harm; the attuned carer reacts, which has the effect of breaking the attunement; the infant, visibly shocked by this break in relationship, experiences shame. All affects, according to Tomkin, are recognised from the change they produce in facial expression; shame produces a characteristic hiding of the face, with downcast glance and lowered head. This response is visible in babies and infants from an early age if there is an abrupt break in the attunement relationship, but achieves full expression in toddlers, who constantly test the boundaries of safety, and constantly need to be patterned through shame to regulate impulse and preserve their own safety.

For the secure infant and toddler, however, this experience of shame which leads to the regulation of impulse is swiftly followed by the attunement being re-established. Carer and child both contribute to this reparation (Hughes, 1997, p. 18). Shame which follows this pattern has been called reintegrative shame. Braithwaite (1997) suggests that at the level of whole societies, those communities proficient at reintegrative shame have low rates of crime, while those who experience and transmit shame as disintegrative tend to have high crime rates. Disintegrative shame, which gives rise to a range of disorders of thought, feeling and social functioning, is considered further when examining the results of unmet attachment needs and also when exploring the phenomenon of rage.

Hughes (1998, p. 299) considers that this process of socialisation and formation of impulse control through reintegrative shame begins at about nine months and continues for about nine months more. By 18 months the brain is developed enough to allow more complex structures of feeling and thinking to emerge in relation to social behaviour, social discipline and self-discipline. These fundamental patterns of response to impulse, however, are as persistent, and as resistant to later cognitive or emotional intervention, as the earlier structures of response to stress. Again we see that the development of human beings is inherently social; we do not exist as isolated individuals, nor even as separate but linked actors in an unfolding shared drama. Rather we are both the product and the producer of our shared environment, shaped by our experience of others even as we shape our own destiny and contribute to the shaping of our world.

Older children

Children who have been fortunate enough to live in an environment promoting secure attachment and who have had no impairment in their ability to interact with that environment will have developed the capacity to regulate both stress and impulse adequately. They are engaged with others and their environment, experience empathy, are emotionally expressive and will have internalised the social inhibitions and taboos of their cultural milieu. By the time they reach school age, they will already have a rich command of language to which they have been exposed, and will be able to give verbal expression to internal states as well as describing external objects. Liberated from the excessive anxiety and excessive shame of children with unmet attachment needs, they are able to explore their world with curiosity, playfulness, imagination and joy.

The general approach of securely attached older children to other humans is one of interest (Howe, 2011), and they are open to the possibility of trust-based relationships while able to make judgements about the trustworthiness of the other. They distinguish between types and degrees of relationship, have relationships which are close, confiding and intimate, and are able to form new close relationships if they meet someone with whom attraction to intimacy is mutual. In moving through the dance of forming and exploring relationships they use and understand language and non-verbal communication precisely, gracefully and in culturally appropriate patterns.

Insecurely attached children
Babies
Lacking a secure attuned relationship, babies are unable to develop regulation of stress. At this stage of development there are only two alternative responses available to the infant subject to unregulated stress in order to promote survival – dissociation or hyperarousal. Even at this early stage of brain development, awareness is not unitary but is split into different components functioning at the same time; dissociation is the process by which the brain protects the organism from becoming totally overwhelmed by generating patterns of auto-matic splitting of awareness in response to repeated experiences of an overwhelming nature. Perry (1999) shows how such splitting pro-gresses from being a trait to becoming a state of brain function impervious to further adaptation. Babies who respond to stress with dissociation will continue to have that as a patterned response to stress throughout life.

Hyperarousal, by contrast, is the state in which unregulated stress continues to affect the entire organism; it is, at the level of the organism, a less despairing response than dissociation, directed towards maintaining the energy to keep trying to defend against the devastation of being overwhelmed. In older children, hyperarousal will lead to a fight or flight response, while younger hyperaroused children will freeze and regress as the only effective defence for them is to engage a rapid adult response to protect them. Thus freezing in response to threat is an extreme attachment behaviour, demonstrating to any available adult the urgent need to attend to a child too threatened to cry out.

In general, Perry (1999) suggests, there is a continuum of pro-bability as to whether children become dissociated or hyperaroused when subject to overwhelming stress. Many factors affect the outcome, but there is a tendency for children who are younger at the time of trauma to dissociate, while older children are more likely to remain hyperaroused; girls are more likely to dissociate, boys to be hyper-aroused; children who suffer direct pain or torture tend to dissociate, those who observe the violation of others tend to remain hyperaroused; and children who experience helplessness or powerlessness associated with the trauma tend to dissociate while those who are actively involved in the event remain hyperaroused.

The effects of dissociation and hyperarousal are global. Everything we can observe about a baby will be altered by unregulated stress. Thus we see babies who cry constantly or babies who never cry at all; babies who jump at every stimulus, and babies who are unresponsive even to extremely startling stimuli; babies whose muscle tone is perpetually tense and rigid, and those who are floppy and unco-ordinated; babies who avoid eye contact, and those whose fixed gaze is disconcertingly empty; babies who withdraw from touch, and those who fail to respond to touch (see, for example, Fahlberg, 2008 and Archer, 1999). Every possible response, every aspect of infant behaviour, is altered by the stress disorder.

Infants and toddlers

As children become more actively engaged with their environment, so the need to regulate impulse is added to the need to regulate stress in order for them to survive. Again the child is dependent on the community, which may be the child's parents, wider family or equivalent social system, to provide the structures which shape the child's development. Specifically, children who experience unmet attachment needs will be unable to experience reintegrative shame. For these children shame will invariably be a disintegrative experience. Teicher (2000) found measurable brain injury in adults who had experienced significant trauma in early childhood; one of these areas of lasting brain injury was to the structures which deal with the regulation of impulse.

Disintegrative shame may take a number of forms, according to Kaufman (1992). There may be a generalised experience of excessive and pervasive shame (Hughes, 1998), which results in children establishing shame as part of their core identity. The child does not experience shame as a transitory unpleasant affect – I have done a shameful thing – but as a pervasive area of self-definition – I am a shameful person. This is a structure or pattern which is formed before the brain is capable of emotional processing, and certainly before the brain is capable of cognition. It is therefore a pattern resistant to classic therapeutic intervention. This is a distortion of the experience of shame which is particularly likely to afflict those who have no experience of attuned relationships. For them the global failure of the attunement–shame–reattunement cycle is inevitable, while the experience of the innate affect of shame is equally inevitably a part of human development. They will experience shame, and they will not be able to regulate it; it will overwhelm them.

Children who experience this level of disintegrative shame are likely to be controlling of others and chronically angry. Rage is a common response to shame and will be explored further in its own right; as for issues of control, children who can be so readily hurt and so little comforted are almost always children who need at any cost to be in control of others and of their situation, though they lack appropriate control over their feelings or behaviour. The inability to develop impulse control also leads to other sorts of harmful, destructive and occasionally bizarre behaviour, including lying, stealing, destroying property, and hurting self and others (see, for example, Hughes, 1997, 1998, and Archer, 1999).

Shame may also become bonded to other innate or developmentally generated aspects of the human condition. These shame binds, whenever they occur, are pre-rational and profound; they are all the more powerful and global in effect if they are engendered at the same early stage of development as excessive and pervasive shame. Kaufman (1992) indicates that the socially engendered affect of shame may thus become bound to other affects, or to drives or to needs.

Young children may experience a shame-generating response from others in their environment whenever they express some other affect such as distress or fear or rage. This creates an automatic link between the original affect and shame, and shame is then experienced instead of the original affect. I have lived and worked with children who never experienced one or more of the self-assertive emotions of fear or rage or sadness; situations which might be expected to produce the emotion would instead trigger shame and whatever, for that child, were the emotional consequences of shame, which might be rage, or self-harm, or self-medication with drugs or alcohol.

Similarly shame may substitute for the lived experience of a drive such as sexuality or hunger, a distortion with desperate long-term consequences, as the growing person will feel shame instead of sexual pleasure or instead of hunger. Shame may also be engendered automatically when the child would otherwise experience a basic need such as the need to relate to others, or to differentiate from others, or to provide nurture for others. Trying to relate to a person whose fundamental needs around relating to others are contaminated by shame is infinitely frustrating.

The effects of such shame binds are most powerful when the persons provoking the shame response are those on whom the child depends for their very life, and when the bind is formed before the brain is fully formed. If the growing person experiences excessive and pervasive shame, so that being shameful is a key element of their core identity, and they also are subject to shame binds, then the wounds are deep and serious.

What we observe are children who are inhibited with the force of taboo from experiencing their own needs, or their own basic drives, or even their own innate affects. They are equally powerfully prevented from accepting any interaction which disturbs their core self-definition of shamefulness, they are children who will resist or disengage from any environment or relationship which is inclusive and accepting, or which provides them with positive messages and praise. How do you manage the paradox that a child who may desperately need to do well in school may trash their bedroom or burn their school books if they get a good report? How do you live with children whose response to any compliment is to cut themselves or destroy their possessions?

The inner experience of shame is of painful exposure, transparency and vulnerability. When shame is reintegrative, this momentary pain provides the energy to seek reattunement. When shame is disinte-grative, it provokes instead the urge to hide, to build defensive strategies against the pain, and to attack the perceived source of the pain. Thus we see children who are concealed from those around them by constantly telling lies, often pointless lies, and who may be unable to distinguish fact from fantasy. Children may also be controlling and dominating, or rigidly perfectionist, or may constantly seek to blame or punish others. These are all defensive strategies to control or trans-fer the pain of being shamed. And we also see children who actively seek reinforcement of their own shamefulness, needing constant reassurance that they are as horrible as they believe themselves to be.

When children are subject to developmental disruption during the period when the mid-brain is developing, their motor control may be affected. They may be seen as clumsy and unco-ordinated, or the distortion of underlying development may be reflected in difficulties with spatial perception and sensory awareness. Children in this situation may be identified as dyspraxic, suffering from "clumsy child syndrome", or they may be disconnected from their own sensory interface with the environment, literally not being aware of their own bodily presence in the world. I have known children who did not know whether they were hot or cold, or did not know how to make a choice between simple alternatives when, for example, shopping for clothing or choosing food in a restaurant.

As these injuries in early growth are carried through into the next stages of brain development, language, memory and the construction of meaning are all adversely affected. Children may have difficulty with forming or understanding words or sentences, or may be able to construct language but not be able to use it as a tool to make sense of the world. Distortions of perceptual awareness may lead to difficulties with reading or writing or making sense of pictures or objects.

Other areas of brain function adversely affected by disrupted attachment are linked to the capacity for empathy and social connectedness. Children may defensively protect against social interactions which engender shame for them, but they may also be simply unable to make the social connection in the first place. And children who have experienced disrupted attachment commonly are unable to experience empathy. They are, after all, thinking and feeling with a very different brain from most of those around them. They have no access to the inner experience of others.

Older children
It is when children begin to take their place in a wider social environment that living with a different brain really begins to result in social exclusion. Although children will usually continue to struggle hard to find a way to be true to themselves and still to be part of society, it is often an unavailing struggle for children who are so different from the norm.

Unable to regulate either stress or impulse, they are liable to behave in ways which are seen as extreme and bizarre. Unable to engage with others or with their environment, to experience empathy, or to be emotionally expressive, they are experienced by others as alien and uncomfortable beings. They will be working to a different set of taboos and social inhibitions from their peers.

They will be unlikely to have access to the rich and varied language of their peers, and will probably be unable to express inner states through language, which in turn leads to impoverishment of the ability to feel at all. Non-verbal communication is ignored or mis-understood. They are chronically subject to excessive anxiety and excessive shame, and these effectively preclude the curiosity, playfulness, imagination and joy with which securely attached children approach life.

Children with unmet attachment needs are constantly in survival mode, and have little interest in others except as possible resources to be used. Trust is not an option, but the inability to trust anyone also leads to an inability to distinguish between persons or to discern the degree of trustworthiness of others; indeed those who are objectively most trustworthy are to the child likely to be most threatening, while those who objectively least deserve trust are most likely to feel to the child familiar and unthreatening. It follows that children with unmet attachment needs are also unable to distinguish types and degrees of relationship, and are unable to form genuinely close confiding relationships. Chance acquaintances are perceived as best friends, loving carers may be perceived as overwhelming threats.

Day by day you will be learning the child entrusted to you. Making use of any of these ideas that inspire you, allow yourself to reflect frequently on what the child is teaching you. Theory and research will then be informing your observations of the child. Such reflection will arise from questions that may lead you closer to the experience of the child.

Examples of useful questions

How does this child deal with stress?

Do they turn to others for help when under stress? If so, to whom?

How much stress is too much for them?

Can they express their feelings? When relaxed? When under stress?

Does the child provoke stress in others?

Can they gain comfort from bodily contact with others?

How does the child relax?

What are the basic patterns of sleeping and eating you associate with this child?

Do they get bored easily? Are they comfortable in a low stimulus environment?

Do they try to soothe stress through unusual, compulsive or obsessive behaviours?

Do they try to overcome loss of sensation through stimulating behaviours?

Do they use food, alcohol, drugs or other substances for soothing or stimulation?

How does this child deal with shame?

Do they like to be in control?

Are they comfortable in situations where other people are in charge?

Are they able to accept praise and blame?

Can they take responsibility for their own actions?

Are they able to rejoin the group after they have caused offence to others?

What can we do?: approaches to living and working with children with unmet attachment needs

The four step plan

Step 1: commitment

Each child needs us to commit ourselves to sharing a journey with them, a journey which we undertake in the full knowledge that it will change us forever. It is impossible to provide an authentic and trustworthy relationship without accepting that measure of vulnerability. Unlike the child, you will have undertaken the journey freely and of your own volition. It is important to remember this if the going gets tough and the enterprise seems overwhelming. Sharing for a while the life journey of children with unmet attachment needs can be a great adventure, it can stretch us to levels of creativity and endurance we had not known we could produce, but it can also be destructive. For in human social relationships, the very forces which are creative are also those which destroy.

We will be required to establish empathy with the child. Some of the time, and it must be only some of the time, we will need to experience the world as the child does. This will produce a dizzying sense of dislocation, followed, if all goes well, by an expansion of perspective. We will come to understand that the world may, at a fundamental level, be different from our most basic assumptions about it. This is what Gregory Bateson called "level three learning" (2000); it is learning which disrupts not merely how we think about the world, but the basic mental constructs that let us learn to think about the world. Level three learning changes us radically. It picks apart and remakes the patterns which shape and contain our understanding.

If you are unable to offer this commitment, do not undertake the work. It will damage you. If the adventure is for you, then proceed to step two.

Step 2: personal support

It is essential when living and working with children with unmet attachment needs that we establish and maintain our own close, confiding, intimate relationships. This is the source of our own sanity and is a resource to sustain our own resilience. The work will challenge and may destroy both. It will also challenge the durability and flexibility of our own secure attachments. It is vital that we pay attention to these relationships, giving at least as much attention to relationships which are mutual and reciprocal and sustaining as to those which are more problematic, more demanding and which will be a net drain on our resources.

It is not enough to think about these personal relationships before you set off on the journey with the child and then forget about them. We live in a dynamic universe, and everything changes. You need to keep paying attention to these relationships, and to other close, confiding, mutual relationships which may form, and to treat these as having a higher priority even than your work with the child.

These relationships are not only a source of support for you, they are the check and balance, monitoring that you are not changing in harmful ways. Dan Hughes (1997, p. 214) says that if we join the child everybody loses, but if the child joins us everybody wins. As we keep the child company on their journey, change happens. You will not be the same person at the end as you were at the beginning, and neither will the child. It is imperative that all the change is in the direction of building attachment and not in the direction of destroying it. Yet the powerful experience of this work can result in us losing our way and going with the child into their own cold and frightening world. What we want is to enable a terrified child to enter safely into the warmth of secure attachments.

As well as the changes which occur in your life as a result of your work with the child, close relationships also change in their own right, they have a dynamic life of their own. Again, it is important to keep an eye on all the relationships in your social network, to ensure that you are not overtaken by events, finding yourself alone and friendless just when you most need a supporting presence.

If you do not with reasonable certainty have the protection of close, confiding, intimate relationships to sustain and support you reliably throughout the time you are giving commitment to the child, then do not proceed with the work. It will damage you. If you do have access to trustworthy and intimate others who are reliable sources of mutual support and joy, then go on to step three.

Step 3: professional supervision

Whatever your role in providing for the needs of children with unmet attachment needs, you must ensure that you have access to professional supervision. It is even more important that direct carers – parents, family network caregivers, adopters and foster carers – have access to professional supervision and support than it is for child care professionals whose work with the children is not carried out in their own life space.

Those who are closest to us will provide the core support which will keep us sane and resilient. But they will not be able reliably to provide the essential overview of the system which will reveal the direction in which we are moving, will alert us to any risks, and will propose systemic solutions which will be beyond the scope of our own vision; we cannot see the ocean when we are swimming in it. Only the professional supervisor can take on this function.

You may be fortunate enough to have clear structures of accountability which provide appropriate supervision in your work with the child. If not, it is necessary to find a supervisor for yourself and to submit yourself to a discipline which may often be uncomfortable but which will be essential for your safety and the safety of your family. Since this relationship too will be dynamic, it is important to keep the situation under scrutiny, and to make sure that your needs are met throughout the whole time of your commitment to the child. Over the course of the changing relationship with the child, even people who have access to professional structures of supervision may from time to time benefit from external consultation.

Although professional and external to your immediate relationships, supervision or consultation may be provided in many ways. It may not necessarily be frequent, it need not be costly if you are relying on your own funds, and it should be set within clear boundaries. It may be provided by any agency employing people with the skill and knowledge to assess the health of family systems and the progress of reparative work in the field of attachment.

When you have reasonable certainty of being provided with sources of professional supervision, it will be possible to move on to step four.

Step 4: working with others to build an environment which promotes secure attachment

All those who have made a commitment to the child now have to work together to construct an environment which will enable the child to move from the cold and lonely wasteland of unmet attachment needs to the warmth and safety and supportiveness of secure attachment relationships.

This environment must meet both the need for affective attunement and the need for reintegrative shame. It will be an environment in which all those close to the child are adopting a consistent approach which meets the child's needs, adapting the approach to fit their own role with the child, but providing great consistency in the basic structures surrounding the child. It will be an environment which respects the child as a unique and infinitely valuable individual with certain inalienable rights, and which also assumes that the child is a social being, born sociable and lovable, and able to discover their own sociability and their own lovable nature if liberated from overwhelming anxiety and shame.

Secure attachment arises out of parenting, where parenting is seen as the activities of the community into which the child is born that ensure that the needs of the child are met. When this social structure is in some way disrupted or challenged, there may need to be help for the immediate caregivers from the wider community, which we might consider to be preventive parenting. Such preventive parenting will enable the child to develop secure attachments despite the challenges; this may apply when babies are born with some impairment, or when parents or other caregivers experience illness or accident or trauma.

When children have suffered injury as a result of the developmental disruption, however, and have formed insecure attachments, then there will need to be more structured help from the community. This could be described as therapeutic parenting. It is parenting which aims to enable the child to move from insecure to secure attachment. If all else fails, it may be necessary for the child to be placed with new carers, and possibly also in an entirely new social environment. This I shall call therapeutic reparenting.

Parenting which has a therapeutic purpose, where there is an intentional effort to promote change in attachment patterns, is, like all parenting, a social phenomenon. It consists of the activities through which the community provides for the needs of the child to be met, but those needs now include the need for reparative work in relation to attachment. It is what is provided when those who have committed themselves to the child work together to construct a therapeutic environment for the child.

Therapeutic parenting and reparenting both require the creation of a formal care team around the child. The informal social structures which will sustain child development and prevent injury for securely attached children are not adequate to meet the needs of children with unmet attachment needs. Parenting insecurely attached children is often counter-intuitive; carers have to *learn* how to approach children who beyond infancy are unable to regulate stress and impulse, and they have to be reliably sustained in maintaining that approach. That is the task of the care team.

The child will need insightful interventions at every level of the social system. Health care, education, community activities, the justice system, counsellors and therapists, and every other service provider right through to central government, where the legal structures are created within which these services are provided, will all be contributing to the outcome of the reparenting. This is the ecology of human development described by Bronfenbrenner (1979).

Therapeutic reparenting

Thinking about the most extreme level of parenting intervention allows us also to develop an understanding of what will need to be the elements of a safe environment for children who have experienced less catastrophic disruptions of their social world. This section explores ideas for effective intervention with children who need reparenting.

Working with attachment issues

It is necessary when living and working with children with unmet attachment needs to maintain both stress and shame at manageable levels, while also providing the maximum possible opportunity for the child and the carers to develop a relationship of affectional attunement and reintegrative shame.

The child's ability to manage both stress and shame need to be constantly appraised and reappraised. Initially the environment should be constructed to keep both to an absolute minimum, and then gradually more everyday stresses and ordinary shame-inducing experiences can be added for the child to learn self-management in a setting increasingly similar to that of their peers.

In the composite children portrayed in Part I, Jay was unable to manage the stress of contact sport in school, and needed to be temporarily removed from that environment for the safety of others; he was also unable to manage the stress of other children coming home from school, and needed that stress to be defused and strategic alternatives to be provided. Shane was unable to manage the shame of having his gift apparently rejected, or the shame of his theft being discovered, and in the one case responded with rage and in the other with dissociation. In both cases he needed help to stay connected to what he had done, and to accept some logical consequences for his behaviour.

The environment should be one which enables carers to produce and sustain a certain attitude towards the child (see Hughes, 1998), and all those committing themselves to the welfare of the child will take their part in creating and maintaining such an environment. Above all, reparented children need to be, and to be able to feel, safe in their new setting. I shall use this word SAFE as a mnemonic for the required basic attitude of carers; it is just an aid to memory, the important thing being to grasp the nature of the underlying attitude which carers need to maintain throughout their time with the child. They need to have, and to hold through all adversity, an attitude towards the child which is Secure, Attentive, Friendly and Empathic.

Carers commit themselves to be:

Secure   Whatever their own attachment history and life story, by the time they are living and working with insecurely attached children, carers must be able to function as stable and adaptable persons, with a stability which cannot be destroyed by any disturbance the child may bring into the household. I have thought of this as creating a still centre to which the child can always return.

Attentive   The carers should be interested in the child, curious about this other human being sharing their household. They will be learning the child as a unique person, and deeply re-spectful of the child as a whole person whose very survival in the face of profound adversity demonstrates courage and resourcefulness. This attitude of benign interest will carry carers through many storms.

Friendly   Children need us to love them, but are likely to find the experience overwhelming. I find the concept of friendliness as an attitude helpful; not friendship, which comes from others, but friendliness. We do love our friends, and we also can be light and playful with them. These qualities of love and joy, combined with passionate commitment to their well-being, is what children need from us as carers.

Empathic Carers must be able to be empathic with the children. Many people unconsciously avoid empathy with children who have suffered such intense early adversity. To place ourselves inside the experience of such desolation is disintegrative, and we protect ourselves against disintegration. So carers need help to maintain empathy; the rest of the care team should commit themselves to keep the empathic carers safe.

Promoting affective attunement

The shape and structure of an effective environment to address the needs of children with unmet attachment needs and promote affective attunement will vary considerably according to the age and developmental stage of the child; the degree of dissociation and hyperarousal; the physical structure and location of the household; the needs of all members of the household; the wider family and social network; and locally available facilities.

The insecurely attached child lacks brainstem state regulation, social connectedness and empathy. Whatever their chronological age, these are functions of human personality laid down as patterns in the earliest period of brain development. Reparenting allows the child to acquire new patterns, but since the brain has optimal periods for such development, and these have passed and gone, the new patterns will be acquired much more slowly than they are in infancy.

Moreover, each child will be unique in terms of their genetic heritage, temperament and early experience. The journey which the carers and their supporters will take with the child will involve working hard to learn the child, and to adapt general principles to fit this unique person's developmental needs.

In principle, therefore, the aims of therapeutic reparenting are to compensate for the lack of stress regulation, to allow the child to adapt to their acquired or innate developmental injuries, to learn mechanisms which work for them to regulate stress, and to learn to relate to others in this new world where they are liberated from overwhelming stress and can explore the joys of sociability and conviviality. Here are some ideas to illustrate these basic principles.

Promoting reintegrative shame

Children who have not experienced reintegrative shame as part of the attachment cycle during the critical period of limbic brain development remain unable to regulate impulse. They are also subject to overwhelming stress when shamed. These children are out of control of their own impulses and at the same time are dominant and controlling in relation to others.

They need an environment where it is both safe and necessary for them to allow adults to be in control, an environment where shame is kept within bearable limits and is followed by overt reintegration into the group. The environment must be safe so that they can learn to trust the adults and it must be structured so that giving up the overwhelming need to be in control is the obvious minute-by-minute choice the child will make.

Choice is itself an issue. During the toddler period of limbic brain development, the establishing of autonomy and self-determination are key tasks for the toddler (Erikson, 1963). Children who have experienced disruption of this process will have difficulty, sometimes extreme difficulty, with choosing. I have known children in their late childhood for whom choosing between drinks on offer, or choosing food in a restaurant, or choosing clothes, are overwhelming tasks. The result may well be an older child producing a toddler tantrum in a very public place, which does not endear them to anyone.

The care team needs to work together to construct an environment in which the child can survive and begin to lay down new patterns of behaviour. Again this will be a slow process, much slower than it is in infancy, for then the brain is just developing as brains do, whereas

Examples of interventions to promote affective attunement

Environment	Activities for carers	Agency interventions
Physical environment Sounds, smells, colours, images, lighting, and fabrics: notice what soothes and what stimulates, and design the physical environment accordingly.	Provide rocking, rhythmic sounds, touch, massage, holding as appropriate. Establish routines for eating and sleeping, and step-by-step bring them in line with the rest of the household and the wider community.	Provide supervision and consultation for carers as needed. Assess and treat any illnesses. Provide appropriately for any specific impairment.
Time The child lives in time; structure the time environment to promote step-by-step normalisation of the key states of sleeping/wakefulness and stimulation/soothing.	Help with hair and skin care. Help with dressing, either actively helping the child to dress or symbolically helping by offering guidance and praise.	Provide routine health care and develop checks and monitor progress. Provide access to appropriate education.
People People are also part of the environment. Notice how the child reacts to different people in terms of stimulation and soothing. Design contact with those people to meet the needs of the child	Encourage playfulness, singing games, physical contact games, but within the limits of stimulation the child can currently tolerate. Talk to the child and establish mutual vocal, verbal and non-verbal communication. Provide interesting food, and encourage the growing child to form personal likes and dislikes around tastes and smells.	Provide equipment for carers to promote stress regulation and affective stimulation for the child. For example: special equipment used to promote development in children with impairment, toys, games, books, recorded music and so on.
	Establish rituals, celebrations and family stories and games which include the child actively within the limits of current tolerance for stimulation.	Provide respite for the carers as needed.
	Provide contact with the natural world, and encourage the child to experience and enjoy the rhythms of nature.	

These key elements of building an environment to promote attunement will need to be provided for all children, whatever their chronological age, who have not experienced the benefits of affective attunement in infancy.

now we are asking the child to invent patterns and connections for which the brain has no template (Miranda *et al*, 1998).

For the carers, this part of the work will be even more demanding than the establishment of affective attunement. The child may resist developing the trust to allow the carers to engender patterns for regulating stress, but at least when stress regulation happens it feels good. Here we are asking the child to trust the carers enough to allow these adults to take over control and provide patterns which eventually will allow the child to manage shame and regulate impulse. This will not feel nice while it is happening, and frazzled parents of toddlers will have sympathy with carers who must go through the same processes but with much bigger children and for so much longer.

Examples of interventions to promote reintegrative shame

Environment	Activities for carers[2]	Agency interventions
Physical environment Safety is the first priority. Children need to be safe even when they are out of their own control. Design the environment to allow constant unobtrusive supervision of children. Be clear about physical boundaries in the use of the house, and exclude children from private space such at the bathroom when others are using it. Consult children about decoration, furnishing and so on, but do not allow choices until the child is ready for them. Be clear that it is the adults who are making all the decisions in the home, but that	Ensure that adults and not children establish the emotional tone of the household. Encourage children to express thoughts and feelings, and accept them. Greatly limit choices. Explain to the child that choice is too hard for them at present, because they did not learn to make choices when they were a baby, but that they will be making more choices when the adults who care about them can see that they are ready. Show steady, friendly concern for the child's struggles to accept the discipline of living with other people.	Provide supervision and consultation for carers. Make sure that everyone is aware of the day-to-day care plan for the child, and supports the structures which will support the child. Monitor the situation carefully; ensure that every adult concerned is able to maintain the SAFE attitude. Provide clear structures for complaints and for maintaining the human rights of the child. If therapists are

---

2   Ideas drawn from experience and from the work of Dan Hughes (1997, 1998)

Environment	Activities for carers	Agency interventions
children's views are listened to.	Provide clear logical consequences for socially unacceptable or disruptive behaviour. Ensure that this is not punitive. Ensure that it is always carried through, and that shame is always followed by reintegration.	available to work with the child and the carers, ensure that the therapy and the daily care are integrated, and that the adults work together to provide safe structures for the child.
Time Provide clear time structures for days and weeks, and acknowledge or celebrate calendar events. Allow the child limited choices around timings, prepare them for events and then stick to the times given. Alternate restful periods with more stimulating activity.	Practise alternative inclusion. Remove the child from a situation where their beahviour is inappropriate, and keep them close to you. Use temporary exclusion ONLY where no other course provides safety.	Provide material support for activities with the child, and also for making good any damage which a child out of control may inflict on their surroundings at times.
People Ensure that all the children in significant contact with a child with poor impulse control and high shame arousal are able and willing to participate in this approach. The child will seek to divide adult solidarity in order to feel safe and in control; prepare for this and do not allow it to develop. Ensure that the child has free access to protective adults. and can express their thoughts and feelings to safe outsiders.	Express anger, if you feel it, but only in short bursts, not as prolonged irritability. Tell the child how you feel, but always include your commitment to them ('It's a good job I love you . . .').

Use the child's anger to comment on their growing attachment to you ('Only people who really do care get this angry . . .').

Limit the ability of the child to hurt you or any member of the household. | Provide respite for the carers as needed. |

Those who support the carers must therefore be prepared for this work to be demanding and sometimes exhausting. It is important that supervisors monitor the situation and prevent the carers from becoming exhausted. Equally important is for the supervisors to ensure that the carers do not come to accept the dominance of the child, and adapt to living with a child who has taken over the running of the household.

All the adults must understand the situation. Throughout this whole stressful process, they must never forget that eventually the child will be able to relax and trust those who love them and are trustworthy. Then at last they can let go of burdens which are far too great for them, they will be happier than they have ever been, and they will be able to begin to recover from the adversity of their early years.

Relating to self and others: rage, reflection and reciprocity

My toes blue with rage
the top of my head
hot with weeping, I shudder as the axe
comes down, what
will you do with me
when you hear the blow
where will you put me then?
Susan Griffin

Rage is the impulse to destroy what offends us. The child growing in their community of loving carers will have been developing, through the processes of attachment, the ability to regulate stress and impulse. Before the child is ready to take their place in the social setting that nurtures them, they will need to be able to regulate the most dangerous of their impulses.

As they gain a sense of self, so the child distinguishes a world beyond self, a world that can cause unpleasant sensations of frustration and shame and fear. These sensations are offensive, and can provoke a powerful impulse to destroy their source. The interactions between children and those who love and protect them during the period when they are exploring the experience of rage set the pattern for securely attached children to deal with the rest of the world.

Although this interactive system of the growing child and the social network is wonderfully adaptable and can absorb many chance occurrences and setbacks, it is also clear that there are many ways in which the process can go seriously awry, so that children develop insecure attachments. Not all insecurely attached children will be significantly impaired in their social functioning, but insecure attachment does lead to impairment and for some children the injuries are severe. These children will be considerably compromised in their capacity to regulate stress or impulse.

Children unable to regulate stress or impulse are not going to be able to manage rage. These are children who are at risk of becoming impulsive, aggressive and violent individuals. As adolescents and as adults they are significantly more likely to engage in violent acts (de Zulueta, 1993, Chapter 5). They will also be denied the other side of the social equation which unfolds itself as the child develops the patterns in the brain that inhibit rage, for the laying down of these patterns also lay down the origins of true reflection and reciprocity.

In experiencing the impulse to destroy the other, the child is confronted vividly with the reality of the existence of another being, a being who can be loved and hated, desired and destroyed. 'Aggressivity is therefore a technique or mode of love-seeking . . . and . . . heightens the sense of the other's presence' (Suttie, 1988, p. 63). Children are able for the first time to reflect on themselves as social actors, people who can make a difference in the world. And they are also confronted with the need to negotiate with the other, to re-establish attunement. The impulse to destroy is the most powerful of the impulses to be regulated through reintegrative shame. It makes a demand on the child to be active in seeking re-attunement. When you have really wanted to kill someone, you will later want to check that they are still alive and unharmed. In doing so, you re-establish dialogue. The child discovers the delights of reciprocity.

What happens?: theory and research about rage and anger

In terms of survival, rage is the third active option when confronted with an aggressor. The first option is appeasement; if we become small and still and harmless, and smile, the aggressor may be deflected. Amplify the activity of the limbic brain a little and the impulse will be to run away; flight can be an effective way of staying alive. Finally, if neither of the above is effective, the increasing stimulus to the limbic brain will produce the impulse to attack; if all else fails, try fighting. These are the three basic survival strategies all located in one small area of brain tissue called the amygdala (Carter, 1998, p. 90).

In the adult brain, the responses of the limbic brain are being continuously mediated by thinking. The survival strategies which are the 'quick and dirty' (Ledoux, 1977, quoted in Carter, 1998) responsiveness of the amygdala are kept in their place, to be activated only under extreme threat to life. The infant brain is not stable, however, and is not fully developed yet. The immature cortex does not have the capacity to regulate these responses. The young child can experience rage in relation to any offence.

There is a fractional time lag between the limbic system response to the offensive or threatening stimulus and the information about the stimulus event reaching the cortex. We have already started to react before we can start to think about what we are reacting to. Whatever the automatic limbic system response – appeasement, flight or fight – once the thinking brain gets hold of it, that response will be overridden unless the threat is intense. In almost all situations we meet as adults in everyday life, none of those responses is appropriate. Instead we will consider the situation on its merits, and make a judgement about the response we want to make.

The cortex can fail to regulate the outburst of rage in three different situations. Firstly, in traumatic events the intensity of the stimulus overwhelms the thinking brain; the cortex cannot regulate the response. Secondly, after certain illnesses or injuries, including some lasting injuries following intense trauma, the limbic brain spontaneously generates the impulse to attack; since nothing is happening in the outside world, there is no information from the environment to the cortex, and it is impossible for the cortex to inhibit the action of the amygdala. Finally, the signals from the cortex to the limbic system, the mechanism to override the fight response, may just be too weak or too diffuse to be effective, which is what happens in the brain of the toddler.

In young children the cortex is still developing. They are not able to override the powerful activity arising from the amygdala. They simply do not yet have the connections between the cortex and the limbic system in place to transmit clear focused inhibitory signals of sufficient power to restrain the activity of the amygdala. The cells in the prefrontal cortex do not mature fully until adulthood, but the process of gaining management of the activity of the amygdala can be accelerated.

Yet again, it is the response the child gets from the social setting that actually shapes the developing brain. The child who is helped to manage and later to inhibit rage is the child who grows the brain cells in the prefrontal lobe to inhibit the action of the amygdala more rapidly. Activity in brain cells also makes them more sensitive and easy to activate; in terms of the power of the brain, practice really does make perfect. The cells in the prefrontal cortex that specifically act to inhibit the activity of the amygdala are most effective in children who develop them early as a result of interaction with secure attachment figures and then use them often.

> The interactive process most protective against later violent behaviour [is] the formation of a secure attachment relationship . . . Here in one relationship lies the foundation of three key protective factors that mitigate against later aggression: the learning of empathy or emotional attachment to others; the opportunity to learn to control and balance feelings, especially those that can be destructive; and the opportunity to develop capacities for higher levels of cognitive processing.
> (Karr-Morse and Wiley, 2013)

As social beings violence both fascinates and terrifies us. Originating in the limbic system, violence is one of a limited set of basic survival strategies. These limbic system responses, and the emotions that accompany them, induce a focused state in humans, which may be called a trance state. Such focused states are an ordinary part of life; they are states of mind in which the entire frame of reference for thought, feeling and action is focused. Driving a car induces a driving trance; the focus of the driver is totally (we hope) on the road. Anything perceived while in a trance state which would break the focus is either not noticed or is reinterpreted to fit the trance. Occasionally driving trances deepen, and people travelling well known routes may find that they have "lost" a bit of the journey as their conscious mind gave way to the trance state.

The result of this focus is that we are unable to use processes of rational thought while in a trance state. Advertisers rely on the fact that trance states make us stupid, or at least highly suggestible about anything that can be linked to the trance. The four basic functions of the limbic brain – food, fear, fighting and sex – are all regularly to be found linked by advertisers to oddly irrelevant objects they want to sell to us. These subjects fascinate us, we can be entranced by them.

So anger, the emotion linked to rage and violence, is a trance state. We are not clever or resourceful or flexible or kind or thoughtful while we are angry. We are just angry. Yet the fascination with anger has led to many myths and fantasies developing around it.

There is, for example, a myth that it is dangerous to suppress anger. Given that the brain has specific pathways to ensure that anger can be inhibited by the cortex, this seems unlikely. Indeed, the safety of individuals, groups and whole societies depends on the ability of the human brain to override the limbic system response to threat. The amygdala is not clever or subtle; it may save our lives in situations of extreme danger, but it is not able to distinguish between extreme danger and many of the stimuli often present in our complex social world. Not only is it not dangerous to inhibit the response of rage or anger, it is socially essential that we do so.

To inhibit is not to deny or repress. We gain control of our responses, and in so doing we process the response in a different way. As we open our minds to a new frame of reference which includes but is not enclosed by the anger, the trance state alters. Different theoretical frameworks would interpret the phenomenon differently, but the important truth is that afterwards nothing is left. The process is complete. Unexpressed rage is not stored up waiting to do us harm, it has simply ceased to exist. The physiological changes that accompanied the anger can do harm to the body, but those are not alleviated by acting out the rage.

Another myth about anger is that repressed anger leads to depression. Both depression and anger are trance states, but they are not mutually exclusive. Some of the most depressed people are also the most angry. After traumatic stress, people often alternate in a disordered fashion between depression and rage, yet neither excludes the other, but they co-exist even in relation to the same set of events. It is also odd that anger is seen as the cause of depression; it is equally likely that if they exist at the same time, the depression causes the anger. In fact there is no evidence that suppressed anger causes illnesses or injuries provided the stress leading to the anger is manageable (Tavris, 1989, Chapter 4).

There are also myths about expressing anger. There has been a pervasive idea that anger must be acted out. The analogies used are those of dams holding back floods, or volcanoes waiting to explode. This sort of analogy is inaccurate. Expressing anger makes us more angry. Violence breeds violence. Pretending that we do not feel angry is also inappropriate. The effective approach is to struggle to find some prosocial way of saying who we are and how we are and what that might mean for other people.

If we feel angry, and our life is not being immediately threatened, then the anger is our problem and no one else's. Basic assertiveness can help greatly in dealing appropriately with angry feelings; I-messages, and being clear about personal responsibility for actions can do a great deal to resolve conflicts. Empathy helps; being aware of the preferences of the other person about anger makes a great difference. Some people like having arguments, others hate it. If two people like having a heated discussion, then no harm is done if they indulge their shared preference. If you are the only one in a group that loves a conflict, then you will not be popular.

It seems likely that the majority of human beings now live in a stressful environment. Noise, excessively stimulating visual images, chemical pollutants, overcrowding and rapid change are disturbing. Power and freedom and choice are restricted and unevenly distributed, which is disturbing. Under these conditions the impulse to hit and kick and bite other people is common. Most adults probably know the ache in the muscles of the back and shoulders and neck and jaw that follows meeting certain people, or being in certain situations. When the impulse to attack is inhibited, the muscles tell the story.

The problems arise when the inhibition is missing or distorted. The impulse is arising from the limbic brain interpreting complex stressors as extreme threat. The prosocial response is to have access to a wide and flexible range of mechanisms to do something else with the energy generated. The antisocial response is to attack. If the inhibition is missing, this antisocial response may be a straightforward physical attack causing harm to the person of another or the environment. If the inhibition is distorted, the attack may be against the self, or it might be a non-physical attack against another causing emotional harm through verbal and non-verbal communication.

In human beings, as in all animals more likely to be prey than predator, the impulse to survive, through attack if necessary, is benign. The impulse is benign but almost always misplaced in a world too complex for the simple limbic brain. The response to the impulse may be equally benign, utilising the energy for creative and prosocial activities. Or the response to the impulse may be harmful, in people who have not been able to develop the powerful and flexible links and pathways in the brain needed to inhibit the impulse constructively. Children, whose brains are still developing, will need the help of adults in their community to create such graceful and flexible responses; thus each unique personality develops in the interaction between the person, the social system that contains them, and the wider environment (Bronfenbrenner, 1979).

What do we observe?: signs and indicators of rage, reflection and reciprocity

Rage
Attacking others
Children who are unable to regulate rage adequately may be subject to sudden outbursts of violence or chronic anger or both. Sudden violence may erupt apparently out of the blue, and be very frightening

for all concerned. It sometimes involves considerable harm to others. The precipitating cause will always seem out of all proportion to the response, but will involve frustration or shame or fear on the part of the attacker.

Two children playing together amicably enough; one makes a mistake in the play, the other smiles – sympathetically? mockingly? – and within seconds the smiling child is on the floor and the other is on the run. The combination of frustration and shame for the first child provoked an instant and intense response. The explanation – 'he was laughing at me' – is recognised by everyone concerned to be inadequate.

> . . . many children who become impulsively violent had, as babies, subtle neurological abnormalities . . . But these begin-nings are not in themselves causal. Neurological differences only render a child more vulnerable to negative environmental circumstances. Whether children become poets or ax murderers depends on the interaction of biological and social factors . . . Though the processes are complex and often the injuries are unintended, when it comes to our babies, we reap what we sow.
> (Karr-Morse and Wiley, 2013

If sudden rage is frightening to live with, chronic anger is wearing. Living with children who are constantly expressing angry feelings is abrasive and can erode the fun and laughter in any household. Chronic anger may be expressed directly as physical bullying, or irritability and fault finding; the level of physical, verbal and non-verbal violence may be sufficient to cause significant harm to others. Or it may be expressed indirectly as tale bearing or innuendo; again this may reach extreme levels of predatory attention to the weaknesses and vulnerabilities of others.

Angry children who dissociate may get others to be angry for them. Watch out for the child who never seems to express an angry word, but somehow is always surrounded with furious people. Children who needle others until they provoke a response against a third party can disturb the equilibrium even of very stable groups.

And children who need others to be angry will find that the world is full of angry people in every setting.

Attacking the self

Young children who feel angry and are unable to regulate rage experience a dilemma. The people around them with whom they feel angry are the very people on whom they depend for survival. If they attack those on whom they are dependent, they may remove the source of their survival, yet the impulse to attack is arising from survival responses. Alice Miller (1990) discovered in her practice of psychoanalysis that children confronted with such a dilemma often resolve the problem by shifting the focus of the rage.

If the parents are the source of survival, yet the child feels the impulse to destroy the parents, then the child may decide that the parent is good and the child is bad. The proper object of rage then becomes the child and not the parent. This self-directed anger, like anger directed at others, may be expressed physically or symbolically.

Some self-harming behaviour is the result of this sort of rage against the self. ' "I hate myself", Lukas says unequivocally. "It's almost an insult for people to refer to it as a self-esteem problem. I'm talking active, passionate hatred . . . " ' (Strong, 2000, p. 12). Self-loathing is common among children who have been able to keep themselves safe in their dependency only by finding an alternative object for their impulse to destroy their parents. Lukas, a 43-year-old lawyer at the time Strong wrote about him, cut himself so savagely that he had recently needed a transfusion of two pints of blood.

Children who direct non-physical violence against themselves may be constantly self-derogatory. They experience and express self-loathing. Personal appearance is an indicator of self-hatred; children who hate themselves find it difficult to care for themselves, and may present in socially unacceptable ways that invite the rejection they feel they deserve. Hygiene, skin care, hair care, clothing are all likely to be neglected by the angry child.

Where the rage is triggered by shame, the anger may be related to intense perfectionism (Kaufman, 1992, p. 87ff). The child may attempt to hold the shame at bay by never doing anything to be ashamed about. Since this is doomed to failure, the child is then angry about their own failure. This provides a very compact mechanism for explaining, justifying and reinforcing the chronic anger the child feels. Children in this situation will set themselves impossibly high standards and then punish themselves for failing to reach those standards.

The shame-related rage may be a response to a particular aspect of the child's existence. Children may, for instance, set themselves the task of being the protector for their siblings or for one of their parents. They may then harm themselves whenever they fail in that self-appointed task. It is a task often first taken on during the period of development when children engage in magical thinking. This will mean that the responsibility extends far beyond the boundaries of physical space and time. Children who have not seen or heard from siblings for years may still harm themselves as punishment for failing to protect a child who has been hurt.

When fear is the trigger to rage, children who deflect the rage onto themselves may attack themselves when frightened. Here is a profound paradox – children who, in response to threatened harm, will harm themselves. Such children will experience self-loathing in any situation that provokes anxiety. This has a harmful impact on their social development, and prevents the building of social resilience. Anger and fear are both trance states that prevent the child from being open to the curiosity and interest in the world that will promote the growth of resilience and joy.

Attacking the environment
Sometimes children avoid feeling angry with dependency figures or with themselves by directing the rage at the wider environment. This rage may be expressed physically or it may be communicated verbally or non-verbally; it can be acute or chronic; and it is sometimes directed against the material environment and sometimes at the containing social group in an anonymous and impersonal way. The linking factor is the experience of the impulse to destroy, felt as anger.

Children may be destructive of their environment as an expression of rage. Sometimes this takes the form of outbursts of destructive behaviour. Older children and adults may continually trash their surroundings, either directing the violence at their most intimate spaces (a form of self-harm) or engaging in acts of vandalism and havoc (when the impulse to destroy is directed at the now anonymous other).

Alternatively, the anger can be directly expressed towards other people insofar as groups of strangers form the environment for the self. A young woman in a crowded tube train carriage sits down beside me. She looks around at the group of hot and weary travellers surrounding her and then turns on her personal stereo at such a volume that her eardrums must have been in peril. I watch other people register the aggressive act and recoil from it. Touching her arm I try to get her attention; she ignores me twice, but finally faces me. 'What?' she snaps. 'That's too loud,' I say, holding eye contact and indicating the personal stereo device. 'So?' – furious rage expressed in a word. I look at her a moment longer and then look away. After a minute, as I check off the seconds on my watch, she turns the device off. 'It's finished now. Satisfied?' she growls. For the rest of the half-hour journey we share I am the target of non-verbal anger of great apparent force, although when she gets up to leave she carefully avoids physical contact with me (a little accident would have been quite easy, and I half expect it). Other passengers break their own rules of non-verbal contact to offer silent thanks, though I know they find my behaviour almost as unsettling as hers.

Reflection

Some time in the second year of life, unless prevented by impairments of function, the child begins to develop a sense of self. Damasio (1999) refers to the development during the second year of the autobiographic self, the self that both exists and tells itself the story of its own existence. This is a step on the way to the development of the reflective self, able not only to act and to tell the story of that activity, but also to evaluate the emerging narrative in a social context.

Social accountability

This social accountability, the capacity to account for ourselves within and to our social milieu, is considered by Shotter (1984) to be the foundation of selfhood. It is clear that the child who is acquiring through social interaction the ability to inhibit impulses, including the impulse to destroy, is also acquiring the capacity for self-conscious reflection.

The impulsive behaviour of the young child provokes a response which interrupts the affective attunement that is the background state of securely attached children. The caregiver thus reflects to the child a sense of self as separate from the carer, an active self whose activity can be evaluated. At the same time, the carer provides the securely attached child with much evidence of approval and joy in their existence as a distinct and effective other. Episodes of shame are balanced with experiences of delight in socially acceptable and interesting behaviour. And the child who has developed through shame the sense of a separate self, can now share in that delight. They can acquire the beginnings of selfhood, discovering the joy and the anguish of a self-aware life.

Social unaccountability

Children with unmet attachment needs have restricted access to this reflective world. Distortions in the social construction of inhibition lead to difficulties with relationships, both with people and with the wider environment. Language development will be affected; securely attached children by the second year are beginning to be able to talk about who they are and how they are; insecurely attached children lack such inner state language. They tell us about the harm they are enduring through their inability to tell us how they are.

Reciprocity

As children discover self through interaction with others, so they can begin to relate to those others as beings like themselves. If the first step on the road to personality is trust, as Erikson believed (1963), then the next, autonomy, is equally a product of the social context in which the child is growing. Once the child can begin to regulate impulse, there is the possibility of choice, and of the making of right choices. Then, for the securely attached child, their trust can be reciprocated.

The child trusts the life-sustaining caregiver, providing that fundamental experience of reliance on a reliable universe which will carry most humans through even quite devastating experiences. Then, as the child becomes more effective as an active participant in this exchange, the caregiver trusts the child. This provides the child with the foundation for the second great assumption that secure humans make about the universe; they are able to believe that they are individuals worthy of respect from self and others. The third basic assumption (Janoff-Bulman, 1992) is that the universe has meaning, which arises as the reflective individual engages with the puzzle of relating to others and creating both a personal and a shared narrative from the experience.

Choice

Children who trust others, are trusted by others and trust themselves are able to make choices. They can reflect on those choices, and in evaluating their own decisions ascribe meaning to their world. No such graceful experience is open to the insecurely attached child. Children who have not experienced secure attachment are likely to be overwhelmed by choice.

As creatures dependent on social networks, every choice for us humans is a social negotiation. Every time we make a choice about anything, we create a change in the environment. Insecurely attached children will be restricted in their ability to negotiate these changes. Avoidant children generally will limit the social interaction of choice-making through dominance and attempting to control outcomes. Anxious ambivalent children often escape making choices through dependency and clinging, getting others to make choices for them and then sometimes raging about the outcome. Children with no organised pattern of attachment at all are often bewildered by choice even over simple things, and can remain perpetually in the role of victim as a result.

Choice generates unpleasant affect responses in children with unmet attachment needs. Their ability to inhibit the impulse to destroy what offends them is limited, so that being confronted with choice can result in rage. Enabling children to develop patterns of self-regulation involves carefully limiting the choices available to them, expanding the range of choice as they grow in their ability to manage choice without being overwhelmed (Hughes, 1998).

Sharing

Children who are discovering the pleasures of sociability and recognising the otherness of the rest of the human world are motivated to experiment with social behaviour. Taste this biscuit I've been sucking, hold this toy for a moment, and always with eyes locked on the face absorbing every nuance of affective response; this soon transforms into real social experimentation. By the third year of life, securely attached children are actively seeking reciprocal social interaction, and are willing to share both experiences and goods.

Sharing requires trust, however, and the ability to make reflective choices. It is not an option for children with unmet attachment needs. Children who are unable to share need to be protected from the experience of being overwhelmed, otherwise they will again be plunged into rage they cannot manage. It is important not to demand that insecurely attached children share with others, but instead to provide opportunities for them to do so and 'catch them doing something good' (Fahlberg, 2008). Then they can reflect on the double benefit of gaining the pleasures of sociability and praise from the same simple action. It is also important to keep the praise to a simple low-key affirmation, since praise can be overwhelming stimulus for children with unmet attachment needs. 'I can't bear it when I get praised in my review meeting,' says one young man, 'I usually have to break stuff afterwards.'

Respect for self and others

Developing sociability provides so many opportunities for mutual mirroring and reflection that the securely attached child rapidly develops a capacity for respect. Whatever their temperament, shy or outgoing, timid or brave, secure pre-school children show already well-developed capacities to manage social situations. They form and can articulate an assessment of the strengths and weaknesses of others, and they relate to others on the basis of that assessment. They treat others with respect and expect to be treated with respect themselves. They have a clear sense of justice and fairness, and demonstrate empathy in their awareness of others.

By contrast, the demands of social interaction are frustrating or shameful or frightening for children with unmet attachment needs. The securely attached child can take the 'I'm OK, you're OK' approach (Harris, 1973) but insecurely attached children are limited to the far less sociable permutations of that formula. Anxious avoidant children are likely to conclude that 'I'm OK, you're not OK'; anxious ambivalent children are more likely to take on the 'I'm not OK, you're OK' approach to others; while those anxious children with no organised attachment pattern are left to conclude that 'I'm not OK, you're not OK' is probably the order of the universe (Howe, 2011).

As frustration and shame and fear trigger the impulse to destroy, children with unmet attachment needs frequently experience rage in situations which for others would generate the experience of respect for self or others. Hence the overwhelming impact of being praised, or of recognising the praiseworthiness of others. Such triggers to rage are bewildering for those around, and frightening for the child.

It is hard to maintain an attitude of friendly attentiveness through the irritations and storms of daily life with children who struggle with impulse, shame and rage. Yet it is necessary to come back to that basic attitude as many times as our serenity is ruffled. It helps to ask yourself informed questions that illuminate your observations of the child. Such a questioning approach creates the space in which it may become possible to reflect on how life is for the child.

Examples of useful questions

How does this child deal with impulse?
How do they deal with anger?

Does the child provoke anger in others?
Are they able to express their feelings in words?
Are they able to be assertive?
How does this child deal with conflict?

What can we do?: approaches to helping children regulate rage

Anger management

There are a number of tried and tested approaches to anger management programmes for adults that can successfully be adapted to help children with managing anger. These tend, however, to rely on engaging neglected inhibitors or creating new inhibitions through learning. Children with insecure attachment patterns do not have established impulse inhibitors, so cannot be helped to engage such existing but underused inhibitions. They will need considerable time and patience before they will be able to develop patterns of self-regulation.

It is therefore important that carers give at least as much attention to the environment as to the internal experience of the child, establishing a safe milieu (Bettelheim, 1974) in which the child can join the carers and begin to develop new patterns of sociability. It is, as ever, vital to learn the child. What triggers rage for this child? What aspects of the environment are soothing? What provides safe stimulation, without provoking a rage response? Once these factors are recognised, and recognisable in other settings, then potentially overwhelming stimuli can be reduced to a manageable level. Then when the child has stabilised, the occurrence of everyday events, which for this child have been overwhelming, can be gradually increased to something more like normality as the child becomes more able to regulate their own responses.

Equally important elements of the environment are the other people who make up the human ecology of the growing child. Children with poorly developed inhibitors for rage need to be able to see those around them managing anger and conflict constructively. This is partly about being with people who are able to regulate their own impulses while being clear and open about their feelings.

Managing anger is not about never feeling angry, nor is it about pretending to feel something else; it is about recognising the inhibited impulse to destroy and transforming the energy to other uses. Similarly, resolving conflict is not about pretending that there is no conflict, but about dealing with others respectfully and openly to sort out the inevitable conflicts that arise when self-aware social beings try to live together. Children also need to have the experience of seeing that people who have lost control of their impulses apologise and make reparation. To err is human, to make good the error is even more human.

For the child, the first step to managing anger will be to recognise the inner experience of the impulse to destroy before acting on it. Insecurely attached children may have little capacity to recognise inner state changes; whatever approach to anger management is being tried, and carers will need to experiment, the aim will be to promote recognition of how it feels to be getting angry. Then the child needs to be able to gain some control over that experience.

It is important to stay with the unique experience of the child. One boy said he got a buzzing in his head when he was about to "blow". He could gain no control over the buzz directly, as a sound, but when asked what colour it was (the limbic brain does not distinguish sense from nonsense) he said it was brown. Once he found he could turn the brown buzz pink he began to feel more able to manage his temper. This sort of modality change, drawn from neurolinguistic programming, is often helpful to children struggling to gain some control over inner states (Beaver, 1997).

Another child, a teenage girl subject to violent tantrums, discovered that she could dissipate the rage if she held her breath and ran to a particular tree. As she wrapped her arms around the tree and exhaled, she felt the rage was taken into the tree and she no longer felt dangerous. Gradually this led to an ability to manage the rage arousal through breath control without the intervention of the accommodating but non-portable tree, and she became socially adept in a range of situations and settings.

The child needs to learn the feeling of the experience of being triggered to rage, not the trigger events. It is helpful for carers to notice what are trigger events for the child, so that they can ensure a low stimulus environment in the early days, but it is of little value for the child to do so. Angry people become increasingly angry, and triggers multiply faster than they can be recognised and avoided; in any case, avoidance is a poor strategy for managing anger.

Anger is the feeling associated with a particular set of physiological changes. Like all such change sets it can become addictive. The body and mind can become habituated to the experience, dependent upon it to feel normal, and need increasing doses to achieve the same sense of normality. People can become addicted to being angry. When this is part of the problem, children who are being helped to manage anger will also need help to accept a different version of how it feels to be normal. A low stimulus, low conflict environment, while essential, will feel very boring indeed for such children. They will need to learn to appreciate the delights of equanimity, harmony and tranquillity.

Agencies have a responsibility to ensure that everyone stays as safe as possible when families are caring for children with limited impulse inhibition. Quite young children can be a danger to themselves and others when they are unable to manage destructive impulses. Families that lack or fail to use supervision are very vulnerable in this situation. Their love for the child can lead to a collusive situation which is actually one of domestic violence. I have known loving foster carers who had so far accommodated to the violence that even when the child beat the carer with a stick several times a week it was tolerated as being part of the price to be paid for being a carer. It is the responsibility of the professional network around the caring family to supervise the situation carefully and to ensure that the family and the child are kept safe.

Assertiveness

Children who are learning to manage anger need also to learn to be assertive. Again there are many established approaches to training people to be appropriately assertive, and again these have largely been designed with adults in mind. Such approaches will need to be adapted to enable children with unmet attachment needs to learn assertiveness.

The first step is always to enable the child to identify their own inner experience. Children who dissociate readily, who are unable to make choices and who lack self-respect are poorly equipped to identify and express their own needs and feelings in any situation. Every possible opportunity can be taken to encourage the child to recognise and communicate both feelings and needs. This will be immensely scary for children who are unable to trust others; to say what we need and how we feel is to make ourselves vulnerable.

Next, children need also to become aware that others also have needs and feelings. The dominance of some avoidant children should not be confused with assertiveness. Demanding what we want is far removed from stating what we need and feel. Being dependent on social relationships, children must learn to recognise their own place in the social network, and to seek appropriately to have their needs met and their feelings accepted. However self-protectively resistant they may be to such dependency, children cannot develop to their potential until they can let go of that resistance and abandon themselves to trusting their social network to support them. They need to join us in the terrifying safety of loving and being loved. Once children can recognise their own experience and acknowledge and respect the experience of others, they are ready to practise being assertive.

Conflict resolution

Being able to express needs and feelings assertively will not diminish conflicts, indeed it may bring to the surface all sorts of underlying conflicts of interests, needs and wishes. It is impossible for people to live together without conflict. We are self-aware beings, conscious of our separate identities and our individuality, even as we are dependent for our well-being on our social network and our intimate relationships.

Learning to resolve conflict is part of preschool experience for securely attached children. By the third and fourth year of life, most children are able to tolerate frustration without misperceiving it as threat, and are able to inhibit the impulse to destroy the source of the

Examples of interventions to promote the beginning of self-control, reflection and reciprocity

Environment	Activities for carers	Agency interventions
Physical environment It requires some thought and constant reappraisal to provide an environment that is both low in stimulus to rage and yet interesting and stimulating to children developing assertiveness and negotiating skills. It will be worth the effort, however, and gradually the need to restrict stress levels can be relaxed as the child develops strategies. The aim is to normalise gradually, remembering that the world beyond home will contain much to make us angry. *Time* Ensure that time structures include periods of relaxation and low stimulus. Help the child manage such times, and be prepared to offer support for children who find low stimulus environments challenging. This support should include helping the child to put into words their feelings, including boredom and ennui, and to identify and value quiet happiness *People* Recognise people who act as frequent triggers to rage and help the child to develop strageties for contact with those people.	Learn formal techniques for anger management, assertiveness training, and conflict resolution and spend time reflecting on how these can be trannslated into useful tools for this child at this time. Practise these skills in your own life, and discuss openly the experience of so doing. Help children find words for affects and feelings, and to distinguish between different feelings in different situations. Encourage children to wonder about the feelings of others, and to explore the effects of negotiating with others. Encourage the use of expressive media such as writing, drawing, painting, and any of the creative and performing arts, and then encourage children to talk about what they are doing. Teach children about listening and taking turns in conversation, and show them that you also listen and value the contributions of others in discussion. Teach children how to apologise if they have hurt someone, and be ready always to apologise if you have been hurtful.	Ensure that carers have access to formal training in anger management, assertiveness and conflict resolution. Ensure that supervisory staff have also undertaken such training, and can supervise carers appropriately in putting the training into practice and in teaching it to children. Assess the well-being of all members of the caring family and ensure that no one is being victimised or bullied. Provide resources for the family to explore self-expression through a range of media and activities. Encourage children and carers to prepare for formal meetings and to express themselves in a range of settings. Promote multi-agency provision to meet the needs of the family. Provide specialist support and consultancy as needed. Provide respite for carers and their families.

frustration, shame or fear. These young children are ready to progress in their social skills as they learn to negotiate with others over conflicts.

Children with unmet attachment needs, however, find it much more difficult to distinguish between unpleasant affect and threat. These children will tend to respond to conflict with appeasement, avoidance or rage. They will need to be taught to confront conflict constructively, trusting that sociable beings can always negotiate a settlement. Such learning will be a slow process for people who have developed neither the foundation of trust nor the social structures of autonomy on which such negotiated settlements depend.

Those caring for insecurely attached children need to learn formal approaches to conflict resolution and to be creative in applying these to family life. They also need to explore ways to teach such approaches to children who struggle to recognise their own feelings, needs and wants, let alone being able to recognise that others have similar claims on the universe.

7 Trauma: transformative experience

You gain strength, courage and confidence by every experience in which you really stop to look fear in the face.
Eleanor Roosevelt

. . . the consequence of a trauma of this kind is that the child tends to regress to an infantile level of behaviour . . .
Gordon Trasler

Fear

Human beings need fear; it keeps us safe from harm. The fear response protects us by preparing us physically, mentally and emotionally to deal with dangerous situations. People who suffer brain injuries which leave them incapable of experiencing fear are very vulnerable to harm (Damasio, 1999, p. 62ff), for we live in an uncertain and often dangerous world, and our survival often depends on being able to recognise, assess and respond to risk.

Like anger, fear is a self-assertive emotion which tends to throw us onto our own resources and alienate us from others. The human characteristics of sociability and conviviality are diminished with the onset of fear. Securely attached people, however, can often retain their inherent sociability even when afraid and then shared fear can be a bond which actually enhances social cohesiveness. Thus fear can be a creative force as it generates energy to handle threat and provokes improved social communication and mutual support.

For insecurely attached people, the isolating impact of fear is damaging to their already fragile social connectedness. Fear is then profoundly destructive of the social fabric and of the individuals who most need the support of those social structures. Fear may strengthen the resilient, and stretch them to exercise their personal and social skills and ingenuity, but it harms the vulnerable.

Trauma hits hardest at those who are most vulnerable, but the overwhelming terror experienced can cause even the most securely founded and resilient personality to disintegrate. For traumatic events go far beyond the limits of ordinary frights and anxieties; they are, by definition, extraordinary. Children who have not been exposed to earlier adversity may still be harmed by the effects of terrifying experience, suffering injuries that leave lasting distortions of personality development.

In this chapter, the consequences of overwhelming fear, the impact of such fear on vulnerable children, and the long-term effects of the post-traumatic disorders which may result from such terror are all examined. The second section explores in more detail the patterns of behaviour we may observe in children who have been subject to traumatic stress, which is another way of describing overwhelming terror. Finally, there are ideas and suggestions for establishing an environment within which children who have been injured in this way may recover and thrive.

What happens?: theory and research about traumatic stress

Trauma

Like all living organisms we generally have an inbuilt preference for survival; for most of their lifespan, living beings seem to endeavour to stay that way. When confronted with a situation which realistically appears to threaten our continued existence, we have an automatic response that greatly enhances our chances of coming out alive. This is known as the traumatic stress response, and the situations which provoke it are known as traumatic events.

Traumatic stress has consequences which can lead to mental health problems. It has therefore been a subject of some interest to the medical profession, and there are a number of diagnostic texts which offer definitive statements about trauma, such as the *Diagnostic and Statistical Manual* of the American Psychiatric Association (1994). Such definitions lead us to conclude that there are two components to traumatic experience.

First there must be an external event, in which the person is confronted with actual or realistically perceived threat to the life or personal integrity of self or others. Then there must be a response to the event which includes fear, helplessness or horror. Thus trauma is by definition a combination of an external event and an internal experience.

Take note that the event may have occurred to "self or others". It is important when looking at the needs of children who have been in situations of domestic violence to recognise that we can be traumatised by witnessing the violation of others. There is some evidence that disorders may be even more common and more severe among those who have witnessed extreme violence, for example, than among the direct victims, however terrible their experience (Harris-Hendricks *et al*, 2000, p. 26).

Traumatic stress

Those fortunate enough to develop through infancy without major disruptions emerge from the toddler period as sociable and convivial people. Whatever their particular heritage and temperament, they will have a preference for liking and trusting other humans, they will find others interesting, and they will be able to live with others in social groups.

Although always adapting and changing throughout life, the brain is fully formed around the time at which, in our society, children are going to school. Under ordinary circumstances children are then, like adults, responding to their environment in a way which engages activity across all levels of the brain (Carter, 1998). In extreme danger, however, the brain responds differently. The limbic system is activated instantly when the threat is perceived, and the body is flooded with stress hormones.

Small doses of stress hormone tone us up and make us more alert and active. But dosage is crucial. In a traumatic situation the stress hormone levels are toxic to some aspects of our functioning; we are actually injured by our own survival response. The organism prefers survival with injury to extinction.

The effect of this stress hormone overload is to alter the functioning of the entire personality. Brain, body and social relatedness are all radically changed. The state-regulating brainstem and emotion-regulating limbic brain take over and critical areas of the cortex and mid-brain are blocked as blood supply to them reduces (van der Kolk *et al*, 1996). Specifically, oxygen to the area known as the hippocampus, which ordinarily has many functions including acting as a communication route between the limbic brain and the cortex, a sort of cognitive map for feelings, is reduced. And part of the brain called Broca's area, in the left frontal cortex, which allows us to express internal experience in words is also deprived of oxygen. 'Thus at the point of trauma there are no words for what is happening to us because the areas of our brains which generate the words are turned off. Trauma is always wordless terror' (Cairns, 2010).

Physically, the body is instantly prepared for flight or fight. All activity is suspended which slows us down or which uses oxygen that will be needed for urgent action. Digestion, elimination (which may occur spontaneously) and sexual arousal are all temporarily stopped. The long muscles of the arms (for hitting) and legs (for kicking and running away) and shoulders and jaw (for biting) tense up in preparation for action. Heart rate, blood pressure and breathing all alter to ensure the oxygen supply to these muscles.

Socially, attentiveness to others is restricted and the capacity to experience joy through social interaction ceases. People who can otherwise engage with others in a mutual and reciprocal relationship which is pleasurable begin to see others much more as means to an end when overtaken by the need to survive. There is a numbing of social responsiveness, and of feeling, so that victims of trauma can seem to be shut behind a glass wall, present in the social exchange, but somehow not really participating. The lights may be on, but in important ways there is no one at home to greet visitors.

In adults and physically mature older children, trauma generates the full flight or fight response. Children, however, are generally flight animals (Roberts, 2000). Adult humans are curiously balanced between being predators and being prey, but children have the responses of prey animals when confronted with threat. The overwhelming urge is to be elsewhere. Given open space the prey animal will run; when cornered they will either switch off, reducing the pain and terror through reducing consciousness, or they may then use teeth and claws in a desperate last attempt to avert catastrophe.

Traumatic stress disintegrates the structures of personality in children whose brains are fully developed. It distorts the developing personality in younger children, whose brain function is not yet fully formed. Younger children subject to trauma are more likely to freeze and regress than to enter a state of preparedness for flight. In terms of survival, the young child is unlikely to be able to escape the source of the terror. Instead they generate an extreme version of the attachment behaviour of infancy; they generate behaviour which will prompt any adult to rescue them who is attuned to the "help me" signals of distressed infants. If this fails, they switch off from the pain, reducing conscious awareness of their environment to reduce awareness of the overwhelming terror and pain.

At whatever age they are acquired, traumatic stress injuries are the puncture wounds of the psyche. Leaving little outward sign, they are in reality deep and devastating, and long after they appear to have healed they may still be festering, producing effects which can be far removed from the original injury.

Spontaneous recovery

Traumatic events are extraordinary, well beyond the ordinary rough and tumble of the world. They are not, however, uncommon. We need only look around at the world, with daily news bulletins of natural disasters, wars, catastrophic accidents and deliberate or casual violence to recognise that, within the global population, trauma is a common occurrence (see, for example, van der Kolk *et al*, 1996, p. 135 for a discussion of the prevalence of traumatic stressors).

Fortunately most people most of the time are able to recover spontaneously from the experience of traumatic stress. Personal vulnerability and the nature and extent of the stressor play a part in the outcome, but these are infinitely variable. Beyond these variables there are three essential factors which make this recovery possible:

1   safety and stability;
2   secure social networks with well-formed attachment relationships;
3   the ability to express what has happened.

We cannot begin to recover from trauma until we are clear of the events which threatened us and in a safe environment. Once we are in a safe setting, we begin to stabilise; stress hormone levels start to fall and a process of healing for the stress-induced injuries spontaneously begins. Traumatic stress is a social phenomenon; it critically damages our capacity to relate to others and to understand our world. Recovery from trauma is a psychosocial process, which takes us on a journey requiring us to find both witnesses and companions who will love us enough to hold us steady as we face our terrors.

In this safe enough space the ever-adapting brain begins to re-establish balance, order and meaning. Our ordinary memory of events has a narrative form; Broca's area is centrally involved in the creation of narrative memory. Not surprisingly, after trauma we have no narrative memory of the events. Instead we have a jumble of sensory perceptions of the trauma, unmodified by any reflection and recorded just as they occurred, captured in the limbic brain. This is not a stable situation for the human brain, which will seek greater equilibrium.

Once stability is established, the limbic system begins to discharge the stored sensory impressions, producing for the recovering victim the experiences of flashbacks, nightmares or persistent ruminations on the traumatic events which characterise traumatic recovery. Once accessed, the traumatic memories can then be processed and rendered harmless through transfer to the narrative life memory. We do this through telling the story. Children will play or act out the story, having less access to language, and will need help to activate Broca's area through talking through the scenes they are acting out.

This process of making narrative out of terror, which enables our brains to function again, can take place because being in a safe place among safe people allows us to take this little bit of memory and relive it safely, without crossing the threshold into being overwhelmed by the totality of the original disintegrative experience.

Even thinking about the trauma raises the levels of stress hormones, however. The next part of the automatic recovery process allows us to recover from that. So there is a time of avoidance, when anything which could remind us of the trauma is carefully and unconsciously avoided. This avoidance part of the recovery cycle continues until the levels of stress hormones have fallen within safe limits again. Then the process of recall, when memories of the trauma intrude into everyday life, repeats itself.

This cycle of alternating intrusion and avoidance continues until the whole traumatic experience has been safely processed and rendered harmless. By that time the victim of trauma has ceased to be a victim and become a survivor. The trauma has ceased to be an ever-present reality dominating life, and becomes a memory of something unpleasant that happened in the past and is now over.

Recovery is not complete yet. The trauma has been consigned to the past where it belongs, but the survivor is not restored to wholeness. For traumatic stress disintegrates the structures of personality, and diminishes the sociable and convivial human being to a defensive and defended isolate. The recovering survivor needs now to undertake a further journey of discovery. They need to find answers to the question 'Who am I, now that I am not who I was before?' to redefine their own identity in the new world in which they find themselves. And they also need to explore their own personal and social power and efficacy in that world, now that they have stopped feeling helpless and hopeless. Finally, they need to let go of the miserable greyness which will have covered them since they entered the gloomy world of terror, and open up to the possibility of joy and delight.

There are three factors necessary for recovery from trauma, all other things being equal. We can see that there are also three phases to the recovery process:

1   stabilisation;
2   integration;
3   adaptation.

Those who have survived trauma are fully reunited with the flow of their lives when they have travelled all the stages of this journey. More than this, many find that they feel that they have been positively transformed in the process (Joseph, 2011). There is a change of perspective and of value which follows recovery from trauma, and many survivors find that they are never the same again. They often feel that in certain respects their lives have been enriched by the ordeal. There are many ways of interpreting this experience, and the shades of meaning are not lost on the survivors, but the fact is that this common though extraordinary experience can have the effect of stretching the personality to explore beyond previous limits. To pass through the black hole of trauma is to emerge into a new world.

Post-traumatic stress disorder

Recovering from trauma is painful and distressing. It may be some small comfort for the survivor to know that not recovering is worse. If we do not have the social environment or personal resilience to process, integrate and adapt to the trauma, or if the traumatic events were so horrific that they overwhelm even substantial social and personal resources, then we face the prospect of being unable to recover.

Then the troubles begin. It is intensely disturbing to go through the process of recovering from traumatic stress when we are in a safe environment, have already established internal processes for regulating stress, have secure attachments, and have access to supportive people with whom we have the close confiding relationships which will enable us to feel safe with them and enable them to commit themselves to keep us company on a difficult journey.

If these elements are missing, the victim of trauma must either bury the trauma and hope it stays buried, a task no more likely to be successful than most of our attempts to dispose forever of highly toxic waste, or enter into the recovery process hoping that it will be effective even in the absence of key essential ingredients. These are not options open to conscious choice. The decisions, if such they are, are made at the level of the organism; whichever of the two equally uncertain courses is taken, survival and health will be the aim.

Recovering from trauma involves allowing the personality to

disintegrate and reform. We need our social network to hold us safe while we fall to pieces, keep us company while we make the journey of exploration which at last leads to a new identity, and act as surety that we have continuity, that even utterly changed we are still the same people they have always known and loved. It is clear that, if vital elements of the equation are missing, that can be a dangerous, indeed a catastrophic process which will disintegrate the personality.

Burying the trauma may seem the more hopeful course. Unfortunately, traumatic stress is highly toxic and tends to penetrate even the strongest psychic defences. Trauma can be contained, but the container will always leak. Thus people may live their life seeming to have recovered from the trauma but in reality living with symptoms for which the cause is deeply buried. These symptoms can have a severe impact on life, including a whole range of physical, mental and emotional symptoms of severe stress apparently without cause. Even more serious is that the buried trauma makes the outwardly stable personality critically unstable under pressure. The person who is unable to recover from their first experience of trauma is much more likely to disintegrate when further trauma strikes.

Post-traumatic stress disorder (PTSD) seems to happen when the victim of trauma lacks the resources to recover, but the recovery process gets going anyway (Joseph, Williams and Yule, 1997). Attempting to end the extreme instability of the post-traumatic period, the limbic brain begins to discharge the stored fragments of memory of the trauma despite the fact that stress hormones have not fallen to safe levels. Now the flashback or nightmare or thought of the trauma, instead of being a step on the way to processing the event and transferring it safely to narrative memory, becomes a cause of new overwhelm.

Whenever the system is exposed to the toxic doses of stress hormones associated with traumatic stress, there is injury to brain, body and sociability. With no escape from the terror of being overwhelmed, the limbic system then activates the avoidance part of the cycle in a desperate attempt to stop the increasing injury. This just produces a whole new set of symptoms, however, without in any way solving the problem.

By the time the person exposed to trauma is suffering the three-fold burden of continuing high levels of stress arousal, intrusive re-experiencing of the trauma and attempts to avoid being reminded of, or thinking about, the trauma, they are well on the way to developing PTSD. If these three produce symptoms severe enough to interfere with ordinary life, and the symptoms persist over time, then they will meet the criteria for such a diagnosis.

What do we observe?: signs and indicators of disorder

Post-traumatic disorders are complex and global in their impact. No two children will respond in exactly the same way, for each personality is unique, and it is that unique personality which is disrupted by the traumatic stress. Yet we will see in each uniquely affected child the signs of the four principal elements of PTSD: hyperarousal, numbing, intrusion and avoidance. Each of these will produce symptoms, which the child will experience as disruption of normal functioning and we will experience as behaviour.

Disruption of normal functioning
Hyperarousal: permanent red alert
The underlying state of people disordered after trauma is one of hyperarousal. This produces a range of direct physical, psychological and social symptoms of arousal. Major body systems are affected; heart rate speeds up and blood pressure rises, digestion alters, as blood supply is diverted to functions more vital to immediate fight or flight survival; the long muscles, which will largely contribute to that survival, are primed with increased blood supply and tense up; every body function changes in response to the signal to survive at any cost.

Blood supply to the brain also alters, with oxygen supply to key areas of the cortex and midbrain reducing dramatically, while the limbic brain becomes kindled to respond to every threat. People disordered after trauma jump to every stimulus, however neutral. Patterns of sleeping and eating are changed, and there are great difficulties with concentration and attention, as the overactive limbic brain searches the environment for threat and excludes other sorts of conscious awareness. When everything is threatening then everything is more or less equally threatening. Hyperaroused people seem to be very alert to threat, yet in reality are very poor at assessing risk.

Socially the hyperaroused person is unable to connect with others. Social connectedness relies on intentionality (Shotter, 1984), the capacity we humans have to relate to others not only on the basis of what they do but according to our assessment of their intentions. Traumatised people are unable to have intentions of their own beyond the will to survive; this supersedes all other intentionality (Cairns, 2010, p. 61). They are also unable to judge the subtle intentions of others, for their whole being is focused on the possible threat others may present.

Numbing: cutting out all distractions

Trauma also produces physical, psychological and social numbing. Survival is the aim, and anything which slows down vital responses is dispensable. So self-generated opioids provide relief for the pain which may be produced by this threat to existence itself; an average sized adult male triggered to trauma will spontaneously generate the equivalent of eight milligrams of heroin. Pain slows us down, and however useful its function under ordinary conditions, threatened with extinction it is a luxury.

Emotional responsiveness is equally a luxury of safety. It can be dispensed with under extreme threat, and given that it will take time, energy and attention away from surviving, that is just what happens. Feelings close down, and the parts of the brain which provide words for feelings, allowing our language-based brains to process the feelings, are also deprived of oxygen (van der Kolk et al, 1996). Instead of the usual rich mixture of affects and feelings available to humans, the disordered person is reduced to an emotional range which goes from extreme fear to extreme rage with no points in between. The rate of acceleration from rest to terror would be the envy of any sports car fanatic. Rest being, of course, itself a relative term. What the trauma victim thinks of as rest would be uncomfortable for non-traumatised people.

Trauma produces a condition called anhedonia, the loss of the capacity to experience joy (van der Kolk *et al*, 1996, p. 421). Joy is vital to human beings, it is the prime motivator for non-essential activity – which, of course, is why it is turned off under extreme threat. In particular, interaction with other people beyond the most basic F-words (fight, flight, feeding and . . . reproduction) is motivated by the possibility of joy. Conversation, intimacy, discourse, playfulness and simply keeping company with others are activities which humans find pleasurable, except when the capacity for joy has been excised from their lives by trauma. Then life is a dull grey wasteland, days are to be got through, and other people are threats or resources or just not of any interest at all.

Intrusion: living in the past

Trauma is not over when it's over; it will not leave us alone to get on with our lives. Once disorder has set in, it is as though the trauma is perpetually present, even when there is no memory of it at all. Nightmares, panic attacks, obsessive thoughts about the specific trauma, or if that is out of awareness, then about anything catastrophic, strange compulsions to re-enact what cannot be remembered, all these are the everyday experience of those who must live with the effects of unprocessed trauma.

Deprived of emotional responsiveness, and unable to process experience, the disordered person has only two responses to events which trigger re-experiencing of the trauma – terror and rage. People whose attachment history has given them perfectly serviceable mechanisms for regulating stress and impulse lose those controls under the impact of traumatic stress disorders. They are then subject to the primal terror of annihilation and the dizzying sense of being out of control in response to stimuli which may be more and more objectively neutral.

For once in the grip of disorder, the intrusive re-experiencing of trauma may be triggered by events far removed from the original traumatic experience. An abused child may register the sound of a stair creaking as associated with the onset of abuse; later they may have no recall of the abuse itself, but may be triggered to a traumatic stress response by sounds reminiscent of a creaking stair. It is clear that the range of possible stimuli of this order is vast.

Such triggering can also become progressively further removed from the original traumatic events. A child hears a trigger sound while painting a picture at school and suffers a panic attack; later, the same experience of panic may be triggered by the smell of paint, or the prospect of an art lesson, or seeing the art teacher in the street. It is very easy for false conclusions to be drawn about the origins of traumatic experience, and the original experiences may be buried under many layers of secondary trigger incidents.

In the end the kindled limbic system, desperately struggling for equilibrium in dealing with unprocessed traumatic material, may be generating such a stream of catastrophic inner experience that the victim is effectively being retraumatised by their own disrupted internal processing. This is the vicious spiral of PTSD. Without any external stimulus at all, the nightmares, flashbacks and catastrophic thoughts can be enough in themselves to create new traumatic stress.

Avoidance: how to feel safe on The Titanic

I once knew someone who was very short sighted and lived in a building with floor to ceiling windows looking out onto a pathway much used by tourists. My friend had no difficulty with the lack of privacy; if she wanted to change her clothes, or just to feel alone and unobserved, she simply took off her glasses.

Living as we do in a world where many things are beyond our control, and yet needing a sense of control in order to feel safe, our minds provide an escape route. If things are truly unthinkable, we are able not to think them. This is much more difficult than it sounds. Try not thinking about your tongue, for example. Can you do it? If we decide not to think about X, then we have already thought about it.

Avoidance is therefore a very complicated process. It involves cutting out all possible reminders of an uncomfortable or dangerous topic, and then hiding not just the topic but also the process by which we have avoided the topic out of reach of our consciousness. The cost of avoidance is very high. We lose the risk of being overwhelmed by the fear, but we must also lose part of our integrity, splitting our awareness so that we no longer know what part of us knows.

Like everything associated with trauma, avoidance is not just an individual but also a social phenomenon. Groups, communities and whole societies have shared avoidance topics, areas of reality which are unthinkable and therefore are taken not to exist. The penalties for individuals who expose the existence of things whose existence is socially denied may be extreme. The little boy who laughed at the invisibility of the emperor's new suit may have survived in Hans Andersen's story, but in real life history tells of many who have paid a high price for simply showing the unacceptable truth.

The curious consequence of our social need for avoidance in order to maintain an illusion of control, is that the very existence of avoidance as a defensive strategy against fear is denied. Traumatised people in the grip of complex patterns of avoidance and denial are treated as though they were behaving rationally and with intentionality. To acknowledge that they are unable to see the origins of their own driven behaviour is to become aware that we too are much less rational than we like to think.

One test for the existence of avoidance is the existence of inappropriate passion in relation to the topic ('methinks the lady doth protest too much'). Some traumas are more socially acceptable than others. Victims of socially acceptable traumatic events are more likely to have their behaviour noticed and attributed to the trauma; victims of less acceptable trauma are more likely to be defined as individually bad or mad. These labels are rarely assigned dispassionately; victims of socially unacceptable traumas are often treated harshly and vindictively by the rest of society.

The social acceptability of traumas varies across communities and across time. The history of the uncovering of child sexual abuse is a prime example of this change over time. When Freud first wrote about the sexual abuse of children, he quickly discovered the social consequences of confronting avoidance, and entered into denial of his own insights (van der Kolk *et al*, 1996, p. 53ff); it was many years before the topic was to become publicly acknowledged, and there are still many areas of avoidance and denial around this previously taboo subject.

The behaviour tells the story

Children who have lived through trauma and lacked the environmental support needed for recovery will be different from their peers in many aspects of daily life. The disorders that follow trauma are so global in effect that disorder becomes the new normality.

Children in this situation often say that they just want to be normal; what they mean is that they want to be like other children, children who have not been radically changed by traumatic stress, for in truth it is normality itself which has been distorted for traumatised children. The children portrayed in Part I, composites of many traumatised children, illustrate the day-to-day impact of such distortion. For the child this experience of perpetual fear is seamless. One way or another, it is the fear that produces the whole range of signs and symptoms we can observe. It may help to think of these behaviours under different headings, but it is important to bear in mind constantly that these divisions are meaningless to the child, who simply has the thread of their daily experience to live through.

More significant still is that our willingness to think of the problems under different headings and from the perspectives of different agencies often contributes to the fragmentation of the personality which is the most devastating result of traumatic stress. We struggle to discern aspects of the needs of the child which qualify for an intervention from an agency, and so we ask the wrong questions. Is this a health problem? A mental health problem? An educational problem? A drugs problem? Or is it perhaps a problem for the criminal justice system? We go on adding to the number of ways the behaviours may be institutionally addressed, and in so doing we add to the burden of disintegration. Until we can achieve as a society a deep integration in our approach to trauma, we will continue to see problems multiply.

With all of that in mind, a few illustrative areas of behaviour we may observe will be considered.

Hyperactivity: life in perpetual motion

Sleeping patterns are disturbed, with nightmares and night terrors being frequent. Children may be unable to get off to sleep, or they may wake up at irregular hours. Some children find it hard to go to sleep, but then are exhausted in the morning and find it hard to get up.

Children may be constantly on the go and constantly seeking a high stimulus environment, having a space between inactivity and boredom about as long as the patience span of city drivers at a change of traffic lights. Attention will be limited and carers learn to speak in short sentences if they hope to keep the whole sentence in the child's awareness. Concentration will also be difficult, as perceptual fields are attuned to threat, and both vision and hearing tune out from tasks which are not threatening. It is hard for traumatised children to see a page of print, when their peripheral vision is scanning the environment for threats. And they will lose the natural human preference for the human voice, as their hearing automatically tunes out non-threatening sounds.

Hypervigilance is a symptom of traumatic stress, and it makes for very jumpy children who find it difficult to feel settled anywhere. In a new or strange setting, they will be scanning every aspect of the environment for potential threats, so any change to daily living patterns is exhausting for them. Others cannot be taken for granted as trustworthy, so that any accident, injury or illness may lead to a breakdown of the fragile structures of trust. I have seen children well established in placement who became terrified when carers needed to remove a splinter or wash a wound.

Dissociation: splitting up is sometimes not so hard

There are various defences the beleaguered mind may try to protect against the continuing stress injury. One which some children may already have in place as a result of their attachment experiences is the defence of dissociation. Whether it is an existing strategy, or newly discovered under the impact of the trauma, it is an effective defence to get through the immediate impact of the stress. Unfortunately it has longer term effects which can be devastating to the personality.

The capacity to split awareness so that at least part of the self is kept safe through even the most painful and destructive experience means that humans are able to be very resilient. Unfortunately it also means that we can disintegrate and still function. We are self-aware beings and we relate to our environment through our consciousness; when that consciousness splits apart the personality is radically fragmented.

Sometimes the splitting, although persistent, is purely trauma related, the self creating a fragment to contain the trauma that will exist alongside the everyday consciousness but only be active when confronted with another traumatic event. People thus affected speak of entering a different type of consciousness, which they recognise as continuous with previous trauma-related consciousness (van der Kolk *et al*, 1996, p. 191ff), but not continuous with everyday awareness. This is a relatively benign level of dissociation, although any dissociation at the point of trauma is a risk factor increasing the likelihood of disorder.

For others the impairment of ordinary functioning as a result of dissociation is much more profound. These are people for whom the separated parts of personality become as it were persons in their own right. These victims of disorder are likely to attract the label of dissociative identity disorder (DID). The outlook is particularly grim for children who dissociate in response to trauma, for they are much more likely to develop lasting disorders, and even more so for those for whom dissociation is already a fixed response to stress as a result of early attachment experiences.

Children who dissociate are, to quote van der Kolk (1996, p. 423), a 'clinical challenge and a forensic nightmare'. Not only are they difficult to engage in a real therapeutic relationship, but it is also almost impossible to ascribe responsibility to people who cannot communicate between the different parts of their personality. These are children who are seen by adults to do something, caught red handed as it were, who say with total innocence 'but it wasn't me!' And they are so clearly convinced of their innocence that stable, sensible adults may still be left with the uncomfortable feeling that perhaps their own senses are letting them down.

Children do tell lies to save face in awkward situations, but children who dissociate tell the truth as they see it. It is the utter belief in their own innocence which can fracture the sense of reality of any adult trying to make sense of the situation. These fragmented parts of personality can be observed in everyday life for some children, and it is disconcerting to be with children who may speak in different voices, like different foods, use a different vocabulary, have different habits and tastes, and generally give the impression of living with several people at the same time all wrapped in one skin.

Again it is the social self that suffers most. If it were possible to imagine a child surviving alone, isolated from the rest of humankind, then that child could be as various as the sky at sunset and no harm done. It is in our relationships, the people we are in relation to others, that we need some sense of continuity, some assurance that there is a person there to know. The work of relating to others is complex and puzzling at best, and it becomes impossible if the other seems to have no steady centre to engage with.

Avoidance of trigger stimuli: what you don't know is there can't hurt you

Avoidant children will avoid any thing, situation or person that may trigger the re-experiencing of traumatic stress. Since PTSD leads to so many objectively neutral stimuli being experienced as triggers, this becomes an increasingly disabling aspect of the disorder. At its extreme it could be seen as 'a phobia of life itself' (van der Kolk *et al*, 1996, p. 419).

Children may avoid certain lessons at school, or they may avoid school altogether. They may avoid lunches, or certain foods, or eating. They may avoid having baths, or going to the toilet, or going to bed, or getting up, or people in green cars. In short, anything at all that might ever have acted as a prompt to a highly sensitive limbic system may come to be the next object of avoidance.

Remember, that for avoidance to work, it has to be internally explained so that the avoidant person never suspects that they are not-thinking about the trauma. These explanations will then be clung to with passion. 'I hate that teacher', 'I felt ill', 'I forgot', 'I had to do something else', and so on and on go the reasons why it was impossible for them just to behave like other children. And if it is pointed out that hundreds of others manage to go to the lesson each week whatever they think of the teacher, the response will be overt or covert distress. The children know that they are behaving differently from their peers. They want to be normal. It is their normality which is distorted, and that is deeply painful if they must confront it.

Transference and counter-transference: what doesn't hurt you can hurt someone else

Dissociation works as a defensive mechanism to enable the child to survive disintegration. Avoidance works as a defence by making it possible for the child to not-think about experience. The phenomena of transference and counter-transference allow the child to survive by transferring to others in the social environment the now absent emotional experience. The child is able to live through dangerous times without having to feel the overwhelming emotions associated with disintegration, but also without losing the reality of those emotions.

The child cannot feel their own emotions, but they can observe the emotional experience of others. The feelings come to be held, and often vividly expressed, in the other people who form the child's social network and human environment. Traumatised children often seem to be surrounded by people who are extraordinarily angry or very sad. The impression, in terms of emotions, can be of the child as the unmoved centre of a raging storm. The immensely restricted affective range of the child, who can register little beyond terror or rage, is reflected in the heightened anxiety and anger expressed around them.

First, in a process of transference, the child sees in us the absent other, the missing carer or the abuser, who would have been the object of strong feelings had those feelings not been excised by trauma. Then, through the power of counter-transference, we feel in ourselves the powerful feelings which are denied to the child. So traumatised children can come to generate quite irrational and unreasonable rage and misery in those who live and work with them.

Traumatic identity: defined by disaster

Trauma shatters the core assumptions that define human consciousness. Survival requires that babies make certain assumptions about the world. Ronnie Janoff-Bulman (1992) describes these basic and necessary illusions that enable us to function as the assumption that:

- the world is benevolent;
- the world is meaningful;
- we deserve good things.

Traumatic events rapidly unravel these beliefs. This leaves a vacuum in our most fundamental cognitive constructs about the world, and nature always abhors a vacuum. Human identity is founded on beliefs about ourselves formed as the environment reflects back to us an image of who we are (Shotter, 1984). Once traumatic stress disintegrates the core of our personality, the busy mind quickly forms another set of beliefs more fitting to the world as we now perceive it to be. These new beliefs or schemas become the foundation for a new identity which may be thought of as traumatic identity.

Traumatised people invariably develop temporary or permanent identity beliefs which are trauma based. The resulting cognitive schemas have a pervasive effect on all other personal constructs. The victim of PTSD may state and live out such beliefs as: 'I have no control over my life'; 'I am the sort of person to whom bad things happen'; 'People who love me always hurt me'; and 'I don't deserve anything good to happen'.

Children who hold core beliefs like this are not likely to have happy lives until the beliefs change. Yet our core beliefs structure our identity, and it is no small matter to change our sense of our own identity. In so many ways we work with children to enable them to form and retain a strong sense of identity, but here we actively invite children to let go of their identity as victim, and to search for a new sense of self. They will resist accepting the invitation.

Memory disturbance

Traumatised children often have no memory of the traumatic events which have disrupted their lives. Sometimes they have fragmentary memories, but they are not able to have formed narrative memories of the events until after they have recovered from the trauma. This traumatic amnesia distresses the child, and we see children struggling to make sense of the gap in their thinking. While on the one hand being avoidant of trigger situations, on the other, and confusingly for the observer, they may seek out situations which seem reminiscent of the past, apparently in an effort to reduce the painful self-doubt that plagues all of us when our memory lets us down.

At other times children are unable to forget the trauma, or more usually certain sensory aspects of it. This hypermnesia takes the child into a perpetual inner world of tormenting images and experiences of the trauma as though it were happening in an eternal present moment. We can see the child present in body but absent in spirit, living in a perpetual daydream – although living nightmare would be a more accurate description of the experience. The child may be said to hear voices, which may be an uncontrollable inner replaying of the voices of abusers, or may be subject to visual images or overwhelming feelings which have no prompt in the present external environment but are internally generated.

The third type of memory disturbance after trauma arises from the reduced oxygen supply to areas of the brain, and particularly to Broca's area. Ordinary memory relies on the formation of links and narrative, and without Broca's area we are unable to create the narrative. The result is a distressing disturbance of short-term memory.

Children whose short-term memory is poor are frustrating to live with. Ask them to go upstairs and perform a simple task, and by the time they have climbed to the top they have forgotten what it was you asked them to do. These are children who never have the right kit for school, cannot remember changes to routine timetables, forget appointments, and always fail to bring home the vital letter seeking permission for them to go on that school trip they have been looking forward to.

Loss of short-term memory is so distressing that children almost always cover up. They feel stupid to find such difficulty with tasks that their peers perform with ease. They feel critically unreliable and therefore unsafe. Then they dissemble: 'Someone stole it'; 'Nobody told me'; 'I didn't want to go anyway' and so on in the hope that, if they are convincing enough, no one will notice they are different.

Learning difficulties
Children who find it difficult to think, to construct narrative and meaning and to remember are obviously going to struggle more than their peers when it comes to learning. Yet the global disorders which follow trauma have an impact on learning which goes even deeper than these disruptions of cognitive functioning. For learning is a holistic process, involving the whole person in changing and adapting to our developing understanding of the world in which we find ourselves. The entire bio-psycho-social injury which is the result of trauma has a destructive effect on the capacity to learn (Cairns, in Jackson, 2013).

Traumatised children may be diminished in their capacity to learn physically, finding co-ordination and balance difficult and possibly having problems with spatial awareness and laterality. They are likely to have difficulties with cognitive skill development in the areas of language, the creation of meaning, making sense of numbers, and so on. They are almost certain to have difficulties with socially-based learning, whether it is co-operating in classroom groups or under-taking learning which relies on empathy and an understanding of the inner world of others, such as understanding literature. Finally, they are sure to have difficulties with learning based on emotion; emotional numbing and the loss of the capacity for joy will put all aesthetic appreciation, response to beauty and delight in living out of their reach. These will be experiences which they can observe in others but never share.

It is frustrating for children to be at school with their peers who can do with ease so many activities that for traumatised children are difficult. It is frustrating for schools to cope with children who may be obviously intelligent but who find it difficult to learn and difficult to manage school as a social setting. The results of these frustrations are vividly displayed in the statistics on the educational attainments of children in the public care system (Jackson, 2013). Here is a group of children who might be expected to be among the most traumatised in the population; they are vastly over-represented in those excluded from school, and are shockingly under-represented in those achieving good, or even average, results at key examinations. These are children whose learning needs are not being met in the education system.

Aggression against self and others

Terror begets aggression. The inner state of the victim of PTSD is physiologically one of permanent terror. Self-harm is common. Sometimes this is related to the altered sense of identity after trauma, which creates self-loathing. Children may harm themselves because they hate themselves.

Other children may become addicted to the self-generated pain-killers which go with trauma. Then they may hurt themselves as a way of getting a fresh dose of opioids. These children often say that they only feel normal when they are cutting or otherwise hurting themselves. This is the language of addiction, and it should alert us to the possibility that they have become dependent on their own self-generated chemicals. Many victims of trauma become dependent on substances, and this is often a form of self-medication to ease the pain of permanent physiological arousal.

Aggression and violence against others is also common. Primed for fight as well as flight, perceiving harmless things as threats, exhausted with constant vigilance, traumatised children are both irritable and unpredictably violent. At best they are uncomfortable companions, and often they are downright frightening to be with. Carers and schools often put aggression and violence at the top of the list of challenging behaviours they find most difficult to cope with.

Efforts to achieve control

It is important to human beings to have a sense of being in control. For most children this sense comes through a gradual development of self-control, as they become able within secure attachments to regulate stress, shame, impulse and rage. Even when this self-control has been achieved, however, PTSD destroys it. People who previously could manage their own physiological responses, emotional experience and behaviour are deprived of this ability by the gross physiological changes arising from unprocessed trauma. Being in a permanent state of high stress arousal prevents self-control.

Since a sense of control matters, children who cannot achieve self-control often become very controlling of others. This has the added bonus of making them feel safer, since other people are part of the environment and everything about the environment seems threatening, therefore other people are a threat.

Children may also be stuck, or have reverted, to the "magical thinking" of early childhood under the impact of trauma. They then feel that they have to be in control of everything or it will stop working. They may believe that they can predict or control the future, or that they are responsible for the safety of others which can be assured by magical acts. One child had to perform six rituals at bedtime to keep his absent mother safe; another needed to stay awake until after midnight every night otherwise someone in the house would die before morning.

Efforts to reduce dissonance

Safety is essential for people to be able to recover from trauma. Yet if we simply take a traumatised child and place them in a safe environment, after a while they start to feel crazy. Their inner experience is of being terrified. The outside world no longer matches their inner experience, for it is safe. When our inner world and our outer world fail to match we feel crazy. This is one of the most uncomfortable feelings for a human being; it is like being annihilated as a person.

We have taken note that the child cannot control their inner experience when in the grip of PTSD. The only way the child can stop feeling crazy therefore is to make the outer world unsafe enough to make sense of the inner experience of terror. Traumatised children will make their world chaotic and dangerous in order to feel sane. Just when everyone around them is feeling that things are going well for them, they will press the self-destruct button.

Psychosomatic and psychogenic disorders

Children living with this level of permanent overwhelming stress may suffer a range of illnesses and ailments. Every body system and organ is affected by stress. The results of long-term exposure to traumatic stress can include headaches, breathing problems, digestive disorders, pain in the joints, backache and immune system disorders.

Children also express their absent feelings through bodily changes, a process called somatisation (van der Kolk *et al*, 1996, p. 183ff). Thus when another child might feel excited, a traumatised child may produce an asthma attack or a headache, and what would be mild anxiety may appear as diarrhoea or indigestion.

Children who have been victims of abuse, especially sexual abuse, may suffer health-related anxieties, even when they have no conscious memory of the abuse. They may be anxious about bodily functions, or the changes of puberty, and will need special care to be taken to provide them with good information and reassurance about their bodies, their developing sexuality, and their changing sexual identity. They may also suffer sexually transmitted diseases for which they will need treatment.

Fear begets fear. It is very difficult to maintain the still centre of adult security when living with children who live with such terror. The basic SAFE attitude, in which the puzzle of relating to other unique persons is addressed with friendly interest and curiosity, is a protector against the stress of daily life with such disorder in the household. Informed questioning of your own observation can generate the reflection on the experience of the child. Then common ground is discovered without needing to be sucked into the vortex of trauma yourself.

Examples of useful questions

Is it likely that this child has experienced a traumatic event?
Do they seem easily startled?
Are they readily overwhelmed by stress?
Can they relax? How?
Do they suffer nightmares or night terrors?
Do they experience panic or terror in everyday situations?
Are they easily provoked to rage?
Can they express their feelings in words?
Do they provoke fear or anger in others?
Do they suffer disturbances of basic patterns such as sleeping or eating?
Do they suffer physical illnesses or conditions related to stress?
Do they find it hard to concentrate?
Do they find it hard to remember things? From the past? Short term?
Do they put themselves at risk?
Do they hurt or harm themselves?
Do they find pleasure in the company of others?
Do they enjoy life?

What can we do?: approaches to living and working with traumatised children

The three phases of treatment

PTSD is global in its effects – those who suffer from it are injured physically, psychologically and socially. Treatment needs to address all of these aspects of functioning. Clinicians seem generally to agree that there are several phases of treatment, and that all must be completed before recovery can be seen as reliable and lasting. Brown, Scheflin and Hammond (1998) suggest three phases of treatment, and since these correspond to the processes of spontaneous recovery this is a helpful structure. The three phases are: stabilisation, integration and adaptation.

Each of these phases of treatment has three components:

1   Stabilisation
    • establish safety and stability

- learn about trauma
- learn or relearn words for feelings
2 Integration
    - control and manage physiological reactions
    - process the traumatic material
    - rebuild cognitive constructs
3 Adaptation
    - re-establish social connectedness
    - re-establish personal efficacy
    - accumulate restitutive experience

Children who are recovering from PTSD will need to be able to work through all these phases, but the complexity of the traumatic experiences and the severity and depth of the injuries they may have suffered mean that children often circle back and revisit earlier phases, or carry on several parts of the process over the same period of time.

Phase 1: stabilisation
Establishing safety and stability
All children who have lived through trauma need to be in a safe environment. Again, it is important to move beyond thinking of the child as an isolated unit separate from their social network. The impact of the trauma affects the entire child/community/society which is in reality the location of the traumatic events. It is not enough to remove the child from a place of danger to a place of safety. Rather, we need to examine the strengths and weaknesses of the whole ecological system that includes the child in order to enable the community to construct an environment safe enough for the child to recover from harm.

Once we see children as a part of their environment, it becomes clear that the setting has to be safe for them and also has to be safe enough to contain any risks they may pose to others. This will mean constructing a deeply integrated approach to contain the disintegration of the traumatised child. Such deep integration can only be achieved when everyone who has anything to do with the child is contributing to the containing milieu from a position of knowledge and understanding.

The whole first phase of effective treatment for traumatic disorders is often missed out when planning for the needs of children. It is not helpful to embark on therapy with the child until the social structures are in place to contain the chaotic processes of integrating the trauma.

These social structures may be provided from anywhere within the social milieu, including the safety of a committed therapeutic relationship, but there must be that minimal stability before the child can progress. This is not an argument for delaying help for the child until they are in a stable placement – a familiar Catch 22 situation – but it is a plea for ensuring that therapy is preceded by the provision of at least minimal safety and stability.

Learning about trauma
The child and everyone who is concerned with the child must be able to understand what is happening. Knowledge is power, and anyone who has suffered the effects of traumatic stress needs to know what has happened to them, what is happening to them and what the future may hold as they recover. This knowledge normalises the situation and helps children to understand that they are not mad or bad, but have been injured by events in their lives.

Similarly, as people around the child come to understand even the most bizarre elements of their behaviour as indicators of the injury they have suffered, it becomes much easier to work together to keep everybody safe. This does not reduce the responsibility of key agencies to carry out their own core tasks; the education system must provide for the educational needs of all students, the criminal justice system must protect the public from crime, and so on. But it does mean that these agencies will recognise the needs of traumatised children and young people as radically different, in some ways, from those of their non-traumatised peers.

It also means that these and all other agencies will need to acknowledge that the trauma does not reside within the child, it is the social system that has been injured. Such injuries require a systemic response (Apter, 1986). If we do not provide structures that promote the healing of traumatic stress injuries, we perpetuate the injury to the social fabric. People who are disintegrated, socially disconnected, terrified to the point of unpredictable violence or self-harm, and terribly compromised in terms of their own mental health (Richardson and Joughin, 2000) will be both a drain on, and a threat to, the life of our community.

Learning or relearning words for feelings
Like the other two steps in this first phase of treatment, getting the brain engaged or re-engaged with the processing of feelings is often forgotten. It is of little value to start working with a child on processing trauma until they have begun to be able to feel and to process those feelings.

Again, this is a part of the treatment programme which will involve everyone associated with the child. When the child is constantly encouraged to recognise and put words to feelings, when emotional literacy is encouraged in every setting and by everyone concerned, it becomes a matter of course for the child to practise what is initially so hard.

Children need to be encouraged and enabled to speak the feelings, and adults also need to be open and authentic with the children about their own feelings and thoughts. Carers and teachers, social workers and therapists, play leaders and child minders all need to be aware of the need to keep exercising the words-for-feelings bits of the brain. Games, stories, mealtimes, bedtimes, rides on buses, playtime in the park, anything and everything can be an entry point to speaking the feelings.

Phase 2: integration
Fuses, switches and safety valves: controlling and managing physiological reactions
If children cannot begin to process trauma without having words for feelings, equally they cannot safely process trauma until they are able to regulate their own physiological reactions. This may be a point where medical intervention is needed; there are drugs which seem to help (van der Kolk *et al*, 1996, Chapter 23).

There are many other approaches which may help different

children. The key factor is the child gaining their own sense of control over reactions or sensations which previously seemed unmanageable and led to overwhelm. Relaxation techniques help some children, including breathing exercises which teach the child to alter physiology by gaining some control of autonomic functions and progressive relaxation exercises which create awareness of the state of the long muscles. Massage, SHEN therapy (a physical therapy designed specifically to address the physical and emotional effects of trauma) and biofeedback (a method of enabling people to monitor their own physiological responses) might also be useful.

Staying very close to the metaphor of the child's behaviour may dissolve the sense of powerlessness in the face of their own impulses. It may sound simple to notice that, if a child is banging their head against a brick wall, they could benefit from discovering the metaphor in words, but it is a truth that for our brains the words prevent the need to act out the problem. Stories which take the metaphoric content of the behaviour and translate it into parallel narrative (remembering that this is metaphor and not simile – resist the need to interpret) are always useful. These can provide the child with genuine alternatives which have the power to change the uncontrollable and the unnameable into things no more terrifying than a fairytale dragon or storybook monster.

A child who had been in institutions since the age of six once assured me as we drove home that he was 'one of the mad children' and I should give up on him. Arriving at the house I noticed a living metaphor and pointed it out to him. Just beside the door was a daffodil uprooted in some over-enthusiastic attempt at weeding. Disturbed and upended, it was doing the only thing daffodils know how to do – it was growing just as it had been left, with its roots in the air and its head underground. Together we tenderly picked it out of its disintegrated world and offered it soil for its roots and sunlight for its bedraggled flower. Fortunately it thrived, otherwise we would have needed another story about the differences in resilience between flowers and humans.

Putting the past in its place: processing the trauma
Although the whole of the social milieu will need to be engaged with this part of the treatment of trauma, it is the part of the programme which will largely take place in more traditional therapeutic environments. There needs to be an active deconditioning of the traumatic memories and responses, and this will involve the help of a therapist. The aim is for all the traumatic material to become part of the narrative memory. It will be consigned to its proper place in history, a part of the life of the child which was very unpleasant when it was happening but which is now over and done with.

Some children go through this process smoothly in childhood. Many have suffered multiple trauma, and will revisit some version of therapy a number of times before they feel liberated from the burden of symptoms. And some children wait until they are adults and have adult resources to carry them through the traumatic recall before they are able to enter fully into therapy.

As well as the now traditional psychotherapeutic, behavioural and cognitive approaches to therapy, some other techniques seem to be promising in bringing relief to people suffering from PTSD. These might include imaginal flooding, eye movement desensitisation and reprocessing (EMDR), systematic desensitisation, non-directive hypnosis, time line therapy, visual/kinaesthetic dissociation, implosion therapy, and so on (see Glossary).

The important thing is to assess very carefully the needs of this particular person at this point in time. The assessment will emerge from the social network, so again it is of the utmost importance for everyone concerned to work together to consider the child in their community and make a recommendation for the next appropriate therapeutic intervention that draws on all the strengths and abilities of every part of the social network including the child.

New beliefs for old: rebuilding cognitive constructs
Traumatic stress shatters our core assumptions about the world (Janoff-Bulman, 1992). The traumatised child is left with the trauma-based belief schemes that replace the lost assumptions. Once the

trauma itself has been consigned to memory and become manageable, the therapeutic milieu must then give attention to the cognitive schemes through which the child will perceive the world and everything that happens to them.

This is cognitive work with the child, and it will probably need both formal therapeutic attention, and the concerted efforts of everyone who makes up the child's social environment. It involves enabling the child to generate choices in relation to central cognitive constructs and then to let go of the damaging schemes and hold onto the constructive ones.

Trauma-based cognitive constructs usually make no sense to anyone who is not the victim, since others are not locked into the unremitting pain which is the daily experience of the traumatised child. An obviously attractive young person who firmly believes they are revoltingly ugly, a clever child who believes they are stupid, an able child who believes they are unable to have any power or choice in their lives, a child who believes that they deserve to be harmed, or that anyone who loves them will hurt them, all these are liable to find that people around them constantly contradict their most basic beliefs about the world.

Such contradictions do nothing to help the child overcome the false and destructive beliefs. For the child these are not beliefs but facts. Anyone who contradicts an obvious fact cannot be taken seriously. When we deny what for the child is evident reality, we simply lose all credibility with the child. At best we will then be seen as out of touch and not worth listening to. At worst we will be perceived as sinister and threatening, since it is hard to understand the motives of someone who keeps contradicting obvious truths, and traumatised people are always predisposed to find others threatening.

The key to helping the child to be free of the grinding destructiveness of negative cognitive constructs is to introduce choice. Without contradicting the original scheme, other possibilities can be introduced. The child can then be invited to think about what for them would be evidence that the new possible belief was valid. For example, what if one person who loves them does not hurt them?

Could this provide evidence for the possibility that there might be some people in the world who can love them and not hurt them? The whole living environment can become the setting for a constant discourse on the nature of reality. If children learn to think deeply about issues less close to the core of their being, then as they progress towards recovery it becomes more and more possible for them to use the developing flexibility of their minds to challenge their own core beliefs. Despite the immense courage required to undertake such a journey, children will do it. For traumatised people, courage is the necessary quality they always develop. It takes courage to live through each day with PTSD.

Phase 3: adaptation

Making contact: re-establishing social connectedness
Children who have emerged blinking from the dark cave of traumatic stress are entering a new world. They will need to relearn important skills, and for those traumatised at a young age, the skills may need to be learned for the first time. In particular, children need to discover or rediscover the delights of social connectedness.

Ordinarily human beings like to be in relationship with other human beings. Trauma damages this predisposition. The child needs to find out that relating to other people is worth the effort, that it makes them feel good. Working with a group of young men who regularly sniffed glue, I asked if any of them had any times when they felt happy when not under the influence of glue. One deeply troubled boy suddenly looked very surprised and said 'I'm happy now!' It was a revelation to him to discover that he was happy just being with his friends in a safe place, without any extra help.

The key thing was to name the happiness. Until he put it into words he was completely unaware that he felt good. He recognised the sensations experienced when sniffing glue as pleasurable, but did not name to himself the happiness of simply being safe and comfortable and with friends, and therefore had no idea how much he was enjoying that basic pleasure. Children need to be encouraged to engage in relating to others, and then they need to be encouraged and enabled to put words to the experience. Without the words the experience will be useless because it will make no contribution to building healthy patterns in the mind.

Making a difference: re-establishing personal efficacy
Only at this relatively late stage of recovery will the child really be able to make use of work to help them build self-esteem. Now is the time for all the activities and interests the recovering child can take on that might have the effect of enhancing their self-confidence and self-concept. Now is the time for praise and congratulation, for now at last the child will be able to hear the positive comments and relate them to their own core self-image.

The entire environment needs to be reflecting this positive self-image back to the child. We can encourage children at this stage to take a real pride in their own personal space. Valuing the space that is identified with the child is also giving a message about valuing the child. Children who have been wreckers of bedrooms and of their own property often become quite house proud at this stage of their recovery.

Clothing and other aspects of personal appearance can be very confidence-boosting for the recovering child. Children who have been self-neglecting may become able at last to take pride in choosing their own clothes and keeping them smart, or to make choices about personal hygiene and appearance that mark a real ability to feel in control of their own self-presentation.

A lot of what you fancy does you good: accumulating restitutive emotional experience
This is quite the most enjoyable part of needing treatment for PTSD. It involves being prescribed anything which would be expected to make you feel good, and then consciously setting out to enter into the experience and to translate it into words. It is a fitness programme for the entire brain, engaging the whole sensing/feeling/thinking organism in a programme of development through practice and repetition.

Attention should be given to every aspect of personal experience to provide, and create a map for, pleasurable experience. Physically, any healthy activity the child finds pleasurable may be encouraged. Exercise and sport, massage, relaxation exercises, swimming, brushing and combing hair, dancing and so on might all contribute to a sense of well-being which must then be anchored and named to make it easily re-accessible.

Intellectual exercises might include reading, word games, tactical games such as chess, writing poetry and prose, using a computer, mathematical puzzles, and so on. Aesthetic activities could include painting, making and listening to music, theatre, opera, visiting beautiful places. Practical activities can all be enjoyed in this conscious way: cooking, craft work of all kinds, gardening, building, decorating, vehicle maintenance are all potentially pleasurable activities that can contribute to the recovery process.

Finally, attention should be given to spiritual activities which can contribute to the discovery of joy in living. Children need to know that meditation, prayer, shared worship and religious ceremonies are an important part of life for many people, providing inspiration, peace of mind and a joyful sense of community with creation.

The linking factor in these very diverse activities is that they can all generate the experience of joy in the lives of human beings. It is not enough to do them, it is also necessary to bring the experience into conscious awareness. As we name the activity and our delight in it, so we establish a pathway to retrieve that delight. Then the joy becomes a source of strength and resilience on which we can draw forever.

Examples of interventions to promote stabilisation

Environment	Activities for carers	Agency interventions
Physical environment Attention needs to be given to those elements of the environment which make this particular child feel safe or feel threatened. Living areas need to be warm and welcoming. Bedrooms and bathrooms need special care. Kitchens and eating areas must be safe and comfortable. Colours, materials, type and distribution of furniture can all contribute. Assess and minimise triggers to trauma in all aspects of the milieu.	Remember at all times that you are dealing with a frightened flight animal. Establish constantly that you are trustworthy. Quietness and gentleness are essential. Avoid sudden movements and loud noises. Find soothing activities the child can accept. Physical contact is needed at a level the child can tolerate. Look for opportunities to show that touch activities can be safe: hairdressing, tending small injuries, treating head lice or athlete's foot, and so on.	Ensure that the physical environment around the child is adapted to soothe terror. This should apply to any setting where the child spends significant time. Home, school, playgroup, hospital, surgery, and so on should all feel as safe as possible. All professionals dealing with the child need to be aware of the implications of traumatic stress for their practice.
Time Safety and stability are enhanced by clear routines and structures. Patterns for eating and bedtimes should be relaxed but stable and clear. The child needs to know what to do if sleep is disrupted, and how to get help if frightened.	Talk to the child. Provide a commentary as you might with a toddler. Use reassuring tones and teach the child to use your voice to soothe fears. Be prepared for the child to need actual or symbolic regressed activity. Special foods or drinks prepared and offered by the prime carer have symbolic value. Bedtime rituals may be needed. 'Magic touch' may be sought for pain (the equivalent of 'rubbing it better' or 'kissing it better' for a toddler).	Teach the child and others about the effects of trauma. Promote emotional literacy in every setting that contains the child. Supervise and support carers fully. Watch for signs of secondary or vicarious trauma in carers (carers becoming symptomatic as a result of looking after trauma victims (Figley, 2002))
People It helps at first to keep just a few familiar people around the child, while allowing for the child's own choices about who feels safe and secure to them. Check for anyone who triggers a trauma response, and try to keep the triggering to a minimum. Similarly,	Teach the child about the effects of trauma in an age-appropriate way. Teach words for feelings all the time. Help the child to identify and name	Be alert for signs of stress throughout the caring family and network, and respond to relieve any early indicators of the

Environment	Activities for carers	Agency interventions
take notice of anyone who provokes a relaxation response, and encourage that soothing relationship.	feelings. Be prepared to name and talk about your own feelings.	system being over-whelmed. Provide respite for carers as needed.

This stage of recovery needs frequent revisiting throughout the recovery process. As the child progresses, each new stage of recovery may destabilise and produce new terrors. Then there needs to be a new period of grounding and stabilising for the child to re-establish their sense of safety and the assurance that they will not be overwhelmed.

Examples of interventions to promote integration

Environment	Activities for carers	Agency interventions
Physical environment The environment now needs to promote and contain the therapeutic process. Safety and predictability are central, but the child will also need to begin to feel in control of their own space. Children should have their own room and be allowed to let that space reflect their fluctuating relationship with them-selves. Mess and muddle may reflect the chaos inside. Attempts to clean up or decorate show the beginnings of self-care, and so on. Art materials, musical instruments, mood altering lights and music, slightly increased stimulus in the environ-ment in terms of colours, materials, changes and surprises can all be useful at this stage of recovery.	Having established safe activities, now use these to' enable the child to establish control over their own physiology. Teach appro-priate activities to soothe stress and to manage shame and rage. Allow and encourage the child to join in pleasurable activities of all kinds with you. Cooking, gardening, house maintenance, vehicle maintenance, cleaning, painting, craft work, music making. Be prepared for storms during periods of formal therapy. When children return to the household from therapy sessions traumatic material will have been activated and the reactions may be extreme. Contact with people who remind the child of traumatic events, and with places associated with trauma, may be part of the	Assess therapeutic needs carefully and provide therapy as needed. Set measurable out-comes for therapy and ensure that the process is regularly reviewed and moni-tored. It is easy for therapy for trauma-tised children to become part of the problem instead of the solution. Maintain clear role boundaries between agencies. Ensure that carers are clear about their role during periods of therapy. Provide regular inter-agency contact and ensure that each agency concerned with the child is kept fully informed about the work of the others.

Environment	Activities for carers	Agency interventions
Time While travelling the integrative stage of their journey, children will find that time distorts and it is hard to keep to routines and patterns. The time environment needs to be structured but flexible. Children should never be penalised for lapses of time awareness while recovering from trauma. Instead they need reassurance that it is hard for them to manage time structures, and invited to join us in finding ways to help them maintain a safe structure. *People* Children will be highly dependent at this stage, and will be disturbing to others. They need encouragement to relate to adults, and to let adults meet their dependency needs.	therapeutic process. Allow for strong reactions. Take steps to ensure safety. Actively seek and use supervision and consultation. Stay in close touch with therapists and be informed about the processes and predictable outcomes of therapy while maintaining confidentiality on content. Keep boundaries around roles. Carers are not therapists, they are providers of a therapeutic environment. Children need to have safe spaces and safe people where they can try to live in the present. It is hard enough for traumatised children to keep the past from intruding into the present when those boundaries are safely kept.	Provide regular supervision and support for the carers. Watch for issues of safety, and ensure that carers, families and wider networks are not put at risk when children are acting out during periods of therapy. Take care of the entire care family. Check who is being affected by the changes in the child during therapy. Provide respite as needed for carers. Provide therapy for carers or any members of the care family network if they are affected by secondary traumatisation. Provide consultancy as needed.

Examples of interventions to promote adaptation

Environment	Activities for carers	Agency interventions
Physical environment Now the environment needs to promote and encourage sociability, stimulate interest and enjoyment of the physical world, and provide restitutive experience. Every sort of material to encourage	Allow and encourage children to develop friendships and promote social activities. Encourage children to reflect on relationships and issues arising from living with other people.	Provide a full range of opportunities for social and personal development within the community. Sports, games, recreation facilities, youth clubs and childrenís organisations, drama, music,

Environment	Activities for carers	Agency interventions
creativity and shared activities should be provided. Animals are interesting and promote social responsibility and empathy. Books, art materials, musical instruments, ingredients for cookery, stuff to make things with. Children need to be encouraged to make much of themselves and the space they inhabit. Scents, colours, and textures can all be enjoyed. Posters and art work enhance the environment. Music and lighting can be explored for their mood-changing properties. *Time* Now children need to begin to take responsi-bility for their own grasp of time and their own use of time. Negotiation should be encouraged. Strict time structures should be relaxed in favour of the child taking control of their time while negotiating sociably. *People* Social effectiveness means relating to all sorts and conditions of people. Encourage the child to expand their horizons, and learn to relate to others with interest and empathy.	Fill the environment with oportunities to enhance self-esteem. Provide activities that can be enjoyed alone and those that are best shared with others. Offer a wealth of materials and opportunities to use them. Outings and adventures are essential at this stage of recovery. Praise and affirmation can now be accepted and should be used whenever appropriate. Show children how to enjoy life by enjoying it yourself. Encourage children to keep a record of their discoveries of the delights and joy living may bring. Keep journals. Take photographs. Make recorded notes of events and feelings. Compose music. Write poetry. Draw and paint pictures. Pick up mementoes and treasure them. Apply these new skills in awareness to more painful experiences. Encourage expressiveness at sad times, and promote discussion and resolution of conflict. Let children know what wonderfully sensitive and responsive beings they are.	arts of all kinds should be freely available for recover-ing children. Ensure that all agencies are aware of the needs of children recovering from trauma. It is import-ant to put enjoyable activities and emo-tional literacy together, so that enjoyment and achievement are reflected upon. The whole brain needs to be engaged as far as possible. Provide resources for carers to enhance the range of activities open to children needing restitutive experience. Encourage carers to widen their own range of interests and activities, and those of other members of the care family Encourage family holidays and outings. Provide continuing supervision and support.

Grief

Grief is the experience of finding yourself standing alone in the vacant space with all this torn emotional tissue protruding. In the rhythm of grieving, you learn to gather your given heart back to yourself again. This sore gathering takes time. You need great patience with your slow heart. It takes the heart a long time to unlearn and transfer its old affections. John O'Donohue (1999)

Grief is more or less universal. Pain and suffering arising from troubled early attachments affect a minority of people, and a smaller minority suffer intense disorder of their feelings and affections as a result of their early experiences. Traumatic events are common in our shared human life, but only a minority of people experience more than passing pain as a result. But loss is part of the human condition, and grief afflicts everyone who lives long enough to be conscious of their losses. It is impossible to get through an average life span without suffering loss. And losses that change the fabric of our lives lead to grief. Like trauma, loss is a transformative experience; it shakes and shifts the patterns of our lives, and we emerge from the experience changed. The process of that change is the process we call grieving.

Some losses lead to culturally structured processes of transition and adaptation; these would include mourning and ceremonies of initiation. Grieving is universal, but such rites and rituals are culturally specific to different communities and traditions; what they have in common is that they provide a way for people to accomplish the personal transformation of grief within the protection of the community as constructively as possible. Rites of mourning and of transition allow and encourage the dislocated self to rediscover a place within the group, marking and containing the absences that are grieved.

What happens?: thinking about loss and grief

Art, literature and music point to the truths of human grieving. Every place touched by human life has evidence of the human relationship to death, loss and bereavement. As a child I sat on ancient tumuli and thought about the ancestors. Archaeology suggests that humans have linked themselves to the dead since the earliest times. In one afternoon I watch my kitten forget his mother, so far as I can tell. My twenty years fostered child comes to ask me to help him find any trace of his. We can, it seems, let go but not permanently forget so long as consciousness and memory interact.

Our grieving takes many different forms but there are common threads. Loss shakes us so that we are often numb at first, simply failing to register the evidence of our senses that our world has changed forever. Then there is often a time of denial, when we minimise the loss and convince ourselves that our new state is really better than the old. We may spend time searching frantically then for alternatives to what has gone, before at last we are strong enough to allow ourselves to confront our truth and know that we can never be exactly as we were. Then sadness takes us over, and despair as hope of recovering the old order disappears, and rage that we must at last remake ourselves and acknowledge the real imperfections of our old state as well as the absences in the new. At last we rediscover the blessings of affection, as our friends who have stayed with us through the darkness help us forward through the maze and out into the familiar new world. Thus humans negotiate the journey of grief (Fahlberg, 2008).

Since Bowlby, we have known that children also grieve though they may take a different path (Bowlby, 1991). Young children may have little concept of the adult concepts of bereavement and loss, but they do have affectional bonds as we have seen, and their own sense of meaning and purpose in the world. All these can be lost, and such losses will produce the personal and social upheaval of grieving.

They tell me I stood in corners burning-in my mourning. Re-strained myself against their embraces. I was three years old.

... I have known other women with cancer – other women who died ... She becomes the model for them all. (Michelle Cliff, 1980)

Children who suffer losses while they are in the shelter of their own families will be able to grieve in and through the embedded patterns of ritual and mourning that every family, community and culture shares. Displaced children, children separated from their families for any reason, will inevitably be grieving and will probably also be deprived of the familiar structures for holding and containing that grief.

Securely attached children who are grieving within the safety of their own families will find comfort and strength, and be developing resilient patterns of mourning and adaptation, through their attachment to those who love and protect them. Children with unmet attachment needs recovering from losses while remaining in their own families will struggle more, but may still be contained safely within the cultural structures of mourning in their family and community.

Securely attached children who suffer separation from their attachment figures will experience both loss and fear (Fahlberg, 2008). If they can find safe enough carers, however, they may draw from them the comfort they expect and trust to be provided by loving adults, and so remain resilient and able to mourn. This will be more likely if the carers are within the same cultural community so that grief and loss are dealt with in ways familiar to the child. Separated children whose patterns of attachment are insecure will be less able to draw on the comfort of substitute carers even though they accept those carers as offering parenting, for children who have not experienced reliable relief and comfort from their own parents will not recognise that parenting might provide such benefits.

Children deprived of anything they recognise as parental care at the same time as they experience loss and grief are much more vulnerable, however secure their primary attachments may have been. Adults, however kindly, who are not accepted by the child as parenting cannot supply the needed comfort and reassurance. They are benevolent strangers who can do nothing to relieve the isolation and confusion of the bereft child, even though the child is accustomed to seeking and finding comfort through parental care.

If the original attachments were insecure then the children will be struggling indeed to find the resources to face this multiple deprivation and loss. Children with unmet attachment needs will not even have the basic attitude of trust and connectedness to appreciate the benevolence of the substitute carers. For them, loss comes to a world already relatively bleak and unreliable, and the fear is an intensification of the persistent anxiety that dominates their experience. Avoidant children may try to manage the grief they avoid through controlling the situation; they may attempt to do this actually, by dominating those around them, or magically, by creating rituals that they can believe will hold the world together. Ambivalent children may become clingy and dependent on anyone who will accept the burden of their need, while at the same time drawing no real comfort from the passive acceptance of the support they are offered, or angrily lashing out at their helpers for failing to supply that comfort. And for children with disorganised patterns of attachment, the loss adds to their burden of confusion and despair, although they may give little outward sign of having noticed that life just became even more bewildering.

What do we observe?: life with the grieving child

Grief is the experience of loss associated with changes that are fundamental to our lives. Grieving is the process of adapting to such changes. Mourning is the cultural structure that our community may provide to contain our grieving. Trauma always includes grief, but not all grief is traumatic. Changes that are anticipated and prepared for will grieve us but need not injure us. Young children moving into a new family structure in a planned way will need to adapt, they will grieve, but can develop without injury. Most children who need therapeutic parenting or reparenting, however, will have suffered the biological, psychological and social injuries of traumatic stress. They will need to recover from those injuries, and grieving will be part of their recovery.

The first impact of grief is to dislocate our world. The world continues but we have stepped aside from it. Then we turn in upon ourselves. Social and sociable in our origins, we become deeply self-absorbed as we explore the new shape of our inner territory. Children and adults alike, grief transforms us into pioneers who must step out into new and unexplored areas. Nobody else was in quite the same relation to that which has been lost, and it follows that nobody else will experience quite the same grief.

Grief is a journey we make alone. Yet at the same time we are profoundly dependent on others, for we can no longer rely upon our old habits and routines to carry us through the day. Children who are grieving will be very varied in their responses; each person must pick out their own route on the journey. What they will have in common is this sense of being both disconnected and dependent, of being self-absorbed to the exclusion of those around them and yet also needing and demanding the attentiveness of others.

Adults are usually, though not always, aware that they grieve. Children rarely grieve in full awareness. Change is what children do. As they develop, so they are changed by their world and in turn they change the world around them. Adults generally have a more formed and settled inner construct of the world; they notice the unsettling effects of changes that will require a reformation of thought and feeling and behaviour. Children may notice the changes, but are less likely to be able to account for the impact on their way of being in the world.

We therefore live and work with children who are unaccountably sad, or angry, or disorientated, or depressed, or agitated, or withdrawn, or hostile. They need us to help them to be accountable, to enable them to account for themselves, so that they can absorb and adapt to their changed and changing environment.

Grief also can bring with it a heavy weight of guilt. As we let go of old patterns and relationships in order to be able to live in our changed world, so we feel the pain of breaking old promises and abandoning past commitments. All grief involves some sense of betrayal, of others or of a previous self. Every discovered joy in the changed world carries the reproach of faithlessness.

Children who grieve need us to be responsive but not intrusive. They need us to be prepared to engage with them in the dance of grief, a dance to music they alone can hear. And finally they need us to lead them back from the isolation of grieving into joyful connectedness with a world that is, after all, full of light and sound and colour and delight and other people.

It is important to be clear about the location of the grief when living with children who are grieving. Everyone experiences some grief in a lifetime, and the grieving children can easily trigger feelings of unresolved grief in us. Again, generating a reflective space through the use of your own informed questions may help you to stay in touch with the child's experience without it becoming your own.

Examples of useful questions

Has the child experienced significant loss, or changes in life patterns?
Are they able to express their feelings about these?
How do you know what they are feeling?
Do they often seem disconnected from the world around them?
Do they seem self-absorbed?
Do they need help to cope with ordinary tasks that other children of their age could manage unaided?
Are they often sad? Irritable? Withdrawn?
Are they able to cry and to take comfort from others?
Are they able to talk about their life before their loss?
Are there signs of progress or do they seem to be stuck?
Are they able to enjoy new experience yet?

What can we do?: approaches to living and working with grieving children

We do not know how to deal with people who have been bereaved. Should we speak or stay silent? Would they like our company, or would they prefer to be left alone? Do they want us to encourage them to re-establish old patterns, to try new things, or to rest from activity and let the emotions flow? There are no formulae to tell us what to do, and our guesses, intuitions and best intentions may all be wrong.

It is true for all human interaction, of course, that we can only do what seems good to us at the time and see what happens. We will make mistakes. Yet somehow we feel that the simple fact that loss is universal ought to make us more accomplished in dealing with it. Practice does help, of course, but only when it is accompanied with a basic humility in the face of the vast and unfathomable range of response of human beings to the experience of loss. First give yourself permission, therefore, to make mistakes and courage to acknowledge them.

There are also good practical approaches to dealing with those who grieve. It is helpful to get training in dealing with bereavement and grief – better still if the training relates specifically to living and working with bereaved children. It is important not to hurry the child through the processes of grieving, and equally important to be active in encouraging the child to talk about what they have lost from their lives. Allowing children to be sad, and giving them opportunities to allow themselves to be happy, are both part of the dance of grief.

The child needs you to take the time and trouble to learn them, and having learned them to accept them with all the feelings of thoughts and feelings and behaviour that go with grieving. You will also need to be aware of the losses and bereavements in your own life. As we live with those who grieve, our own wounds can be reopened. Children need us to be able to separate our losses from theirs, so that they can stay connected to their own experience without feeling inhibited by the need to protect us from being hurt. You have to be strong yourself to bear the grief of others.

Examples of interventions to enable children to grieve and recover

Environment	Activities for carers	Agency interventions
Physical environment Allow the child to create a safe space which is their own personal cocoon to retreat to. Provide plenty of stimulus to engage the child, but also have quiet areas for relaxation. Offer pictures, objects, books, music, poetry that reflect a full range of emotions, including sadness and despair, as well as hope and joy.	Learn about grief and mourning. Be aware of the losses in your own life, and the strength and resilience that have carried you through. Be willing to share some of this with grieving children, while knowing that every grief for every person is unique.	Provide training for carers. Provide supervision and support for carers. Provide access to grief counselling and other similar resources needed. Make sure that life story work is done with the child, and is repeated as needed to allow for the changes in perspective that go with the process of grieving.
Time The rhythms of grieving are different from those of other parts of life. Learn what best meets the child's needs in terms of eating, sleeping and structuring time. Try to fit meeting those needs into the time structures that suit the rest of the family.	Allow the child to be sad at times. Provide opportunities for the child to express grief, including access to art materials, writing, drama, music, and craft activities. Work with the family group and the network to support the child sensitively through the time of their grief which may be long and recurrent.	Plan contact around the need of the child to grieve, and facilitate contact that works through all the stages of grieving.
People Other members of the family may need help to recognise the needs of someone who is grieving. Children who grieve may find themselves someone to confide in; that person may then need support to carry the load cheerfully.	Be aware of anniversaries and be willing to mark them with a ceremony that has meaning for the child. Be willing to visit places and people who can help the child with the process of grieving, including visiting places from the child's past. Help with formal life story work, and be aware of the life story the child is always building.	Provide a stable resource for the child so far as possible; prioritise stability in providing a named and known social worker for grieving children.

8 Resilience: affirmative experience

Solitude

This truth – to prove and make thine own:
Thou hast been, shalt be, art, alone.
Matthew Arnold

And if he doesn't turn away, if his eyes don't turn to stone,
I'll ask him – is he scared to be alone?
Dory Previn

Que no haya soledad. (Let there be no isolation.)
Silvio Rodriguez

What happens?: thinking about the development of personal resilience

Sociability is so rooted in our human personalities that in most cultures to be solitary is seen as an extreme punishment or as an extreme religious or spiritual discipline producing altered states of consciousness. Yet grief isolates us, and mourning rituals generally support a process of separation, self-discovery and re-integration into a changed social order. As children become reflective they develop a sense of being a self distinct from their environment. If they are to thrive, this recognition that they are in some sense alone, separate from all other living beings, will become a comfortable solitude. A child who can be comfortable with solitude is a child who can develop personal resilience.

Resilience is a growing field of thought and study in child develop-ment. It is evident that children who seem outwardly to have been through the same experiences have very different patterns of survival. The same events will lead to completely different outcomes for child-ren, or, since resilience is a dynamic concept, may also lead to different outcomes for the same child at different times. We are all vulnerable, but some are more vulnerable than others, and all of us are more vulnerable to some events than to others.

Resilience is not the same as invulnerability (Schofield, 2001), but in beings who can never be invulnerable, and human beings can never be that, resilience is the obverse of vulnerability. It is closely linked to the internal working model of the world generated through attachment experiences. Children ascribe meaning to their experience based on their personal internal working model, and it is the nature of the meaning they generate that will determine their resilience to that experience. Once children are able to generate meanings that lead to creative and constructive responses to events, they are set on the road to developing resilience.

Children who believe that they are to blame for the losses and hurts in their life will experience new loss and hurt as evidence confirming their own lack of worth and helplessness; they will be less likely to be able to respond to such events with creative energy. Children who believe that adults, or men, or teachers are to blame for their pain will experience fresh pain as confirming or extending those beliefs; they will be unable to draw comfort and strength from their relationships with adults, or with particular types of adults. Our internal working model of the world provides the basis for adaptive or maladaptive personal and social responses to events.

A young man who has grown up with drug-using parents interprets any adversity in his life as a reason to seek medication for the pain. When he experiences stress, he reaches for the heroin. As he progresses towards recovery, his belief systems change. Now the many difficulties in his life – homelessness, lack of money, being a victim of violence – begin to be interpreted as evidence that he needs to change his lifestyle. The pain that previously was the evidence that he needed drugs becomes the evidence that he needs to let go of drugs.

In constant interchange with the environment, the child develops more or less creative and effective ways of building their experience into their developing personality. Key attachment relationships provide the raw material out of which the child constructs a perceiving and interpreting self, a uniquely vulnerable and resilient self. As Maggie Ross says in her study of her life as a religious solitary: 'We are all, each one of us, solitary; that in the end each is a unique creation of God, and alone because of that uniqueness . . .' (Ross, 1988, p. 3).

Aspects of personal resilience include insight – the capacity to reflect on our own sensation and make sense of it (Wolin and Wolin, 1993, Chapter 4) – and independence – the capacity to negotiate enough separation from others to create a safe personal space (Wolin and Wolin, 1993, Chapter 5). Children who have been able to develop insight and independence are in a good position to be able to form a coherent and balanced narrative of their lives. This will provide them with a continuous sense of self, with a sense of personal identity and with the basis for self-esteem.

One of the greatest difficulties with the concept of personal resilience is also one of the most encouraging. The building of a personal construct of the world is very hidden; we can never be sure how another person is experiencing the world. Children may sometimes pick up on tiny clues that they are loved, or respected, or valued and thus transform their self-concept so radically that they begin to perceive their whole world through different eyes. It will be very hard for the observer to know that this critical transformation has happened.

Karr-Morse and Wiley (2013) show in the true story of two brothers how small influences may create large effects. In a life full of distress and trauma, one brother had some experience of being valued and encouraged, the other did not. Among many slight differences in apparently similar lives, these contributed to very great differences in outcomes for the two boys. By the age of 20, one was a convicted murderer on death row and the other was a student in college. Yet these things were so slight: a loving tone in the voice of a grandfather, a grandmother who could relate encouragingly to one brother but not to the other, a brief experience of foster care in a home that offered love and respect recognised by one of the brothers but passing unnoticed by the other. Another example of the power of small interactions:

A young care leaver . . . was asked . . . what had made him a "success" despite the difficulties he had experienced growing up in care. He cited as an example someone who had listened to him, a doctor who had seen him as a child. He asked the doctor, 'Do you sometimes give people drugs just to keep them quiet?' The doctor replied that he did not, but went on to say that it was an interesting question and that he should keep on asking questions. This had made him feel valued . . . and this very brief remark had given him positive encouragement. (Mather and Batty, 2000, p. 11).

What do we observe?: life with children who are developing personal resilience

How are we to notice that children are developing resilience in their solitude? Whatever their temperamental differences, secure children can generally play happily alone or with others. They are able to talk about themselves reflectively, and in doing so they indicate an active imagination and a general sense of well-being with their own inner world. They will use their surroundings as the landscape of their imagination, telling themselves stories and building rich metaphors as they transform the outer world into a varied and resourceful inner universe. As they grow they dance and draw and sing and construct and narrate their experience to create an internal model of astonishing complexity. We watch the child constantly testing this developing model against the world. We also see the genetic templates of their potential unfolding and taking shape through this dance of interaction with the environment.

From the earliest days of life the child is alternating outward experience with inner processing. As the growing personality becomes more and more complex through this constant reshaping of the inner territory, so the child becomes more able to be comfortable with solitude. Happy children may be outgoing or more withdrawn, may be highly active or more reflective, and may be impulsive or more restrained, but whatever their personal characteristics they will be able at some level to tolerate both solitude and company. They will also find, beyond mere toleration, some measure of enjoyment in being alone and in being with others.

Children with unmet attachment needs, however, are much less able to tolerate, still less actively enjoy, their solitude. Their anxiety about the world and their place in it interferes with their ability to explore and enjoy their environment. The first indicator of discomfort with solitude is a diminished ability to enjoy time alone. Outgoing children will tend either to seek perpetual high stimulus activity when solitary, or to seek to end the solitude by never being alone. More withdrawn children may endure rather than seeking to end the uncomfortable experience of solitude; it is not unusual to see anxious children spend periods alone just gazing sadly into space, or, if they do engage with an activity, to find that their engagement is curiously joyless.

This lack of spontaneous fun or joy in living is a marked characteristic of anxious children, however different they may be from each other in their approach to life. The frenetic activity of the anxious outgoing child may seem like the pursuit of pleasure, but those around the child are usually well aware that joy is not the result. Instead there is likely to be a sense of something being actively avoided, of the activity as a diversion from some unnamed and unnameable absence.

Quieter or more withdrawn children may seem more obviously in touch with that terrifying emptiness than their more active and outgoing peers. Solitude is the space in which we may feel our own presence and reality. Children who have not had their existence cherished and confirmed from the beginning often struggle to feel any such sense of presence. One young man said, 'I feel empty in the place where other people have feelings. I don't know what it would be like to have fun.'

Children who dissociate may also feel that even when they can find a sense of being, they can never be sure that it will persist. Their sense of self is likely to be fleeting and uncertain, or scattered and diverse. They feel either unformed, as though they have no boundaries, or broken, as though they have many internal boundaries separating fragments of the self. Solitude for such children is a torment; without others to provide a structure they often have a sense of dissolving or disintegrating that terrifies them.

When children cannot feel safe in solitude they cannot concentrate for long on absorbing tasks. It is hard for them to get into a state of "flow" (Csikszentmihalyi, 1993). It is a paradox that people who are most at home in themselves, most confident of their own existence and identity are the very ones who are most likely to be able to enter the self-forgetfulness of utter absorption in some solitary activity. Children who lack a clear sense of self are less able to let go of self-awareness in concentration on activities. They are restless and find it hard to focus. At the same time, they often feel bored, and usually feel just on the edge of boredom; it takes very little drop in stimulation for them to feel edgy and dissatisfied.

Children who struggle with solitude are frightened of separation. Once they begin to trust those who care for them, they may find it frightening to be left. Going to bed may also give rise to high anxiety for children who are frightened of being alone. Children who have previously been punished by isolation may be especially vulnerable to anything that seems to echo the ordeal of being separated from others and forced onto their own overstretched resources.

When impulse regulation is difficult for children, they may find the physical presence of the carer helps them to control destructiveness. If they are left on their own, they may set about destroying their environment. Parents and carers often comment that they had only left the child untended for a moment, yet something in that brief time had been destroyed, stolen or damaged. Children with little sense of self become quickly overwhelmed. If their carer is absent, they seem to lose their sense of being an effective individual able to make choices and act upon them. Instead the impulsive emotional mind takes over, and chaos rules.

Children who are subject to excessive and pervasive shame are also unable to find comfort in solitude. Introspection is harmful when it leads only to self-blame and shame. Then the child may become locked into an experience of overwhelming shame which must be either absorbed into the growing personality or transferred to others. Neither of these is healthy, and the child will often avoid solitude after experiencing once the corrosive effects of introspection in the presence of pervasive shame.

When children who would prefer to avoid solitude find themselves alone, they may try to soothe the stress this evokes. Rocking, thumb sucking, stroking fabrics, masturbation, and making rhythmic or humming noises may all be an attempt to soothe or distract themselves for children who find solitude stressful. Others may try to alter the numbing effect of the fear of loss or abandonment with self-stimulating behaviours. Head banging, hair pulling, scratching or cutting may all be attempts to engender feeling in a body numbed with stress. Masturbation may be a means to stimulate sensation, as well as a means of soothing stress arousal. Some children when overwhelmed may switch off completely and go to sleep; this is unlikely to be refreshing sleep, however, and they wake up still overwhelmed and still scared to be alone.

Observation is of little benefit until you can make sense of it. In learning the child you will need constantly to ask questions of your own experience of the child in order to get closer to the child's experience of the world.

Examples of useful questions

Does this child enjoy solitude?

Do they still need to be in the physical presence of a carer?

What type of solitary activity might help this child develop?

What are their special interests?

What are their special skills?

Which of their senses gives them most delight?

What can we do?: promoting personal resilience with children who find solitude difficult

Children who have unmet attachment needs benefit from the physical presence of adults as much as possible. At the same time, they need to develop the capacity for solitude. How do we meet these conflicting needs? It is important to spend time with children comfortably in the same space, but not directly engaged with the same activity. Children who become aware that we like to share time in this way can feel that they are acceptable to us for who they are, and not just for the things that they do.

This has a double benefit. The child becomes more at home with their own being in the world, and it becomes more straightforward to deal with matters of discipline when children are more confident that we accept them as they are. It is a delicate negotiation to be with someone while they explore their own solitude. Parents of secure toddlers do this, however, without difficulty. The preoccupations of very young children are rarely of gripping interest to adults. Carers produce just enough interest and engagement to allow the toddler to know that there is a connection, and just enough distance to ensure that the young child is also discovering their own unique perspective on the world.

This intimate negotiation with babies and toddlers will meet the needs of older children who have suffered early adversity. It is rarely intuitive, however. Carers have to learn to behave with older children in ways that might be immediately evoked by being with infants. Generally, as children grow older, adults interact with them in ways increasingly similar to the interactions of adult life. There is an expectation that people who are in intimate relationships are either doing something together or they are separate. Although people often share space while engaged in separate tasks, the nature and level of awareness is quite different if one of the people is still a dependent infant. This is the type of separate but alert awareness that insecure children need from their carers if they are to be able to discover and explore a comfortable solitude.

Then they will need as much stimulus as possible to explore, express and enjoy the developing self they discover in their solitude. Fill their world with light and sound and colour and movement. Notice the sharp intake of breath, the moment of wonder when something catches and engages the attention. Children who have unmet needs, who have lived through adversity, who live with profound anxiety or active terror, are deeply preoccupied. We must be alert for the moments when the cloud of preoccupation lifts, when the contingent beauty of the world breaks in. Those are moments of personal growth.

Children who cannot tolerate solitude well, and yet also cannot relate well to other humans, may benefit from caring for animals. The relationship between a child and their pet can be an effective bridge to learning to relate to other people, and it can also provide a suitably engaged yet separate presence for the solitary child to feel able to explore the gifts that solitude may bring.

Personal exploration in this aspect of development is not about achievement, and it is not about self-absorption. It is the journey Narcissus failed to make. It is the journey towards that warm and humorous acceptance of the self that is attractive to others precisely because it has no need of others. It is the growth of the independence that must precede the reciprocal interdependent relationships of adult life.

Yet although the development of personal resilience is not about achievement, it is important for children to be able to reflect on their lives as they discover their own acceptability to themselves. Formal and informal life story work may be useful. Helping children to think about the qualities that have enabled them to survive such hard times will help. Noticing and encouraging children to notice the attributes, strengths and virtues they bring into the family will help.

Children can also be encouraged to discover and develop new skills and interests, and to practise these privately in the quietness of their own space. Art, music, drama, poetry, journal writing, building and making things – anything that can grab the attention of a pre-occupied child can be explored and made available. Physical activities that promote balance and self-knowledge may be tried. Yoga, massage, dance, gymnastics, and a whole range of other activities may help the child feel at home in themselves.

Finally, carers need to lead by example. Children will learn to be at ease with themselves as they live with others who are comfortable in their own skins. It is helpful for troubled children to see that life can be joyful, that pleasure in simple things can be spontaneous, and that human beings can take delight in being in the world.

Severe adversity in early life distorts the perceptions. It may take many years before children can understand what they are seeing. Those will be years in which carers who are not aware of the difficulties involved in living with joyless people may lose the joy from their own lives. It is vital for caregivers to retain a sense of personal integrity and self-acceptance. When carers enjoy their own life it will enable them to help the children in their care to find the unique grace and dignity that belongs to them and that is the gift each child brings to the world.

Compassion

What happens?: thinking about the development of social resilience

From the first moments of life, children are interested in other people. In the early years, however, it is hard for them to distinguish between self and other. Even when they begin to be able to use language about their own inner state, they may fail to differentiate between their experience and that of other people. For some people this difficulty in distinguishing between self and other may persist or recur, with results ranging from the disastrous to the comic. 'Put your coat on,' my grandmother in her later years used to say, 'I'm cold.'

Examples of interventions to promote personal resilience

Environment	Activities for carers	Agency interventions
Physical environment Plenty of personal space to explore their own solitude (it may not be the space set aside for them in the home). Children often choose a location that is special to them for this exploration – a den, a particular tree, the space under a work bench or table. Children exploring solitude will benefit from a rich and stimulating environment with access to many materials and media to help the exploration.	Children need to be with people who are at ease with their own solitude. Active engagement with your own self-discovery and self-development helps the child to make their own adventure, to set out on their own journey. Commit yourself to activities that bring you joy and contribute to your growing sense of identity. Allow children to see the pleasure and uncertainties of such personal journeys of discovery.	Families will need supervision and support to provide an environment that allows the child to move from dependence towards autonomy. Provide access to respite care if necessary to allow carers to model self-development and self-discovery. Carers who have been absorbed with earlier stages of child development may need encourage-

Environment	Activities for carers	Agency interventions
Time The rhythms of solitude are different from those of the social world. Children who are really making the journey of self-discovery will need those around to keep an eye on the clock for them, and to keep them in touch with the requirements of every-day life.	Establish a family atmosphere in which it is ordinary for people to make discoveries, to express them-selves in many different ways and through many different media, and to have periods of solitude and reflection.	ment to engage with activities that are just for them; physical exercise, classes, art, poetry, craft, reading, organised religion, spiritual exercises – anything that allows them to explore and express themselves can be encouraged.
People Children who are making this exploration withdraw a little from the social world. It is important that they do not lose contact with others. If children have issues to work through about contact with their birth families, these will surface whenever they are engaged with the question: Who am I? They may need special contact with members of their birth family at such times, or if this is not possible or appropriate, they will need help to work through the issues they cannot address directly.	Make available private spaces and quiet corners. Encourage children to keep journals and photographic records of their life. Provide access to physical activities, musical instruments, art materials, books, journals, newspapers, poetry, craft materials, gardens, animals, cultural experiences, whatever may contribute to the journey of exploration this unique child will be making. Promote and encourage formal life story work, and appropriate contact with or learning about birth family.	Provide resources to enable carers to create an environment that encourages self-discovery. Ensure that agencies work together to promote self-discovery for the child. Liaison between different agencies working with the child and family is vital when the child is addressing these issues. Provide formal life story work as appropriate. Enable and encourage contact with birth family as appropriate.

Generally children in the primary school years have made the extra-ordinary leap from egocentricity to awareness of the reality of perspectives other than their own. The developing brain has become a social organ, and the child is able to move from primary attachment relationships to group membership. Carol Gilligan (1998) has observed that girls and boys develop differently in terms of this decreasing egocentricity and increasing consciousness. She describes the stages of development in girls as being concerned with care, which moves from self to others at around the age of seven, and then during adolescence shifts again towards universality.

The child at first is centred on care of the self, which may include being interested in the care of those she sees as an extension of herself, her attachment figures. Then she is able to experience the separate and alternate perceptions of others in her immediate community. This produces a sense of group membership, and a capacity to share the views of others. It also leads the child to be very sensitive to those views, and this stage of development is sometimes called conformist or conventional, reflecting the strong group identification of children at this point in their lives. In adolescence, however, the child may develop a wider perspective, and become able to put their sense of group identity in a more universal framework. These stages in the development of compassion have been described by Ken Wilber (2001, p. 20) as egocentric, ethnocentric and worldcentric.

Boys, according to Gilligan (1998), take a different developmental path in the growth of compassion. As children of primary school age they tend to be more concerned with justice, fairness and rights as issues, compared with the greater preoccupation with relationships and care shown by girls. Both sexes follow the same developmental path from egocentricity towards social consciousness, and Gilligan suggests that, after they reach the postconventional or worldcentric phase, men and women have access to the male and female voices in themselves. Justice and caring unite to produce mature compassion. As Wilber (2001, p. 22) puts it: 'The spiral of development is a spiral of compassion, expanding from me, to us, to all of us.'

All of which is much more difficult for children who have unmet attachment needs. How is the child who has not fully experienced being cared for, who has not experienced reciprocal fairness and social reciprocity, to develop group connectedness? We see again the layers of interlinked disadvantage that gather around children whose basic needs have not been met. For social connectedness is a strong factor in building resilience to adversity (Gilligan, 2009). Children who can form strong social connections become more resilient. Children who have already suffered harm can become increasingly more vulnerable to further harm because of their difficulties in connecting with others.

Resilience does seem to have a truly chaotic quality. Small differences at early stages of development can lead to enormous differences in outcome. Small differences at any stage of development can have significant effects. Steven and Sybil Wolin (1993) and Jane and Robert Coles (Coles, 1986, 1990) offer vivid portrayals of the lives of children who show extraordinary resilience in the face of adversity. It is clear that children can survive, and thrive, even in terrible conditions. It is also clear that we must be able and willing to help them develop the resilience they need to do so.

What do we observe?: life with children who are developing social resilience

Compassion and comparison go hand in hand for the growing child. The unfolding of the brain as a social organ allows the child to make sense of the world of others, and to join with others to form groups. It also allows them to make comparisons. Attachment figures are no longer seen as the universe within which the child is safely contained. Instead they become important figures in an expanding landscape, but figures that can be examined and may be found wanting.

Parents of school age children know well the experience of being subjected to these unfavourable comparisons. 'My teacher says . . .', 'Jamie's mum can drive a fork lift truck . . .', and, most crushing in intent, 'All the other children have got one!' It is all part of the growing ability to be part of a group. In the process of developing compassion the child will inevitably be making comparisons; in order to join a group, the child needs to be able to grasp the essential elements of membership. Social awareness is the key by which children enter the world of the human group.

When children have developed through secure attachments the capacity to regulate stress and impulse, when they are not in a traumatised state in which they interpret neutral events as overwhelming threats, then they are able to develop social connectedness. For such children it is a seamless development; they move from playing alongside, to playing with, to being friends with other children. They move from unquestioning and undifferentiated connectedness to their primary carers to a position of enhanced consciousness in which carers and self can be distinguished from one another and each can be criticised from the perspective of the wider group.

Secure children are amassing new experience and new skills very rapidly at this stage of their lives. In doing so, the wider group reflects back to them an image of self-efficacy and so they develop a realistic self-esteem. They begin to take on specific social roles, and to take their place in a variety of groups, giving them the opportunity to try on a range of such roles. Respect gained within this range of settings generates self-belief and the ability to be flexible and creative in new settings and situations. Telling stories, and telling their own story to others generates clarity and meaning, and the ability to reflect on the question 'Who am I?', a question of immeasurable importance to human consciousness.

By contrast, the lives of children with significant unmet attachment needs or unresolved trauma are profoundly impoverished. Difficulties in regulating stress and impulse lead to groups being an often overwhelming challenge. Pervasive and excessive shame leads to self-disclosure and reciprocal story telling being an experience of overwhelming shame and self-concealment. Diminished capacity for empathy leads to socially inappropriate responses and behaviour. All these lead to exclusion from the group.

Human groups are unforgiving of difference, especially in childhood. The group will exclude those who are not able to fit in. Extremely anxious individuals, whether actively anxious or avoidant, will protect themselves by self-exclusion. Even if we do not take our most vulnerable children away from society and shut them up with others of their kind, they are likely to be excluded or to exclude themselves. And like calls to like, for the child needs a group to belong to, so we see socially vulnerable children finding peer groups of other socially vulnerable children. Policies of social inclusion are ineffective unless and until we address these dynamics.

What can we do?: promoting social resilience with children who find compassion difficult

Encourage social inclusion

Children will need help to be included in the groups that will help them grow. This is work that will involve a response from the whole community. Schools, health workers, activity groups, cultural and religious groups, neighbours, shopkeepers, police and anyone else who may encounter or be encountered by the child will need to be alert to the part they have to play in helping. They need to understand that in these encounters they contribute to the growing or diminishing resilience of the child, and that it is in the best interest of the whole community to promote the resilience of our most vulnerable children.

Schools in particular have a key part to play in developing resilience. Sonia Jackson has shown that, above all else, staying within mainstream schooling is a predictor for successful outcomes for children looked after in public care (Jackson, 2013). This is not surprising once we recognise that school is the centre of life for most school-age children. The attention of the school-age child is appropriately shifting away from the primary attachment group to wider social groups and groupings. School is where they spend a large proportion of their time, and it also provides a range of social experiences.

Other groups also matter, however. Carers may need to work hard at promoting inclusion for children whose behaviour may lead them to be excluded from the wider community. There is work to be done with the child, to help them to develop social graces that will be enough to carry them through. There is also work to be done with the community to help people understand the needs and responses of very anxious and easily overwhelmed children.

Encourage personal and social efficacy

Here the work is first to strengthen a sense of identity and to build self-esteem in the child, giving them a more settled base from which to venture into social relatedness. Then the child will need to be encouraged to develop new skills and abilities, both personally and socially. Finally the child will need their moments of empathy, areas of insight and understanding, and positive group roles to be recognised and valued, so that they can begin to feel that they have something to contribute to groups.

Identity work will include and extend earlier life story work. Now the emphasis in such work will be on the strengths and resiliencies that the life story has provided for the child to use as a foundation for daring to enter into new social groupings. It will also need to include the preparation of an appropriate cover story for the child, so that they can tell their story to others without being damaged in the telling. It is important at this stage that life story work enables and encourages the child to join identity affirming social groups beyond the immediate attachment group or family (Gilligan, 2009, pp. 16–19).

Such life story work will allow the child to create their own truth from the bare facts of their life. It will also explore and sustain key elements of social identity such as ethnicity, religion, language and culture. There are particular issues for life story work with black children in a predominantly, and dominantly, white society. Ryan and Walker (2007) provide helpful advice on enabling children to develop their own life narrative.

Everyone connected with the child has a part to play in enabling the child to build appropriate self-esteem. Noticing and commenting upon the child's aptitudes, abilities and personal qualities are of immense benefit to the developing personality. This is not to make the child into a bumptious self-advertiser. Indeed, sensitively and appropriately done, it will have the opposite effect. Many very anxious children protect themselves from overwhelming feelings of worthlessness and insignificance with an apparent overweening arrogance. In our family we used to call this "the Zaphod factor", after the Douglas Adams character (1988) Zaphod Beeblebrox. It is the factor at work in people who are so defended against their own insignificance that, no matter how broad a perspective they are offered, they will still remain quite certain that they are the centre of the universe.

True self-esteem, however, will allow children to let go of the need to protect themselves against insignificance. They will then feel better about themselves and more at home in the universe. They will also be much more acceptable to others. Again we see the paradox that those who are most vulnerable are least able to gain resilience. Those who have least self-esteem are least able to acquire it from their interactions with others. They need us to help them.

Encouraging the child to build on existing skills and abilities is important. It is equally important to allow and encourage children to seek and develop new interests and skills. Activities, hobbies, sports and group adventures such as school trips and camps are all opportunities for children to develop a sense of personal efficacy. So are any opportunities that can be given for children to contribute to group planning and decision-making. Children also need to learn the art of planning for their own lives, and to discover that they can make plans and carry them through. Again, it is likely that they will fail to notice their own growing competence unless it is explicitly commented upon. Anxious children need to be alerted to the occasions when they have managed to make a plan and stick to it.

Encourage continuing change

The present preoccupation in the public care of children is with outcomes. This redresses the balance on a long period when we have seemed to have little interest as a community in what actually happened to children we received into our corporate care. It is, however, a concept with fundamental difficulties when we apply it to human lives rather than to mechanistic processes or the products of computer programmes. For human life is a continuing process, and the outcome is always, in the end, death.

This is not to diminish the need to keep track of what we are doing to our children. It is outrageous that so few of the children we have committed to the public care system have achieved educational results at school that bear any relationship to those of their peers (Jackson, 2013). All the images of our most vulnerable children being looked after only to be vastly over-represented in those young adults who are homeless, or in prison, or in need of mental health care, or using drugs, or otherwise continuing to be involved in chaotic and harmful lifestyles are true. But they are only part of the truth.

We do need to give children time to recover. It is very important not to set outcome dates too early. Or not to set them at all, unless we regard outcomes as only a snapshot at a particular time of the state of being of a complex person who is still developing, and who will continue to develop. When thinking about educational outcomes, I wrote the following anonymised case study with one of my children; we include it in the hope it might add to the debate about outcomes.

Bonita's story

The eldest of five children, Bonita was looked after at home for most of her first seven years, although she had many short episodes of foster care in that time. There were many moves and changes in family composition during that time, and there were also repeated concerns about neglect and possible abuse of the children. Bonita's school attendance was very irregular during these early years.

When she was seven, Bonita was removed from home as a result of abuse and neglect, and a care order was sought and granted. She was placed in foster care, and the other children remained at home. Foster placements continually broke down for Bonita, and she was placed in a children's home when she was nine years old. No further foster placements were found. At the age of ten, so her social worker told us, she was turned down for a place at a special boarding school for being 'too old and too difficult'. She was placed with us as a permanent foster family when she was eleven.

We had an approach that we believe helped to contribute to a good educational outcome. It included ground rules: treat one another with respect and kindness; school attendance is an expectation; everyone who has had a troubled start in life may show this in their feelings and actions at times, but we will try to keep such troubled behaviour at home and not at school. We also made a promise to our children: for the rest of our lives we will take a parental interest in you so long as that is what you want.

For the next three years, until the age of 14, Bonita was reasonably settled in placement and catching up at mainstream school. She developed many new interests and activities. At the same time she experienced increasing mental and physical health problems, including self-harm, violence, volatility, and eating disorders. She was often absent from placement in attempts to return home. During this period her next younger sibling was received into care, but the others still remained at home.

We maintained the approach of keeping home as a safe arena to contain difficulties as far as possible, leaving school relatively trouble free. We encouraged a range of interests and activities outside the home for Bonita and all members of the foster family. It was a priority for us to establish and maintain close liaison with school and social worker.

By the time she was 14, we felt it was impossible for us to maintain the safety of the placement, and Bonita was removed to a children's home nearer to her birth family. We remained in touch with her while she was at the children's home. Her high-risk behaviour led to her being moved to a special unit in Wales, far away from her family and from us. Once there our letters to her were withheld. Bonita was very unhappy at this placement and asked to return to our foster family. She moved, at our request, to a bridging placement for two months and then returned to her placement with us.

Once Bonita was clear she wanted to return, the interim placement was agreed to allow two months for us to negotiate with school for her to return to them. It also gave the opportunity to set a clear placement contract with Bonita, enabling her to get some recognition of the feelings of others in the family, and giving them time to prepare for her return. She then returned to us, and restarted school on a restricted entry GCSE programme. Very close liaison between school and foster family was set up to try to ensure a smooth transition after six months absence.

Bonita remained with us and at school until she was nearly 16, and took and passed five GCSEs, four at grade C and above. There were still many concerns about her mental and physical health and safety, however. One week after her exams finished, she left the foster home and returned to a children's home near to her family. Three days after her sixteenth birthday she ran away and got married. Her first baby was born when she was 17. Bonita had no contact with us for two years, then when she was 18 she and her husband moved home and were living near to us, her foster family. A second child was born the following year. There were still many concerns about Bonita's mental and physical health.

We warmly accepted the renewed contact with Bonita, but were careful to set clear boundaries about the nature and extent of our involvement with her.

When she was 21, Bonita left the marital home.

The foster family offered support, within boundaries, to Bonita and her husband and children.

At the age of 23, Bonita remarried. Two more children were born over the next two years. Bonita and her second husband set up their family home nearby. Concerns about mental and physical health continued, but Bonita's mental health was beginning to improve by this time. She was increasingly able to seek and make use of therapy.

We offered continuing support to the reconstituted family.

By the time she was 26, Bonita had decided to take an access course at a local college with good creche facilities. She later completed a full time level three access course in four subjects: English, Psychology, Environmental Studies and Sociology, as well as retaking GCSE Maths. She passed in all subjects, her lowest mark being 92 per cent.

It is clear that everyone here made mistakes. We certainly did as the care family. The agencies involved also made some mistakes, with the possible exception of the school, whose staff made heroic efforts to contain and support Bonita (this might be considerably more difficult in the current educational climate for schools). And finally, Bonita herself made mistakes. Yet at this point everyone survives and few people would regard the present situation as a failure, whatever that might mean. An unfolding life is a complex process.

Examples of interventions to promote social resilience

Environment	Activities for carers	Agency interventions
Physical environment Children who are exploring the wider world need a safe base to which to come home. Rules and conventions matter, so families need to provide a home that is culturally appropriate enough for the child to feel able to bring their friends home. They also are at a stage when their personal space begins to be a statement about self. They will need some space that they can own as an expression of their developing personality. Adults need to be able to accept that this may sometimes look chaotic, if chaos is their truth at that time.	Children need to see that social relationships matter to us, and that they sustain our own resilience. Ensure that children can observe the importance to carers of their own relationships. Provide a secure and structured base from which the child can safely venture. Make sure that ground rules are clear and explicit. These can be flexible, but it is important that adults stay in control of the flexibility, providing reasons and explanations for the rules and any variations. Allow children to have some personal space in the home where they can express who they feel themselves to be at any given time.	Encourage and support care families to establish and maintain a wide range of social relationships. Provide resources for children to pursue interests and hobbies. Provide resources for children to engage in group activities, outings and holidays. Engage children actively with planning processes relating to their own lives. Help them to make plans and carry them through. Provide formal life story work as appropriate.
Time Children can become exhausted if they are not helped to put boundaries around their use of time. Even negotiation about time can become an opportunity for more self-understanding or a battleground. Probably both will happen on different occasions. The process is what matters.	Keep a close eye on physiological markers such as eating and sleeping. Encourage good habits in both. Help children to understand the importance of a healthy lifestyle to be able to enjoy life fully. Engage with the child's life narrative, and encourage the creation of meaning and of a cover story.	Ensure that all agencies that are or may be concerned with the child are aware of the issues in promoting social resilience. Work actively to reduce social exclusion for vulnerable children. Recognise that this is

Environment	Activities for carers	Agency interventions
People Vulnerable and anxious children need help to make constructive relationships with others from a broad spectrum. Invite others into the home. Inclusiveness will help the child to make sound judgements about those who hinder their own development. Adults will never be able to get it right in trying to help children make constructive relationships. Keep trying. Even our mistakes help the child to think about the issues.	Promote realistic self-esteem at every opportunity. In particular notice and comment upon every aptitude the child shows for social relatedness and caring about others. Recognise that boys and girls may express relatedness in different ways, and that each child is unique in their social connectedness. Actively promote learning and work with schools to encourage educational success.	an active process to which the child is central. Try to address the dynamics of exclusion and self-exclusion. Ensure that agencies work together to promote the child's social resilience, including particularly working to enhance educational achievement for vulnerable children.

Tranquillity

Maybe, at a certain moment, it's best to think differently about people. Maybe we shouldn't be emphasising so strongly what "problems" they have, but how they get through their lives.
(Marian Putnam, quoted in Coles, 1990, p. 304)

What happens?: thinking about the development of transpersonal resilience

Always, in living and working with children, I have wanted to know how they get through their lives. Children have taught me so much about living with courage and grace and dignity, about doing the best we can with the cards that are dealt to us. It is hard for children to survive the pain of unmet basic needs. It is hard for them to survive the pain of traumatic experience. It is very hard indeed for children who have suffered these pains to feel that they exist as a self connected to other selves, yet they often do.

There are those who hold the view that beyond compassion there are further steps, or stages, or waves of human development. There are those who assert that children have a spiritual life, or the possibility of consciousness that transcends and includes the self. Such views and assertions are found in the work of diverse people including deep ecologists like Bateson (2000) and Capra (1982), developmental psychologists such as Graves (Beck and Cowan, 1996) and Maslow (1968, 1970), and transpersonal psychologists such as Wilber (2000, 2001).

These remain potentially controversial views; I have come to them because of what I have learned from children. Like Jane and Robert Coles (1990), and Steven and Sybil Wolin (1993), I have observed that the children with whom I have lived and worked have deep concerns. I have also discovered that they prosper in their development when we address those concerns as spiritual needs. Making the assumption that children can develop transpersonal consciousness, while not assuming that they will or should, allows for the greatest possible responsiveness to each unique individual.

I have used the term tranquillity to indicate a state of peaceful joy, or perhaps what Treya Killam Wilber (Wilber, 1991) described as 'passionate equanimity'. It is not a state reached by most of us more than fleetingly, but I consider that children do experience such states, and that they are deeply healing.

What do we observe?: living with children who are exploring tranquillity

Before we are able to enjoy tranquillity we need to be able to recognise and value the experience. Children need to be able to learn what peacefulness is and what its meaning might be for them. Initially they will be learning by observation. If they live in a household where quietness is valued, they are likely to learn to value it. Winter evenings in front of the fire, summer afternoons in peaceful places, quiet moments during a long journey. Gentle physical contact such as resting against one another, or brushing and combing hair, may increase the sense of ease and well-being. Quiet music can add to the peacefulness if silence itself is still too threatening to the stressed or frightened child.

Activities can be added that enhance rather than diminish the tranquillity. Reading, knitting, sewing, drawing, making models, sharing poetry, making music can all add to the quality of time spent together. Sometimes children like to learn relaxation or meditation techniques, and can find the practice of these immensely healing. Always there need to be markers to help the children identify and recall the experience. 'I do like these quiet evenings together', 'It's so peaceful here'; any comment or image that holds the experience for a moment so that children begin to develop a pattern for peacefulness.

Children may bombard us with questions about our own spiritual journey, or they may want to make their own exploration in deep privacy. They can be encouraged to keep a journal, in words, or paintings, or craft work. They can gain immensely from being exposed to art, music and natural beauty. It can also help children to connect them with the biographies of others, especially people who have made the journey from adversity to fulfilment.

Children who are beginning to explore transpersonal issues will be full of conversation. I have seen this ignored or diminished in some settings, yet the questions and dilemmas raised by children can be the source of profound discourse if treated with respect. 'Where was I before I was a baby?', 'How do we know we both see yellow?', 'Why does it hurt when people call me names?', 'Why have some people got a lot of money when other people haven't got any?', 'What happens when we die?' – sometimes it can seem that there is no end to the questions.

If these are treated with the weight they deserve, and many of the questions children ask will tax the resources of the greatest philosophers, then children begin to discover a discourse which genuinely assumes that they have as much to give as to take in intimate relationships. We can learn so much from the questions of those who have not learned not to ask.

What can we do?: promoting transpersonal resilience

The former Looking After Children System (LACS) was based on research conducted by Professor Roy Parker and his colleagues into the nature and dimensions of good parenting. The outcome indicators provided by these developmental dimensions and the Assessment Framework that emerged from this research give a structure to the following Part III on how foster carers may, in daily life, promote transpersonal resilience. The framework may also suggest a basis for critical reflection on the concept of outcomes in child care.

Part III

Promoting transpersonal resilience

Brian Cairns

Promoting transpersonal resilience

Health

Developing awareness of our minds and bodies and respect for them

Mindful carers need to adopt a perceptive and thoughtful approach to the health of children they look after. Older children may arrive with their own narrative about health and health care which may not be helpful. All children may arrive with all sorts of previously unidentified health issues that are not immediately obvious, or that have been ignored or misunderstood. They may lack any age-appropriate understanding of how to care for their bodies and stay healthy. They may mistrust or fear health professionals.

We know now that early trauma leaves its marks – often hidden – on body functions (physical health) and brain function (emotional and mental health). It really helps for carers to be alert to these and to ensure that their observations are shared within their professional networks, and often with the child themselves: 'Have you noticed that it's more difficult for you to . . . than it is for a lot of your friends? So shall we think together about how we can help you to make it easier?'

Learning to keep in mind the key factors below helped us in our own time as foster carers, and would help even more now as we have learned more about the insidious and life-changing – sometimes life-threatening – effects of previous traumatic experience, and the equally life-changing – but inevitably life-enhancing – power of building resilience in our children and in ourselves.

Key factors
- *Being aware of the likely health-related consequences of earlier abuse or trauma*
  Learn as much as you can about child development and early brain development, and about how traumatised people of all ages are likely to develop maladaptive behaviours, often damaging to

their immediate or long-term health, in order to function adequately in the moment or to protect themselves against physical or emotional pain.

- *Considering possible health-related reasons for unusual behaviour*
  Some examples from our own history: a child seen as wilful, disruptive and lacking in concentration turned out to have serious hearing problems as a result of recurrent untreated ear infections that had caused permanent damage to the ears; a child who constantly dropped money because early physical punishment had left him unable to rotate either arm to make an upward-facing palm; a child unwilling to walk moderate distances because of flat feet caused by fallen arches and unnoticed through many years of wearing ill-fitting shoes.

- *Remembering to take into account children's mental health needs*
  It is wise to look out, even in quite young children, for signs of eating disorders, self-harming behaviour, stress-related psychotic or schizoaffective behaviour or any indications of behaviour relating to post-traumatic stress disorder. All of these could be dismissed as "naughtiness" or "adolescent rebellion" or "manipulation", but in our experience such behaviours in children and young people are almost inevitably triggered by episodes of intense early childhood stress or abuse.

- *Making health issues part of everyday family conversation*
  We can find no virtue in shielding children from "adult" topics of conversation, provided that they are approached in a matter-of-fact manner and with constant mindfulness of the impact on each vulnerable child. Unsensational conversation around the supper-table about health-related articles read, health-related TV programmes watched, the health, life and death concerns of friends and acquaintances, our own visits to doctors and dentists and pharmacies, experiences of treatments, vaccinations and check-ups, our own efforts to stay fit and healthy – all these help to

normalise health as an integral aspect of life and to develop trust in discussing it.

- *Explaining to children and other important people in their systems and networks the possible roots of their physical, mental and emotional difficulties*
  As far as possible, it's important to practise therapeutic care WITH children, not ON them. A child is more likely to take care of the plaster cast on his broken arm if he understands the purpose it serves and how the broken bone will heal, as well as why it broke in the first place. It's great if the carer can get the doctor or nurse to explain it fully themselves, but the carer will need to repeat and explain afterwards (probably often!). Take a similar approach to explaining why the child finds it difficult to behave in particular ways, or to resolve particular feelings. And make sure that teachers and other people in their network understand as well.

- *Using the strength of the network as a source of acceptance and support*
  With older children (and their agreement!) this can often include their friends and peers. It's also protective of those other network members and of the relationships.

- *Exercising care in choosing a GP who will understand the needs of looked after children*
  It's worthwhile taking time over this and negotiating a change of GP if you feel that there is a block in trust or understanding between the current GP and the child that will be difficult to remove, and that someone more aware of attachment and trauma issues and more open/approachable is available. The GP needs to understand that insecurely attached or abused children may lack conscious awareness of their own bodies, or may experience emotional disorders as physical pain. Once a helpful GP is iden-tified, it's good to be assertive about always having appointments

with that person, unless the situation is an emergency. We found it good to "demystify" the GP by referring to him/her frequently as "John Smith" or "Mary Green" rather than the more distant "Dr Green".

- *Normalising routine medical procedures and check-ups as part of everyday life*
  Not something we did – but something we should have done – was to establish annual health checks for ourselves and our birth children as well as those which were statutory requirements for our foster children. We did go for dental checkups as a family. We also tried not to exhibit undue anxiety about GP or hospital visits of our own and to discuss them objectively.

- *Ensuring that children have access to a variety of people in whom they may confide about health matters*
  This is part of a broader issue of building the child's resilience – and social skills – by working actively to help them build good relationships with a wide range of "safe" adults whom you also trust and who will relay concerns about the child's wellbeing back to you. If there is a school nurse, this is a great relationship to foster for both the carer and the child.

- *Making available varied sources of information*
  It's good to be a bit untidy and to leave helpful leaflets, magazine articles and so on lying about the house along with lots of other stuff that you don't mind the children seeing! It's also good – and we will return to this in the "Education" section – to have plenty of bookshelves in public areas with books on health-related topics mixed in with the rest, to have plenty of useful links bookmarked on the family computer, to look at the synopses of TV programmes and quietly encourage shared watching of those with relevant topics or plots, and to take your child with you when you go to give blood or visit the dental hygienist – be creative!

- *Encouraging children to care for animals and participate in looking after small children*
  This can be fun! Whether the animals are the responsibility of the adults or of an individual child, they bring endless opportunities to discuss unthreateningly how they – and we – care for their bodies, how and why we identify a healthy (or toxic) diet, how they experience stress and how it can be avoided, illnesses, peer relationships, lifestyle and exercise, anatomy, conception, pregnancy and birth, and of course life and death. It is positively good to involve foster children as directly as you safely can in observing and participating in the provision of care to younger children and infants, either in your own household or in others, provided that you and the other adults involved are aware of potential hazards, assess the risks and manage them sensitively.

- *Involving children in the miracles and emotions of birth and death*
  Leading on from the previous point, it is a precious gift for a foster child to be involved in a loving family through a pregnancy and birth, and this can also be true when the foster family is experiencing a terminal illness and a death, provided that the other adults are able to continue to be emotionally available for the child.

- *Providing a nutritious and varied diet without straying far outside cultural norms*
  We found that table d'hote was generally to be preferred over à la carte as an approach to family meals, once individual cultural norms and health needs were taken into account, and the child had developed sufficient trust to accept that we weren't actively setting out to poison them! Keeping it simple and involving the children in preparation of meals (and in the clearing up afterwards) are both norms worth establishing. It's no bad thing to ensure that fresh fruit is always readily available, and as with everything, modelling a moderate and healthy approach to food and drink is important.

- *Establishing mealtimes as enjoyable shared social occasions*
  Mealtimes shouldn't be a frenetic battle. We aimed for a convivial event which was part of the comforting daily household routine, unrushed, as far as possible uninterrupted by phones or TV, at a pre-set, attractive table, including all household members at least once each day if at all possible. Visitors, invited or otherwise, would be expected to join us at the table. There would be plenty of conversation, with encouragement for everyone to take part. We made a little ceremony of starting meals together, joining hands for a few seconds around the table in something approaching silence.

- *Providing the space, freedom and equipment to encourage healthy exercise*
  Children need time and space to exercise, and plenty of opportunity to do this in a spontaneous and unstructured way. Traumatised children may need additional help and encouragement to overcome inhibition or lack of physical co-ordination, and to learn how to use their bodies and enjoy it. We were fortunate to have the use of a large garden in a rural setting with acres of local common land, and we ensured that there were always plenty of bicycles, skateboards, bats and balls and racquets, as well as more structured opportunities to join sports clubs. We also resisted the growing social pressure to chauffeur children everywhere and encouraged them where possible to walk or cycle.

- *Keeping open channels of communication to discuss health issues concerning diet, smoking, alcohol and other drugs, and sex*
  Observation of and comment on life going on around us provides endless opportunities, as does conversation about what we see on TV.

- *Leading by example, ideally one of tolerance and moderation*
  Our children, including our foster children, can be our severest critics, and we should welcome this. There is never any justification for a "do as I say, not as I do" approach. Conversely,

ultra-hardline attitudes are likely to cut little ice, close down communication and entrench harmful behaviour. It can be important to be mindful of particular trigger points for individual children: one may be terrified to see carers enjoy a glass of wine, fully expecting that drunkenness and wholesale domestic violence will follow; another may see an affectionate hug between loving adults as signalling the start of an episode of sexual abuse. Noticing such reactions must lead to reassurance, sensitive discussion, and often modified behaviour on the part of the adults until the child feels fully safe.

- *Recognising that you may be able to advise and encourage, but not to enforce*
  It's easy to feel that you have become totally responsible for your foster child's risky or unwise behaviour in relation to health issues. For the sake of your own health, remember that many of your child's choices are currently governed by events and experiences in which you played no part. Remain loving and caring, in the knowledge that your concern, advice and example may be translated into action a decade or more into the future.

Education

Developing appreciation and understanding of the world around us

Traumatised children are unlikely to find learning easy. We learn best when we feel safe and can build trusting relationships with those around us as they help us to make sense of the world. Children whose experience has led to them being in care may well be unable to do this. They may find both their foster home and their school bewildering and threatening environments. Their experience may have led them to find fear, not interest or wonder, in the unknown. Their world may have been one of chaos in which no assumptions could be made about the patterns and rules that order and underpin much of our growing understanding of the world. Their narrative may have been one of failure and learned worthlessness.

Many children in care have never been "school-ready". As carers, we need to bring them to that stage, whatever their chronological age, carefully taking down the barriers to learning, which may already be substantial and unyielding. Once they can experience it, we need to build their capacity for wonder and their sense of self-worth. And we need to find and support schools that exhibit a sensitivity to individual need and understanding of trauma sufficient to nurture these children through a development as miraculous as that of a butterfly from a larva. These are tasks of which successive governments, seeing education, it would appear, as nothing more than acquisition of a toolbox for economy-boosting employment, have shown little understanding.

Key factors

- *Keeping the long-term perspective – building a framework for lifelong learning and learning for life*
  It helps to turn your back on assumptions that your foster child should be able to do or to understand specific things at a specific age or in an expected order. Building and rebuilding brain connections is a slow and very individual process. The goal is not "passing eight GCSEs by the age of 16", but "making sense of the world and developing curiosity and wonder".

- *Ensuring that there are always quiet, peaceful areas in the living environment*
  Whether for formal homework, for reading, for exploring ideas together, or for quiet reflection, spaces where distractions are kept to a minimum but which can be shared calmly with others are places where learning can happen.

- *Facilitating the development of the necessary building-blocks for learning – concentration, curiosity, wonder, imagination, empathy*
  Keep thinking of new ways to do this that fit with where the child is on their own journey: games, stories, drawing, singing, reciting nursery rhymes and poems, posing rhetorical questions ('I wonder why . . . ?'; 'What if . . . ?'; 'Do you think . . . ?'; 'Did you

know . . . ?'), providing explanations of how things work and why things happen, collecting objects, drawing the child's attention to the natural world, involving the child in shopping, choosing, budgeting, reading out what you see around you and commenting on the passing scene, visiting new places...and so on.

- *Providing varied, stimulating leisure experiences and ensuring that children meet a variety of interesting people*
  A good way to make connections is to link leisure activities with learning – to do things or go to places that the child has heard about in school, or in a book you have read together, or have seen on TV. Use the local library with your child. Go together to performances of all kinds in your community. If you go abroad, try to make opportunities for your child to meet local children and experience something of their lives. When you get to know someone who has knowledge or expertise in something which your child wouldn't otherwise experience because it isn't part of your life, encourage them to share it with you and your child.

- *Extending horizons through wide-ranging conversation and discussion*
  We all learn as small children by listening to conversations that we don't, or don't fully, understand. Children in care may often dissociate from conversations taking place around them, or filter out whatever doesn't immediately appear to apply to them, but they benefit from being accepted as part of a group of people among which conversations and discussions are happening and which they can join at any point. It's good to assume that the child is involved in your conversation with others, whether or not they are actively participating, and for your body language to indicate this.

- *Challenging children to form and develop opinions, and respecting them as they do*
  We are often slow to ask children and young people what they

think, and quick to knock them back if they express a view that is at variance with our own, especially if it is expressed inarticulately or defensively. We need to develop within ourselves the capacity not to feel threatened by what children think, but to develop a relaxed interest in why they think it, and always to be prepared to modify our own view on reflection.

- *Making books, computers and anything else that enhances learning readily and profusely available*
  As foster carers, we aimed to have books of all sorts in every room in the house and newspapers or magazines on virtually every table. Interrupting someone who was reading was seen as similar to interrupting someone who was talking. Nowadays, we would aim to have computers, with appropriate filters, almost as accessible, and for "looking it up" to be a fairly constant activity. Varied music should be readily available too. I remember the wonder of a ten-year-old foster child calling me back from the kitchen to the sitting-room to rewind a tape to a few bars of trumpet solo in a Shostakovich concerto which she had found beautiful – the precursor to her joining a brass band. Embrace distractions: if your child's homework remains incomplete because she was suddenly intrigued by an unusual word which led you into a lengthy shared exploration of connections totally outside the curriculum – rejoice!

- *Enabling each child to identify and develop individual interests that may enhance self-confidence and increase "connectedness"*
  Many new foster carers talk excitedly about being able to involve foster children in their own interests of scouting, horse riding, modelmaking, or whatever. This may have its place, but effort should constantly be made to identify activities that will hook the child's interest, and to facilitate them in taking up those activities, even at the cost of your own pastimes.

- *Modelling reading, thinking and learning with enjoyment*
  As always, children are more likely to attempt or copy something

which they can observe others doing with pleasure, especially when the "others" are people whom they are learning to trust. It's great when carers are undertaking their own learning – gaining new qualifications, preparing for a new job, mastering a new skill, researching new interests, greater knowledge, new places to visit – and being positive about it whilst being open about the fact that they don't always find it easy. Make learning infectious. There are multi-faceted benefits in sharing your own learning about fostering with older children.

- *Exercising reasonable control over access to computers, smart-phones and television*
  There is a balance to be struck and monitored between ensuring internet safety and making online information readily accessible. "Entertainment" use of media demands some strictures on time so that other activities and human contact aren't frozen out. We tried to ensure that television programmes were specifically requested by the child and agreed with the adults, and that, once selected, they could be watched with a minimum of interruption and, if possible, with an adult present to comment, interpret or discuss afterwards. We kept televisions out of bedrooms (including our own, again on the "do as I do, not just do as I say" model) and would probably do the same now with computers and think carefully about how to monitor smartphone usage.

- *Maintaining stability in placement and school settings*
  All the above factors relate to what can be done at home to encourage learning. Patient work with the child at home will help them to feel safer in school and ready for, or more able to benefit from, what the school offers additionally in terms of education. Each disruption is likely to set the process back.

- *Choosing schools with care, with emphasis on a happy, tolerant atmosphere*
  "League tables" tell us little about whether a school will have the flexibility and understanding to nurture and gain the confidence

ATTACHMENT, TRAUMA AND RESILIENCE

and trust of a traumatised child. Whilst the structure, routines and daily expectations within the school may provide the child with helpful boundaries, the ability to develop a recognition of the child's individual personality, needs and sensitivities, and to devise ways of acknowledging these, are crucial. We were attracted to our local comprehensive school (of 1,200 pupils) because the head teacher made it his business to get to know every child during their first term and to greet as many as possible by name each day, and because the ancillary staff were obviously valued, regarded as important members of the school community, and encouraged to relate well to the children.

- *Using mainstream, local non-selective schooling where possible*
  If the child can cope with it, it is good for them to feel part of the community in which they live, to have exposure to as wide a peer group as possible, and to have a wide range of learning opportunities which they can be helped to access at their own pace. In the present educational climate, schools that are still managed by the local authority may have easier access to the services of other professionals, such as educational psychologists and speech therapists, although academies and free schools may have more flexibility to support an individual child creatively.

- *Getting to know school staff well and becoming a trusted part of the school community*
  This is vital. Carers need to feel at home in their children's school and able to talk with staff on a relaxed basis, openly and frequently. We liked being able to get to know them as fellow members of our local community as well as teachers, and, as with GPs, to be able to humanise them for our children by referring to them by their full names rather than the depersonalising "Miss Jones", in a world where children are used to calling their parents' friends, friends' parents, and adult neighbours by their first names.

- *Helping teachers to understand the children's experience*
  On the whole, teachers have not received training about the

effects of impaired early attachment relationships and unresolved trauma. When these things affect our child's ability to conform to social norms or to learn effectively, it is incumbent on us to ensure that as many as possible of the school staff who come into contact with them understand and "learn the child". We need to offer this learning in a spirit of co-operation as colleagues, members of the therapeutic team around the child. This is not about sharing confidential detail about what the child may have experienced in the past, but explaining how the child's brain functions now, and what the child will struggle with.

- *Negotiating with teachers to avoid or mitigate inappropriate sanctions or exclusions*
  Most school sanctions rely on the assumption that the child needs to be made to think differently in a future similar situation in order to act differently, and that the sanction will act as a future prompt to conforming behaviour or deterrent of undesirable behaviour. Children acting in response to trauma are following well-trafficked brain patterns that may be maladaptive and which allow no time to engage a thinking response. They are likely to be unable to make a link between the sanction and the offence, and the sanction may serve only to further distance them from feelings of trust and belonging. Their first need is to feel safe. Only when this happens is it possible for a person with whom they feel safe to discuss with them how they might try to address a similar situation in the future, and how they might be helped to self-regulate before the thinking brain is closed down. Teachers may need help to understand this. The Head of Virtual School for Looked After Children in your local authority may be a valuable support in this.

- *Ensuring that the journey to and from school is stress-free*
  When a child frequently arrives at school "in a state", teachers may feel that things must be going wrong at home. Conversely, when the child consistently arrives home distressed, carers may jump to the conclusion that there are problems at school. Neither

may be true. The problem may lie in the journey – bullying from other children, loud music or insensitive chatter from the taxi driver, over-stimulation, harassment from would-be exploiters. The child is most able to benefit from school if getting up, having breakfast and the journey to school are calm, unrushed, and predictable. If distance and safety considerations allow, a leisurely walk or cycle ride can make for a good transition.

- *Avoiding competition and competitiveness whilst encouraging co-operation in learning*
  We seem to live in an increasingly competitive society, and the apparent imperative of competition and out-performing others in a world presented as one of individual winners and losers can too easily take over as the prime motivator used by teachers – and parents. This is often unhelpful to children in care who have a personal narrative of "low" achievement and expectations. One teenage foster child of ours agonised over completing a "personal achievement record" before writing 'I succeeded in not killing myself'. Achievement as measured in measurable attainment and qualifications can – and often does – come a few years later for our foster children than for their peers. It is less likely to come if they cannot develop a sense of learning as an enjoyable and satisfying undertaking that can be shared with others.

- *Encouraging children to take responsibility for their own learning whilst making extra help available*
  If we start from the assumption that children, as human beings, want to learn, but may lack the courage or the tools and brain function to do so, we can cast ourselves as willing helpers, and find other helpers to complement what we can do. They will learn more effectively if we optimise their opportunities through responding to their emotions and their curiosity; engage with them; remain relaxed in sharing and guiding their explorations; maintain an upbeat approach; help them to put their often tentative learning into words; and indicate that we are sharing whatever delight they can experience from it.

- *Assuring each child that there will be no financial barrier to achieving educational ambition*
  Keeping open the doors of educational opportunity for every young person throughout childhood and into adulthood needs investment of time and resources. It is important for carers to make whatever commitment they can, but also to push hard for assurances and repeated confirmation of those assurances from local authorities, that the child's educational needs will be adequately identified and funded, even if the young person is older than their peers at the point where they become able to benefit from the provision.

Identity

Developing a sense of where we came from, who we are, and who we are becoming

My identity is continuing to develop, and will continue to do so throughout my lifetime. It includes not only my family, culture and ethnicity of origin, but also my likes and dislikes, my opinions and beliefs, my sexuality, my social tastes and preferences, my frames of reference, and all my personal history as I have experienced it or re-experience it as I reflect on it. For it to be true to me, and I to it, I need self-awareness and self-knowledge.

This process has featured a continuing cycle of identification and differentiation. As an infant I identified with my mother, and then with my father and other close relatives. As I developed a sense of myself as a separate being, I began to notice things about me which differentiated me from them and from other people. This may or may not have been encouraged and respected, depending on whether my family or culture valued or feared diversity.

As I entered adolescence, I was more conscious of identification with my peers – and as time moved on further, I differentiated myself from many of them, and identified more with others who shared my interests and views, in turn becoming aware of differences between me and them, and continuing this pattern of identification and differentiation to become increasingly the unique, but still changing, individual that I am today.

The development of a foster child's identity involves facilitating this process, all the time ensuring that the early stages of it, the parts before verbal memory kicked in, or the parts that have been obscured by dissociation, trauma, or simply by separation from the people and places who would otherwise serve as reminders and holders of the narrative, are safely held and recorded without distortion.

Key factors

- *Recognising that many aspects of our identity are not static and that looked after children will need much help and encouragement to develop their own identity*
  We cannot change aspects of ourselves such as ethnicity or genetic inheritance. Neither can we change historical events – but we can learn to view them differently, to manage and regulate unhelpful feelings engendered by them, and to form brain patterns that enable us to act differently in response to those feelings. And we can help our children to do this too, by modelling it in our own behaviour and by using stories and metaphors to prompt reflection and reassessment of the past.

- *Enabling stabilisation in the present, integration of the past, and adaptation to current and anticipated circumstances*
  This is the therapeutic cycle of recovery from trauma, a cycle repeated many times like the process of identification and differentiation. Formal life story work may have a place in this, but the important work is done in informal moments, and in interventions that enhance the child's sense of present safety, the context-building of reflection on the past, and the recognition and expectation of joy and being at ease with oneself.

- *Offering each child a real choice in establishing an identity in which they can feel comfortable and true to themselves*
  Parents and carers often, perhaps unwittingly, close down

identity-building in children by throwaway comments like 'You're just like your brother/mother/so-and-so in *Eastenders*', delivered either approvingly or critically. Experience of varied lifestyles and belief systems and non-judgemental explanations of the assumptions underlying them can help older young people to practise identification and differentiation while still safely held.

- *Offering unconditional lifetime family relationships*
  In order to give a foster child the security in which they can safely explore their identity, it is helpful if the foster carers can commit, on their side, to offering a "family-member" relationship to the child for as long as they want it. This is not a demand for reciprocity. Adults who have derived great benefits from their foster carers may well not wish to see themselves as sons/daughters of the family throughout the decades that follow or as supports for their carers in old age, but welcome the knowledge that the door remains open to them and that their time in the foster family remains remembered and valued.

- *Allowing children the maximum control possible over what name(s) they choose to call themselves – and others*
  This can seem a tricky issue. Our name can be an important part of our identity, but also one which we may change, formally or informally, on our passage through life. Allowing children, particularly children in foster care, some control over this can legitimise for them the ongoing process of building a personal narrative through identification and differentiation. So the child may helpfully exercise choice over which variants of which of their given names they wish to be called by at the current stage of their life, whether they wish to be known informally by the surname of the foster carer rather than by that of their birth family, and know that the foster family will feel honoured if the child chooses to formalise this on reaching adulthood, and similarly unfazed if they reverse this decision at a later date.

- *Establishing recognisable but flexible routines and acceptable individual and family rituals*
  All the rituals and routines of family life – what we do around mealtimes, bedtimes, laundry, Christmas and birthdays, what stays where, whether or not we wear shoes indoors, and so on – can be bewildering to the newly arrived child. Many of those same routines can and do quickly become part of the sense of security and predictability that helps the child to feel safely held a few weeks or months down the line, and part of what the child will rebel against as the need to differentiate arises in due course. But just occasionally – and we should be open to the possibility – there is a detail of the way we do things which the child just cannot deal with, and which we might consider changing, and sometimes any member of the household may question how we do something and come up with an idea that suits most of us better.

- *Assisting children to recognise and identify their own emotions*
  To develop our children's emotional literacy we need to be very aware of our own emotions, and to be able to identify the child's emotions clearly and objectively. We shall return to this in the section on social and emotional development.

- *Encouraging self-expression in personal space*
  There is a balance to be kept here. Many traumatised children need their personal space (usually their bedroom) to be a soothing space with a minimum of stimulating distractions. But the child themselves may not recognise this, and may favour garish colours and loud designs on every surface. So it can be important to find other individual personal space – a workshop, part of the garden, an ancient caravan parked on the drive, even the corner of the sitting-room behind the sofa – where the child has freedom to do (within reason) the thing that is special to them at a given point in time. We even gave over the conservatory for some considerable time to a foster child for breeding rabbits and guinea pigs!

- *Establishing clear boundaries around personal and family space*
  The importance of the privacy of children's bedrooms is as much about issues of identity-building as about issues of child protection. Each child needs a safe space in which they can be themselves, subject to discreet, respectful and appropriate adult oversight. Adults can model the use of personal space by the expectations around the use of their bedroom or a study/office. It always felt important to us that the kitchen was very much a shared family space, and that the boundaries of all spaces (except, of course, bathrooms) were enforced by expectation and not by locks and keys.

- *Using the physical environment to create an atmosphere of calm, comfort and safety*
  Children often come into care from environments that are chaotic, unpredictable and visually discordant. We tried to do a regular "five senses tour" of the physical environment of our house and garden from the point of view of each of our children, thinking about how what they could see, hear, touch, smell, and even taste in each space might affect their sense of safety and wellbeing or stimulate their senses positively, and making adjustments or compromises accordingly.

- *Finding opportunities for developing mutual trust*
  It should go without saying that, as carers, we should never give our children cause to see us as untrustworthy. We should do what we say we will do, be where we said we would be at the time agreed, report accurately our conversations with teachers and social workers, and so on. And we should be honest in our explanations and apologies if circumstances occasionally make this impossible. We should also find ways of showing our children, who may never have been fully trusted before, that we see them as trustworthy people. This can be by asking them to check your purse for pound coins for the supermarket trolley, or to take a message to a neighbour, entrusting them with something

to look after for you, seeking their help to put a plaster on your cut finger. Be alert for opportunities!

- *Minimising arbitrary rules and physical barriers*
  Rules can often be or become purely expressions of power and dominance that have little practical use. Children soon learn that in other households where they don't apply, the sky doesn't fall in. It is useful to check frequently whether rules in your household still have a purpose, or whether they are inhibiting children from doing things in their own perfectly valid way. Physical barriers, such as locked cupboard doors, can perpetuate a belief that one cannot be trusted. Avoid this by locking away only things that constitute a real identified safety hazard, and if the item under lock and key (such as a shotgun) isn't essential to the household, store it securely somewhere else.

- *Finding opportunities for acceptable physical contact*
  We all need gentle physical contact with other people. It helps us to know that we are cared about and lovable. The child care professions have become scared of it in their increased awareness of sexual abuse and paedophilia. We need not to shun physical contact, but to find and foster safe ways of providing it, and of accepting it from our foster children. Hair care provides excellent opportunities, as do hand and foot care and massage. Sitting back to back on the floor is mutually supportive and is a great way to talk without embarrassing or over-stimulating eye contact. High fives are a good way to celebrate a minor or major achievement unselfconsciously.

- *Supporting contact appropriate to the child's current needs with family members, past carers and old friends, whilst acknowledging and accepting the likely subsequent emotional turmoil*
  The need for children to maintain contact with their family of origin (unless it is dangerous in the present or re-traumatising) is better recognised than when we were active foster carers, but the skill required to support such contact in a manner supportive of

positive identity-building cannot be overestimated. Sensitive preparation and debriefing are vital, as is alert and knowledgeable supervision of the contact itself by people who are empowered and equipped to intervene in the best interests of the child. Contact needs to happen in a form and at a level which the child can currently sustain and in awareness of the child's changing and developing needs and wishes.

- *Recognising children's frequent need to identify themselves as part of a group*
  "We" is such a powerful word. Being able to use it allows the child to see themselves as part of a definable entity bigger than themselves. Being able to feel it anchors the child to humanity. As carers, we have to ensure that the child has opportunities to be part of a range of "we's" as well as to recognise when a "we" has become a constraint or a prison, and to offer the child an alternative and the reassurance that the uncomfortable "we" doesn't need to be identity-defining.

- *Using the strengths of the group – in modelling, supporting, caring, indicating acceptable behaviour*
  We had a large foster family. This presented certain practical challenges but brought many strengths, the greatest of which was being able to apply groupwork theory in helping children to embrace and develop positive identity features. It can be good to ensure that children who don't have such a peer group at home are part of an organisation – such as scouts or a sports team or a drama group – where similar group influences can apply.

- *Encouraging contact between children and a range of respectful adults who may be helpful role models or offer moral or spiritual insight*
  This can arise through encouraging children to form their own relationships with carers' friends, neighbours and colleagues, and other adults in the context of clubs or worship groups. It is important for children to have safe contact with adults of both

sexes, varied sexual orientations, and a range of religious and political beliefs and cultures, for the process of identification and differentiation to happen optimally. For children whose ethnicity is different from that of their carers, it is particularly helpful to facilitate relationships with a range of adults who share their ethnic heritage.

- *Helping children to identify a spiritual dimension to life without imposing religious conformity*
  I recognise that this may be seen as a contentious view, both by those who deny a spiritual dimension to life and by those who see their own religious faith group as having a monopoly on truth. I would maintain that a spiritual aspect to identity is important enough for children to be encouraged to seek it and to find their own way of experiencing and expressing it.

- *Retaining carer autonomy through assertive negotiation of clear roles and responsibilities with social workers*
  The Foster Carers' Charter has achieved a great deal in this respect. I am sure that children feel that their carers are more valued and trusted, and therefore that they themselves are more valued and trusted, when they have the autonomy to make more decisions within the care household about day-to-day matters without having to refer to an outside authority.

- *Trying never to say no when it is possible to say yes*
  We all feel deflated and diminished when we ask for permission that is flatly denied. It is so much more supportive to find a way to say 'Yes, provided that ...' or 'Yes, but not yet ...' or 'Yes, if I come with you'. All these responses legitimise the request, and thereby the person making it.

- *Encouraging debate and valuing and respecting a diversity of points of view*
  It adds to our sense of self-worth if we are invited to give our

opinion. It detracts from our sense of self-worth if that opinion is laughed at or rubbished – better to be invited to justify it and for points of common ground to be identified or to be politely disagreed with. The positive self-esteem of our looked after children is often fragile and easily shattered.

Family and social relationships

Developing tools for conviviality at home and beyond

Our adult foster children sometimes tell us of conversations with new friends and acquaintances who exclaim at some point of realisation, 'I would never have guessed that you grew up in care!' Since we can look back at the time when we first met them, and recognise that in many cases any reasonably astute observer might have picked them out very quickly as a child in care, these comments give us pleasure.

Traumatised children do not, on the whole, see the world and their fellow humans as friendly and benevolent. They may not see relationships as fixed or predictable. They may feel themselves to be unworthy and have little expectation that anyone will want to relate to them positively. Our aim over the course of childhood is to help them to overcome these barriers to relationship-building.

The foster home is the practice ground for relationship-building. Once the child feels safe there, foster carers can think carefully about how to help and encourage the child to build successful relationships further afield, including giving thought to the viability of improving relationships within the child's birth family and community.

In order to relate easily to other people, we must develop empathy and the ability to respond to them as they are. We must learn to be relaxed in their presence, and to relate across a context-appropriate range that spans both light-heartedness and seriousness. We need to expect that others are likely to respond positively to us, and that they will behave in ways that we are likely to be able to predict. The conviviality of which we are then capable enables us to negotiate, to be assertive without becoming aggressive, and to gain and maintain employment, as well as helping us to join and be accepted by any social grouping that attracts us.

Key factors

* *Recognising the significance of relationships with birth parents, but being realistic about their limitations and the risks that they may pose*
  It is important to keep very clearly in mind whether or not the child is subject to a care order, and whether the long-term plan is for permanence or for rehabilitation with birth parents. All contacts need to be carefully risk-assessed, with careful thought given to the venue, how the time will be spent, and by whom it will be supervised.

* *Actively looking for opportunities to facilitate helpful relationships with other birth family members*
  Many foster children will derive great benefit from maintaining or advancing relationships with other non-abusing relatives, including half-siblings and step-siblings, and it is worth asking for time and resources to enable these contacts to be made and developed.

* *Understanding when children feel an inappropriate level of responsibility for other birth family members and helping them to let go*
  Children in dysfunctional families may come into care bringing with them a heavy but inappropriate weight of responsibility for their siblings or parents, which distorts their ability to form relationships with their foster family and others. They will need help to give others permission to take on these responsibilities and to explore the freedom that this will bring.

* *Discouraging children from making "child in care" a central part of their identity*
  Traumatised children naturally seek out and identify other traumatised children to whom they can relate. Other children in care will often fit that model. But to become too set in the image of the "child in care" can perpetuate a lack of self-esteem and

ambition. We chose to discourage our foster children from attending many social events that were aimed at "children in care", preferring to find ways to broaden their range of friends and social contacts.

- *Giving children a wide range of models of successful relationships within a family context*
  Sometimes foster children can divide the world into "foster families" (weird, abnormal) and "normal families" (everybody else). So it is good to demonstrate examples of the whole spectrum of household groupings in your area: children who live with relatives other than parents; children of LGBT parents; mixed birth/adoptive families; mixed-heritage families; step-families; three- and four-generation households; families who live communally, and so on.

- *Encouraging children to relate to one another as siblings and to expect a lifelong mutually supportive relationship*
  Particularly where placements are expected to be long-term or permanent, it is worth remembering that although the child should be able to expect that their relationship with their carers will continue on into adulthood, those carers will eventually die, and the more lasting relationships are likely to be with the carers' birth children and with other foster children in the household. It does no harm to foster those relationships as quasi-sibling relationships and to make assumptions that they may also be deep, lifelong and multi-generational.

- *Planning shared and individual celebrations that become a recognisable pattern whilst retaining enough flexibility to meet individual needs, sensibilities and choices*
  It is often through repeated ritual celebrations that children learn and practise social expectations. There are advantages in arranging that the birthdays of every member of the fostering household are marked and celebrated in a similar "special" way, and for

household patterns to be created around the festivals featuring in the family's or child's culture, such as Christmas and Easter within Christian cultures. Hallowe'en, Pancake Day, anniversaries, end-of-term, and as many other regular "occasions" as you can think of can also be opportunities for family celebrations that may, with due caution, be extended to involve extended family and friends. Each of these should have a recognisable but adaptable structure and a relaxed feel.

- *Helping our own extended families to understand our foster children's place in our life and to include them naturally in wider family activities*
It is a responsibility of carers to make clear to their extended families that, in their household, it is the emotional needs of the foster children that are paramount. At the same time, an extended family which warmly accepts the foster child into it without fuss is a real boon. It is worth making clear at the outset that you will not tolerate any arbitrary distinction being made between foster children and others, but you will welcome your relatives taking a real interest in all the children in your household and finding positive ways of relating to each of them.

- *Reducing contact with any of our own extended family who find it hard to accept our foster children as family members*
Sometimes much-loved relatives find it difficult or impossible to accept foster children as "part of the family". They may speak to them in a different tone, ignore them altogether, exclude them from invitations, "forget" birthdays, or send presents that are obviously different from those sent to carers' birth children. It's important to raise the issue with them, to suggest changes in behaviour (maybe no presents for anybody in your household, or one big one to be shared) – and, at the end of the day, to recognise that withdrawal from that person, however painful that may feel, may be necessary while you are fostering.

- *Refusing to make unnecessary distinctions between birth children and looked after children, both in practice and in conversation with others*
  The important word is "unnecessary"! Fairness is not about treating everyone the same, but about treating individuals in equal accordance with their needs. It helps greatly to think carefully about language, and to avoid using any terms that appear to discriminate between household members who are foster children and other household members. This applies particularly in conversation with non-household-members, where you can talk about "my children" and refuse to make assumptions that questions about "your children" may be enquiries about your birth children alone.

- *Recognising and using the strength of the family group to add richness to shared experience, to provide mutual support and to address problems*
  The role of "children who foster" is increasingly recognised, and thoughtful carers will take care to ensure that the burden of being a "child who fosters" doesn't become overwhelming. Where there is more than one fostered child in the household, each of them also takes on aspects of the "child who fosters" role, and the strength and resilience of such a household is often substantial. Such a household provides real opportunity to develop empathy and social responsibility.

- *Being aware of potentially helpful relationships between individual children and facilitating their development*
  This can be of particular benefit at transition points such as the move from primary to secondary school, or from school to employment or further/higher education. Our own foster family provided several examples of very helpful "mentoring" relationships that developed between older and younger foster children, including after the older child had moved on to live independently.

- *Encouraging older children to take responsibility for younger children*
  Children whose own experience of being parented was damaging can learn a great deal from observing their foster carers with much younger children, and from being given appropriate opportunities to undertake some of the caring tasks themselves.

- *Trusting, as far as possible, the children's own choice of friends whilst helping them to recognise the social difficulties that some of their friends may experience*
  Foster children will often, like the rest of us, select friends whom they see as being like themselves. In practice, this can often mean children with similar histories – and similar difficulties with self-regulation and making and maintaining relationships. In a household where the language of attachment, trauma, resilience, stress and emotions is commonplace, discussion about friends' issues may be helpful and lead to spontaneous and helpful reflection about the friendship or how the friend can realistically be supported.

- *Welcoming children's friends into the house whilst expecting them to relate appropriately to all of the family*
  Pushing foster children's friendships underground is not advisable. However, there are many advantages in establishing the convention that friends are normally welcome in the foster home, alongside the expectation that friends, on arrival, will be introduced to, or, if already known, greet and converse briefly with the adults present, and ideally all other members of the household as well. This develops social skills and helps in keeping track of what's going on.

- *Developing our own friendships among people who could relate easily to the foster family*
  Thoughtful foster carers are always on the lookout for other people who can not only become members of their informal

support network, but who will also bring another helpful relation-ship to their foster children. This may be through sharing their leisure interests, experiences or skills, or may be indirectly because of who they are – their culture, their sexual orientation, their work – or simply because they are kind and likeable people who will accept and respect your children and be good role models.

- *Encouraging children to make a wide range of friendships and social contacts with people of all ages*
  Child protection concerns can sometimes lead carers to be over-restrictive on children's opportunities to make relationships with adults. Relationships made in structured settings – school, sports clubs, youth clubs, etc, are fine and can be very important, and we should ensure that these opportunities to relate to a range of adults, with or without carers/parents hovering in the background, are available to the child. But, appropriately monitored, friend-ships with trusted neighbours and acquaintances can also be encouraged, and help to develop skills that come to the fore when the young person is moving on from care into adult life.

- *Accepting the social vulnerability that can accompany being part of a foster family, and working at overcoming it in ways that meet the needs of everyone in the family*
  Becoming a foster carer helps you to see who your friends really are. Some will rapidly distance themselves, and some neighbours may make their disapproval and mistrust of your family very clear. How you deal with these unwelcome developments is important modelling for your children, particularly if you can patiently find ways to overcome the prejudice where you find it and maintain a positive view of society and your community as a whole.

- *Seeking opportunities to be involved in the local community, both individually and as a family*
  Being seen as "different" may lead to some degree of social

marginalisation or exclusion for foster carers and their families. So it helps to take a proactive stance in becoming involved in aspects of community life and increasing the proportion of members of the community who know you and your children and are prepared to be well-disposed and part of a benign network around the child. At the same time, it is wise to be careful not to take on so many responsibilities that your ability to be adaptable to the ever-changing needs of your foster children is compromised.

- *Avoiding placing children in unnecessarily stressful social situations*
  As an empathic carer, you will quickly become aware of what causes stress to your child at a level which they find difficult or impossible to regulate. You may feel that a given situation will be too much for your child to manage, and relieve the pressure by avoiding the situation entirely or restricting the time spent participating in it. In other situations, if you are present, it's best to maintain a discreet awareness of what is happening and be ready to intervene by giving the child additional support, enabling them to self-regulate, or by helping them to withdraw from the situation. For situations when you will not be present, it is good to rehearse with the child beforehand any likely triggers of stress and the contingency plan to aid self-regulation or to find support.

- *Explaining in advance expectations in unfamiliar social situations and being on hand to alleviate stress or help children to withdraw appropriately*
  Much stress in social situations can be reduced or eliminated if the child knows what to expect and is given advance permission to opt out or seek help if stress levels are rising. Any identified points of potential difficulty can be discussed frankly, along with planned ways to negotiate them. A helpful tool is for the person who can usually help the child to regulate stress to entrust to the child an object of personal significance to touch or hold while they put into practice rehearsed relaxation techniques.

- *Helping adolescents to seek and maintain suitable part-time work as well as involvement in school-based and community activities*
  Despite being set about with regulations, the "Saturday job", paper-round, or equivalent, if they can be found, is much enjoyed by many children, including foster children. The advantages are enormous, if there is an open and trusting relationship and good communication between the young person, the foster carer and the employer. They include an enhanced self-image – involving making a contribution, being given responsibility, earning money – and further opportunities to relate to adults on a more equal basis, whilst learning new skills and experiencing the discipline of the workplace.

Social presentation

Developing the confidence to claim social inclusion
Children who have experienced trauma often feel different from the rest of humanity, and excluded from or marginalised by society and the social groupings and situations that it comprises. They lack confidence that they will not experience repeated rejection, and the social skills to overcome their fear and expectation. In consequence, they may present themselves in social situations in ways that appear to invite rejection, and resist learning the social skills that might make a difference.

The resulting difficulties in making and developing social relationships, securing and maintaining jobs and tenancies, and feeling generally at ease and confident in social settings, are compounded in a society that values first impressions, superficial "good manners" and conformity to ever-changing norms of social behaviour.

Carers can help the young people they look after to gain sufficient confidence to feel that they have a right to participate in any social grouping they choose. They can also help them by teaching how others may, and probably will, draw conclusions from dress, body language and manners that they deem inappropriate, and how to weigh up a reasoned choice to stand out from the crowd on principle rather than unintentionally or as a way of inviting rejection. There are strong links here with the process of identification and differentiation already considered under the heading of "Identity".

At the same time, sensitive carers will do their best to remain non-judgemental themselves, and avoid "judging the book by its cover" in relation to people of all ages, cultures, etc.

Key factors

- *Aiming to have children included in as many broadly-based social and community groups as possible*
  Participation in interest groups – sporting, musical, theatrical, or any other group in which most participants are not other children in care – is hugely beneficial, not least because it is delegating some of the work on social presentation from the carers to the group members! For some children in care at particular points of their development, it may be helpful if the carers, or their birth children, are involved as well; for others, or at other times, confidence-building and identity-forming is enhanced if the young person can see the activity and the group as their own personal thing, with carers supporting by provision of transport, membership fees, kit, etc.

- *Modelling a relaxed, autonomous, non-consumerist attitude to matters of clothing and personal style*
  In making their own social presentation choices, carers can demonstrate their own ability to make judgements about whether and how they are accommodating with social expectations day by day – at work, in social settings, and in semi-official settings like school parents' evenings. It is good to talk about our own decision-making processes with our children, and to ask their opinions too. At the same time, it is good to show that you find nothing wrong with cheaper non-advertised brands and bargains from charity shops, and that when you are among people with whom you can relax, it is behaviour rather than appearance that really matters.

- *Respecting individual preferences and not judging by appearances*
  Carers sometimes rush into replacing "unsuitable" clothing that children bring to the placement, or over-reacting to experimentation with hairstyles, make-up, and so on. It is much better to invite children to reflect on how other people may react, and whether that is the reaction hoped for or expected.

- *Helping children to understand appropriateness in terms of the feelings of others and the social consequences of deciding to set aside social expectations*
  This relates particularly to behaviour in social situations and developing skills in greeting, making conversation, and recognising how other people can be helped to feel more comfortable and appreciated. It is good to present behaviour in these terms rather than as a set of arbitrary "rules", and to help children to notice the ways in which some other people are able to make them feel relaxed and valued. The other side of the coin is to draw their attention to behaviour in third parties that has the opposite effect, and to correct yourself in your children's presence on the inevitable occasions when you behave inappropriately in relation to others.

- *Recognising the effects of children's damaging experiences on their choices of clothing and perceived self-image*
  Children's choices may indicate a history of sexual abuse, either through being sexually provocative to gain acceptance, or by seeking to ward off unwelcome sexual attention. Children who have been physically abused may avoid eye contact or greeting in a bid to remain unnoticed, or be totally unable to respond to a question through fear of attracting punishment for the "wrong" answer. A show of defiance and aggression may simply arise out of having needed to appear "hard". Carers need to be alert to these scenarios, and patient both in enabling the child to gain self-understanding and in helping other adults in the meantime to see the child beyond the behaviour.

- *Getting to know local retailers as a family*
  This proved to be really helpful for us, living as we did in a small town. Building friendly relationships over years with shopkeepers and their long-serving staff helped our children to trust them and to engage with them increasingly confidently, and also helped the shopkeepers to be appropriate in their reactions to children who found making choices difficult or, on occasions, found the temptation to shoplift too great.

- *Supporting the school, with qualifications, on school uniform issues*
  School uniform can be a battleground for children in care, because it is imposed on children who may already feel that they have lost control over so many aspects of their lives. It may be wise to choose a school where the uniform policy allows for some individuality. At the same time, the existence of school uniform provides an aspect of life in which discussions about the pros and cons of conformity with social expectations will undoubtedly arise. There will be times when carers will need to advocate for the child against an over-zealous implementation of uniform rules. One particular example for us involved intervening assertively when the school sent a child home because her skirt was too long, unaware of how we had worked hard to persuade the child, who had suffered long-term sexual abuse, to wear a skirt at all rather than trousers.

- *Laundering and caring for children's clothing carefully and efficiently*
  This is one way of showing children indirectly that you really care about them. A pattern of household organisation where clothing goes through the laundry process promptly and is returned to the child neatly presented and smelling sweet, with any needed repairs tidily done, is a constantly-repeated gesture of love.

- *Encouraging frequent bathing/showering as a pleasurable and relaxing activity in a comforting environment*
  Carers can model socially acceptable behaviour here and chill out at the same time! Children will learn to appreciate a bathroom that looks and smells clean and fresh, where towels and flooring are warm and inviting, and where there is a good range of toiletries. The bathroom is also a good place to have a selection of undemanding things to read, perhaps a cheap portable radio, and soakable toys (even when children might be thought to have outgrown them!). Any way in which the link can be made between being clean and feeling good and relaxed is positive.

- *Learning how to give attention appropriately to each child*
  In large or busy households, it can be easy for one child to slip under the radar and avoid important social interaction. A careful carer will ensure that each child is conversed with individually at many points of every day, and certainly around each mealtime and on each occasion of entering or leaving the house. Finding some way of making appropriate and acceptable physical contact is important too. Our family pattern of joining hands around the table at the start of each meal contributed to this, particularly since we discouraged any member of the household from always sitting in the same seat at the table.

- *Enabling each child to make safe and rewarding relationships with adults who enjoy their company*
  Too many children and young people are uncomfortable and ill at ease in the company of older people simply through lack of experience. It is important to encourage them to relate to a range of adults. This can be done by introducing your foster child to every adult who comes to visit you and expecting them to be involved in greetings and farewells. Normalise handshakes, and encourage young people to participate in "adult" conversations without monopolising them. It's worthwhile to notice adult friends and acquaintances who find it difficult to talk to your

foster child without sounding patronising, and give them some tips!

- *Learning how to listen and respond to each child respectfully and without condescension*
  As we learned more about trauma, we became more aware of the importance of responding to what the child is feeling in the first instance, rather than what they are saying (or screaming!). That's not to say that the content is unimportant, and when conversation is possible it is always best to respond to what is being said in a measured and calm way, as you would to a colleague or a customer in the course of your working life. Our own upbringing and experience of education, apprenticeship, etc, may have taught us that derision, dismissal and aggression are appropriate ways of reacting to younger people and their ideas – they are not! Pro-social responses can be modelled, practised and learned.

Emotional and behavioural development

Developing the ability to understand and manage feelings and impulses

Behaviour lets us know that brains are working. Brains affected by stress that we cannot regulate are working in survival mode – fight, flight or freeze. Brains affected by trauma that we cannot resolve push us towards hyperarousal or dissociation.

If we are to help our foster child to change unwanted or mal-adaptive behaviour, we must learn to understand the effects of trauma and to recognise what the child is feeling and when they are under stress that they cannot regulate. We need first of all to help them to feel safe – only then can they begin to use their thinking brain and to think before they act on impulse. We need to help them to identify their feelings and articulate them, and to begin to understand how trauma works. Only then can we hope to help them to learn ways of self-regulating in the presence of stress and being able to develop responses to stressful situations that are both pro-social and effective.

Key factors

- *Never underestimating the long-term effects of early damaging experiences*

  As a foster carer, it is probably worth banishing the term "bad behaviour" from your vocabulary. The behaviour of foster children may often be antisocial, alarming, violent, dangerous, and a host of other similar adjectives, but rather than falling into a value-judgement about the child or the behaviour, it is usually more helpful to ask yourself what the child is feeling at the time and how those feelings may arise out of traumatising experiences that they have had, perhaps repeatedly. The child's behaviour is a stream of messaging about their emotions and their past.

- *Accepting that facilitating emotional and behavioural development cannot be left entirely to other professionals*

  Providing a safe space for the child is fundamental to the task of fostering. A calm and predictable trauma-aware environment in the foster home, with clear routines and boundaries safely held, will underpin all the other therapeutic work that carers and the other members of the professional team around the child will undertake. The most important members of this team are the carers, since they are a constant daily presence and are becoming a crucial attachment figure for the child.

- *Understanding that a punitive approach to inappropriate behaviour will be unlikely to succeed and be counter-productive*

  Punishment is unlikely to help the child to understand the different emotions they experience, why they occur, and how to handle them. It is, however, likely to consolidate a sense of personal rejection and low self-esteem, and to add to the belief that the world is harsh and arbitrary. Reparation is, however, often helpful, if it follows a reasonable conversation with the child about how the child's actions have damaged someone else, and a genuine discussion about how some of that damage can be undone.

- *Minimising use of arcane systems of rewards and privileges, whilst stressing and identifying the social benefits of pro-social behaviour*
  Reward systems rapidly become disconnected from the behaviour to which they are supposed to relate, become a nightmare to administer, and get in the way of genuine loving relationships! The greatest reward for pro-social behaviour is being able to live in an ever-more trusting and relaxed relationship with other people, and it is always worth demonstrating this.

- *Ensuring that consequences of inappropriate behaviour are logical, proportionate, and capable of being understood by children*
  Sanctions (consequences) may be effective, provided that the child can see that they follow logically from the effects of the problematic behaviour on relationships or welfare. It's also important that the child is clear about what they have to do in order for the sanction to be lifted, is genuinely capable of doing it, and knows to whom to turn for help.

- *Recognising that children with chaotic previous experience will need help with understanding cause and effect*
  Many children in care will have come from dysfunctional households where events seem unrelated and arbitrary. Their brains will have had little opportunity to build the patterns that come from experiencing the same chain of events repeatedly with a positive outcome.

- *Recognising that children with attachment disorders will have difficulty in acquiring an understanding of emotion, and a language in which to express it*
  In order to understand their behaviour, children need to gain an understanding of the feelings that underlie and prompt it, and to acquire a vocabulary with which these emotions can be expressed and examined. Carers can help in lots of ways: talking about their own feelings, those of other people and of fictional characters, talking about emoticons, and, most importantly,

engaging the child in expressing their feelings and finding the words to do so.

- *Finding ways through shared stories to undertake this emotional education*
  Telling and reading stories isn't just about helping the child to learn to read or calming them down at bedtime. Stories can be found or made up to illustrate the feelings arising out of any situation, and explored with the child in a way that doesn't feel so emotionally threatening as addressing their own feelings directly.

- *Taking care to model for children the behaviour and values that we expect from them*
  If we are expecting our children to learn to behave in a pro-social way, we must ensure that we behave well towards them and towards others. They will be the first to notice hypocrisy. When our own behaviour, as it perhaps frequently will, falls short of the standards we would want to set, a genuine attempt at apology, reparation, and analysis of how we expect to deal better with similar situations in the future, models what we expect of our children.

- *Learning to recognise when children experience stress and how to help them to reduce it*
  We may have learned how to regulate stress through early attunement with our mothers or other attachment figures. Foster children may need to learn stress regulation from their carers. It is good to develop mindfulness of your foster child – awareness of what will cause them stress, or awareness of the signs in them that stress is building. Then you can develop with them approaches to regulating that stress, both when you are present – a particular smile or gesture, moving closer, a "secret" word or phrase that helps them to attune to you – and when you are not – a tangible reminder of you that they can squeeze in their pocket, breathing or postural techniques that you have practised together, phrases

that they can "hear" you saying. You might also rehearse with them what they can do if things get difficult – who they can phone, where or to whom they can go, what they can say or do.

- *Ensuring that our physical environment is designed to reduce stress*
  When a child has "lost it" in some way, our own level of stress may lead us to plunge straight into "dealing with" the child there and then. But it is usually much more effective to be responsive to the child's feelings and make or identify a space where they (and you) will quickly feel safe and be able to relax. So make a judgement, within the practicalities of the situation, about what that environment might be. It may be indoors or outdoors; it may involve reduction of eye contact (maybe walking together outdoors or sitting at right angles); increasing physical comfort or security (a cushion to hug); an adjustment of light (drawing or closing curtains); moving away from distracting or enervating noise; providing a drink or a bite to eat; including a third party in whose presence the child feels safer, etc. It is also good to make a low-stress environment available for the child at home and to encourage them to recognise when stress is building up in themselves and seek out the low-stress safe place. We probably all need somewhere like that.

- *Accepting that our children may not understand their own behaviour or its effect on others, and trying to explain it to them in a non-blaming way*
  The child who is dissociative, or who has responded impulsively to their feelings, may well be unable to answer the question 'Why did you do that?' Pressing for an answer will be counter-productive; it is better to speculate openly: 'I wonder if you did that because you felt . . .' This turns the whole discussion into a shared attempt to solve an interesting puzzle, and lowers the tension. Once the child is engaged, it's time to look at the effects of the behaviour (which may need a similar approach to move

beyond perplexity, such as: 'Do you think Shannon's leg might be hurting where you kicked it?'), examining why it's not acceptable, and considering together whether and how the damage can be put right, and how similar damage might be avoided in the future.

- *Keeping attention focused on long-term outcomes rather than being distracted by temporary apparent setbacks*
  The cycle of recovery from trauma – stabilisation, integration, adaptation – is not a smooth journey. We are persistently knocked back by new events, and need to restabilise, reintegrate, and adapt once more. The adult human brain is rarely fully formed much before the age of 25, and the previous decade-and-a-half of adolescence is a time of much reshaping and reordering, particularly for young people whose early lives have left them with a great deal to reprocess. This isn't helped by our society's insistence that we should reach certain developmental landmarks at a specific chronological age. It is best not to get too fixated on those age-related landmarks, and rather to think about how we can enable our children to be the best person they can be by the time they are 30.

- *Facilitating through open discussion the development of individual moral codes*
  It is facile to be prescriptive about moral codes. The moral code of each one of us is subtly individual. It defines how we choose our employment and our pastimes, whether and how we vote, how we use our resources, how we behave towards people we know and people we don't know. Once our children have developed some understanding of their feelings, and have started on the process of conscious identification and differentiation, which is building their identity, it is good to be able to discuss issues of morality with some objectivity, whilst also considering the implications of expressed moral positions on relationships and social cohesion, rather than imposing your own position.

- *Valuing appropriateness above consistency in response*
  Carers need to be consistent only in trying to do their best for each of their children. There is nothing to be gained by attempting to apply the same "rules of engagement" to each child, or even to the same child over a period of time. If a chosen sanction isn't effective in helping child A to behave differently, but has been just right for child B, then do something different with child A. The fact that you were happy for child A to stay up until 11 o'clock at the weekends at the age of 12 is not a reason for you to apply this two years later to child B, whose needs may be totally different. Paradoxical approaches can work. One of our children had great difficulty in sharing anything with others: we gave him a huge jar of sweets on the condition that he ate every one of them himself – and he immediately began to offer them around. Another child would have sat in the corner gobbling the sweets until he was sick. A different child couldn't describe how he felt before lashing out at other children: we asked him to imagine the feeling and tell us what colour it was – and to our surprise he was not only able to tell us that it was brown, but also to turn it to pink and neutralise it. Another child would have dismissed us as certifiably mad.

- *Relishing the puzzle of learning how other people tick*
  The clergyman who officiated at the wedding of one of our sons described marriage as a lifelong puzzle in understanding how another person ticks, and recommended it, therefore, to people who enjoy puzzles. Fostering is a succession of similar puzzles. Each child is marching to a different beat – or to many different beats, simultaneously. If we don't enjoy the puzzle of learning the tunes, we need to find something else to do!

Self-care skills

Developing practical skills for 21st century living

Perhaps unsurprisingly, we found that most of the children who grew up with us needed relatively little specific help in gaining "independence skills" in the year before moving on. Our household was a large one, and needed many hands to make light work of what needed to be done if it were to function at all!

If young people have made real progress in the preceding six dimensions of development, the foundations for embarking on adult life will be in place, and if carers make it clear that they will continue to be available for help and advice as new issues arise, they can be reasonably sure that the help and advice will be sought. You might like to reflect on how many domestic skills you had already mastered at the point where you left school – possibly very few! But you are likely to have had a reasonable idea of what you would need to become competent at, and enough confidence to know that you would, with a little effort, be able to pick it up.

Nevertheless, there are specific approaches that can helpfully be adopted through childhood and adolescence that will not only make the practical aspects of the transition to independence easier, but may also help to keep the foster home a place of relative order and calm for more of the time.

There are important riders, however, which may make it impossible for young people to achieve a safe independence at the point where local authority support stops, or indeed ever.

The first of these is that we must now assume that a sizeable and growing percentage of children who come into care will have some level of Foetal Alcohol Spectrum Disorder (FASD) that has caused irreparable brain damage before birth. This remains persistently under-diagnosed, or misdiagnosed as various other conditions and syndromes, particularly as ADHD. It may affect the executive function of the brain, which typically develops from around the age of eight onwards, and enables us to make judgements and decisions on the basis of information received from a variety of resources and then processed. Moreover, people with FASD may be very literate, but struggle to understand what they read – or hear – at anything more than a very basic level, and also struggle to master numeric concepts such as time and money. Deficiencies in these respects may make it impossible for an adult ever to build an adequate range of self-care skills or to live totally independently without the assistance of an "auxiliary brain". We would urge all carers to learn about FASD and to be alert for indications in their child's behaviour and early history that FASD could be a factor.

Another rider is the inescapable fact that social, political and economic circumstances and structures in the UK in the second decade of the 21st century make it much more difficult for young adults to access permanent employment that will provide an income adequate to secure stable housing and social inclusion than has been the case for several decades. Most will need a considerable level of parental support and subsidy over many years – many more than local authorities will or can provide. Long-term carers need to be aware of this, and if they are committed to their children's long-term futures, they will need to be advocating fiercely on their behalf, and/or willing to continue to provide the needed support and subsidy well into adulthood that the state is not providing.

Key factors

- *Recognising the importance of motivation and role models*
  Pragmatism helps. Young people will not be motivated to take on new learning and responsibilities when they are wrestling with really difficult personal issues, nor should we normally expect them to. But they will often respond willingly to necessity – to taking more on when one of the adult carers is ill, or when another child in the household is in obvious need of concerted attention. Older peers or siblings can be helpful role models. Many young people will only be motivated to learn a new skill or take on a new role when they can see a genuine personal advantage (but preferably not a financial bribe – too many aspects of our lives have been distorted into commercial transactions).

- *Sharing household tasks – but not rigidly or oppressively*
  It can be an important part of the ethos of any foster home that domestic tasks are shared unless health and safety considerations preclude it. Domestic independence is best preceded by domestic interdependence. Visible sharing among the adult members is crucial, and although this doesn't preclude one adult taking on the bulk of the responsibility for some tasks for which they have a particular skill or aptitude, it is right and proper that no task is exclusively devolved onto one person, or becomes gender-specific. Although we involved our children quite a lot in domestic tasks, we decided against "rotas" or anything that detracted from an assumption that we would all want to take our part and contribute what we could. And we recognised that there would be particular days or periods of time when a particular child might simply not be in the right emotional space for this sharing and needed to be allowed to return temporarily to a state of "dependence" appropriate to a much younger child.

- *Banishing the labelling of household tasks and responsibilities as "chores"*
  The story of Tom Sawyer and his fence-painting comes to mind. If we make something seem like fun, or at least satisfying, others will want to join in. If we present domestic tasks as wearisome and gratefully avoided, it won't surprise us if they are not appealing to others.

- *Involving children in carrying out any household task in which they show an interest, and making it fun*
  Grasp the moment when the child or young person wants to have a go with the vacuum cleaner, to help with baking, to load the washing machine or the dishwasher, to mow the lawn, or to assemble the flatpack, even if it means that the job will take longer, be less well done, need supervision, or have to be redone later. If there are health and safety considerations, be creative in finding ways in which the work can be done safely, rather than turning the young person away.

- *Striking a balance between domestic chaos and fastidious order, and prioritising accordingly*
  It is our view that children benefit from seeing that household items each have their place. This adds to their sense of order and security. At the same time, enjoyment of the moment is more important than constant obsessive tidying up. Cluttered, messy space is not conducive to soothing, whereas austere, clinically tidy spaces are likely to lack stimulation and inhibit creativity. Sharing space involves thinking of the other person and their comfort and convenience, and for that reason it seems reasonable to me that carers should pay more attention to maintaining the best balance in shared areas of the house than to insisting on particular standards in children's own bedrooms – their private space. However, a counter-argument is that bedrooms need to be soothing spaces, and few households have sufficient space to offer a foster child both a soothing bedroom and a personal creative space that is constantly buzzing with energy and activity.

- *Accepting that most independence skills will be acquired only when the need arises, so being available then to advise and teach*
  Of course, this doesn't preclude engineering the need! But a helpful approach can be to ask the question, 'What are you going to do about xxxx when you have moved away? Would you like me to show you?' Offering a gift rather than imposing a requirement seems like good psychology.

- *Remaining available to young people after they have left home to live independently*
  Of course, this is something that many carers want to do and are increasingly encouraged to do, along with recognising that "leaving home" and likewise, "leaving foster care" is often in the young person's experience not a specific moment in time but a gradual change over time. However, we learn best how to address a problem when the problem is a real one, so the best learning opportunities are in confronting issues as they arise, either when still in the foster home or after moving on, alongside the carers.

- *Being clear and consistent in allocating and defining time, and keeping to deadlines*
  Time management is a skill that can be difficult for newly-independent care leavers, especially if their early lives were marked by chaotic parental lifestyles. So carers do well to prioritise doing what they have said they will do at the time they said they would do it. Apart from providing security to the foster child, this models good planning. It also helps to avoid loose phrases such as 'I'll do it in a minute' when what is really meant is 'within the next couple of hours'. It helps to work with children and young people in estimating the time it will take you to do things, as a game, and checking afterwards to see if you were right or wildly wrong.

- *Using a family diary together*
  This is another aspect of time planning that can involve the whole household rather than being imposed on the foster child. The child can be aware of the adults' personal or work deadlines: "report to be completed"; "MoT for the car to be done"; "boiler service to be arranged"; "insurance to be renewed".

- *Giving particular thought to how children learn to manage money, and allowing for learning from mistakes*
  We gave pocket money only when we had evidence that children could count it, have a reasonably accurate idea of what things cost relative to each other, and could estimate what change to expect. We encouraged them to open bank accounts and to research where they would get most interest on their savings, and entrusted them with their own clothing allowance as soon as we felt they could manage it, whilst recognising that we would take it over again if unwise decisions were made. Similarly, we encouraged financial planning by moving towards receiving their pocket money by monthly cheque, which encouraged actually visiting the bank and getting to know the staff.

- *Involving children and young people in household decision-making and budgeting*
  Throughout our time as foster carers, we kept detailed family accounts of income and expenditure that were always available to be shared in response to questions or expressed interest. We involved them in financial decision-making: 'If we spend £x on that, we won't be able to afford £y for this.'

- *Find opportunities for children and young people to use public transport and find new places independently*
  In a world where children and young people are increasingly transported everywhere by car, especially in smaller towns and rural areas where public transport is minimal, it can be hard for them to develop the skills for finding their own way around. Opportunities have to be made and risk assessments carried out, but the benefits in learning and in acquiring confidence can be considerable.

- *Helping children to use the internet as a research tool for daily living, and fill in forms together online and on paper*
  This has perhaps become the most important of all pieces of self-care learning. As soon as children can read, we can encourage them to use the internet to find out about any query they have, from how to boil an egg to how to deal with athlete's foot. We can ensure that they are aware of where the internet can be accessed cheaply or free of charge. We can accustom them to completing forms and information requests by working together on booking holidays and concert tickets online, or completing an application form for a postal vote.

- *Finding opportunities to teach young people about how public services are run and accessed*
  Another important aspect of helping young people to navigate the adult world is involving them in your own contacts with service providers and taking opportunities to explain simply how, where,

and by whom local public services are administered. Simply pointing out the local council offices to a primary-school-age child as you drive past and telling them something of what goes on there can be the foundation of that tranche of later learning. National and local elections give scope for discussions of public service policies, as do questions like 'Who pays my social worker?'!

- *Ensuring that young people have the opportunity to learn to drive* This is an expensive skill to acquire, but so worthwhile in terms of independence, adult responsibility and employment skills, that it merits being planned for, both financially and in preparing the ground via cycling and cycling proficiency training, driving practice off the public road, and involvement in basic maintenance of the family car, years in advance.

- *Enabling young people to be responsible for their own physical, mental and emotional health* ... which brings us neatly back to where we started, with health. Young people in care who are approaching independence need to have overcome the physical legacy of previous trauma sufficiently to be able to understand their own bodies, to know how to stay healthy, to recognise symptoms of illness or destabilisation in themselves, and to know where and how to seek help. This knowledge should include an understanding of attachment and trauma, and how they have been personally affected by their own attachment and trauma experience. And alongside that, an awareness of how they have achieved a measure of resilience, and of how they can maintain and build further on that, will be the most important self-care skill they can acquire, the one which matters most to every child.

In conclusion

Learning from the questions posed by those who have not learned not to ask will lead us to a perpetual journey of shared development.

The answers children discover also need to be treated with appropriate respect. A child struggling with traumatic deaths confides that he has found something out. 'Look', he says, 'see these conkers?' I agree that I can see them. 'They look all dead, but I found out that if I plant them a tree could grow. Did you know that something that dead could make a tree?' It seems astonishing, I agree. 'Trees are alive, aren't they?' Again, I affirm that trees are living plants, and very beautiful. 'Do you think I should plant these conkers?' I hesitate. 'Not every conker grows into a tree, you know.' A scornful look moves the metaphor forward: 'Of course not! But every one should be given a chance, don't you think?' The discourse is now very profound. My assent is all that is needed to complete the healing metaphor. 'Everyone should be given a chance,' I say.

We hope that our discoveries and our mistakes can help others to ensure that every one is given a chance.

References

Adams D. (1988) *The Restaurant at the End of the Universe*, London: Pan Books

APA (1994) *Diagnostic and Statistical Manual of Mental Disorders*, New York: American Psychiatric Association

Apter S. (1986) *Troubled Children, Troubled Systems*, New York: Pergamon Press

Archer C. (1999) *Parenting the Child Who Hurts: First steps – tiddlers and toddlers, Parenting the Child Who Hurts: Next steps – tykes and teens*, London: Jessica Kingsley Publishers

Bateson G. (2000) *Steps to an Ecology of Mind*, Chicago: University of Chicago Press

Beaver D. (1997) *Easy Being: Making life as simple and as much fun as possible*, London: Useful Book Company

Bettelheim B. (1974) *A Home for the Heart*, New York: Thames and Hudson

Bowlby J. (1991) *Attachment, Separation and Loss* (three volumes), London: Penguin

Braithwaite J. (1989) *Crime, Shame and Reintegration*, Cambridge: Cambridge University Press

Bronfenbrenner U. (1979) *The Ecology of Human Development: Experiments by nature and design*, New York: Harvard University Press

Brown D., Scheflin A. and Hammond D. (1998) *Memory, Trauma Treatment and the Law*, New York: Norton

Cairns K. (2010) *Circles of Harm: Surviving paedophilia and network abuse*, London: Lonely Scribe

Cameron S. and Magill C. (2009) *Achieving Positive Outcomes for Children in Care*, New York: Sage

Capra F. (1982) *The Turning Point*, London: Simon & Schuster

Carter R. (1998) *Mapping the Mind*, London: Weidenfeld & Nicolson

Cliff M. (1980) *Claiming an Identity They Taught Me to Despise*, London: Persephone Press

Coles R. (1986) *The Moral Life of Children*, Boston: Houghton Mifflin

Coles R. (1990) *The Spiritual Life of Children*, Boston: Houghton Mifflin

Cozolino L. (2014) *The Neuroscience of Human Relationships: Attachment and the developing social brain*, New York: Norton

Csikszentmihalyi M. (1993) *The Evolving Self: A psychology for the third millennium*, London: HarperCollins

Damasio A. (1999) *The Feeling of What Happens: Body, emotion and the making of consciousness*, London: William Heinemann

De Zulueta F. (1993) *From Pain to Violence: The traumatic origins of destructiveness*, London: Whurr

Demos V. (ed) (1995) *Exploring Affect: The selected writings of Silvan S. Tomkins*, Cambridge: Cambridge University Press

Erikson H. (1963) *Childhood and Society*, New York: Norton

Fahlberg V. (2008) *A Child's Journey Through Placement*, London: BAAF

Figley C. (2002) *Treating Compassion Fatigue*, London: Routledge

Gilligan C. (1998) *In a Different Voice: Psychological theory and women's development*, New York: Harvard University Press

Gilligan R. (2009) *Promoting Resilience: A resource guide on working with children in the care system*, (2nd edn), London: BAAF

Harris T. (1970) *I'm OK – You're OK*, London: Pan Books

Harris-Hendriks J., Black D. and Kaplan T. (2000) *When Father Kills Mother: Guiding children through trauma and grief*, London: Routledge

Howe D. (2011) *Attachment Across the Lifecourse: A brief introduction*, New York: Palgrave Macmillan

Hughes D. (1997) *Facilitating Developmental Attachment: The road to emotional recovery and behavioural change in foster and adoptive children*, New York: Jason Aronson

Hughes D. (1998) *Building the Bonds of Attachment: Awakening love in deeply troubled children*, New York: Jason Aronson

Jackson S. (ed) (2013) *Pathways through Education for Young People in Care: Ideas from research and practice*, London: BAAF

Janoff-Bulman, R (1992) *Shattered Assumptions: Towards a new psychology of trauma*, London: The Free Press

Joseph S. (2013) *What Doesn't Kill Us: A guide to overcoming adversity and moving forward*, London: Piatkus

Karr-Morse R. and Wiley M. (12013) *Ghosts from the Nursery: Tracing the roots of violence*, New York: Atlantic Monthly Press

Kaufman G. (1992) *Shame: The power of caring*, Rochester, VT: Schenkman Books

Koestler A. (1964) *The Act of Creation*, London: Hutchinson

Maslow A. (1968) *Towards a Psychology of Being*, New York: Van Nostrand

Maslow A. (1970) *Motivation and Personality*, New York: Harper and Row

Mather M. and Batty D. (2001) *Doctors for Children in Public Care: A resource guide advocating, protecting and promoting health*, London: BAAF

McNamara J. (1995) *Bruised Before Birth: Parenting children exposed to parental substance abuse*, London: BAAF

Miller A. (1990) *Thou Shalt Not Be Aware: Society's betrayal of the child*, London: Pluto Press

Miranda L., Arthur A., Milan T., Mahoney O. and Perry B. (1998) 'The art of healing: the healing arts project, early childhood connections', *Journal of Music and Movement-based Learning*, 4:4, pp. 35–40

O'Donohue J. (1998) *Eternal Echoes: Exploring our hunger to belong*, London: Bantam Press

Oaklander V. (1989) *Windows to our Children*, London: Real People Press

Perry B. (1999) *Effects of Traumatic Events on Children: Interdisciplinary education series*, Volume 2, Number 3, New York: Child Trauma Academy

Perry B. (2000) *Brain Structure and Function, I and II: Interdisciplinary education series*, Volume 2, Number 2, New York: Child Trauma Academy

Richardson J. and Joughin C. (2000) *The Mental Health Needs of Looked After Children*, London: Gaskell

Roberts M. (2000) *Join-up: Horse sense for people*, London: HarperCollins

Ross M. (1988) *The Fire of Your Life: A solitude shared*, London: The Lamp Press

Ryan T. and Walker R. (2007) *Life Story Work* (3rd edn), London: BAAF

Salmon P. (1985) *Living in Time*, London: Dent

Schofield G. (2001) 'Resilience and family placement: a lifetime perspective', *Adoption and Fostering*, 25:3, pp. 6–19

Schore A. (2003) *Affect Dysregulation and Disorders of the Self*, New York: Norton

Shemmings D. (2014) *Assessing Disorganised Attachment Behaviour in Children: An evidence-based model for understanding and supporting families*, London: Jessica Kingsley Press

Shotter J. (1984) *Social Accountability and Selfhood*, London: Basil Blackwell

Siegel D. (2012) *The Developing Mind: How relationships and the brain interact to shape who we are*, New York: Guilford Press

Steiner G. (1961) *The Death of Tragedy*, London: Faber and Faber

Strong M. (2000) *A Bright Red Scream: Self-mutilation and the language of pain*, London: Virago Press

Suttie I. (1988) *The Origins of Love and Hate*, London: Free Association Books

Tavris C. (1989) *Anger: The misunderstood emotion*, London: Touchstone

Tedeschi R. and Calhoun G. (1995) *Trauma and Transformation: Growing in the aftermath of suffering*, New York: Sage

Teicher M. (14 December 2000), available at: www.researchmatters.harvard.edu

Tustin F. (1981) *Autistic States in Children*, London: Routledge

van der Kolk B., McFarlane A. and Weisaeth L. (eds) (1996) *Traumatic Stress: The effects of overwhelming experience on mind, body and society*, New York: Guilford Press

Wilber K. (1991) *Grace and Grit: Spirituality and healing in the life and death of Treya Killam Wilber*, Boston: Shambhala Publications

Wilber K. (2000) *Integral Psychology: Consciousness, spirit, psychology, therapy*, Boston: Shambhala Publications

Wilber K. (2001) *A Theory of Everything*, Boston: Shambhala Publications

Wolin S. J. and Wolin S. (1993) *The Resilient Self: How survivors of troubled families rise above adversity*, London: Villard Press

Glossary

Adaptive Tending to increase chances of survival in changing circumstances.

Affect Innate responses to stimulus, producing changes in the face and then the rest of the body. Tomkins identified nine affects and believed these to be the primary motivators of human behaviour. The nine are: interest, enjoyment, surprise, distress, fear, anger, shame, dissmell and disgust.

Affectional bonds Links between individuals that involve strong affect that serve to deepen relationships and ensure they persist over time.

Amygdala An almond shaped structure in the forebrain that is part of the limbic system. It has a major part to play in emotional responses, response to threat, impulses, and emotional memory.

Anhedonia The loss of the capacity to experience joy.

Attachment An innate behavioural and emotional system designed to maintain physical and emotional proximity between a developmentally immature infant and his or her caretakers. From the point of view of an observer, it is marked by proximity seeking. From the infant's subjective viewpoint, it is marked by emotional security. Attachment can be expressed through an intimate persisting affectional relationship between two individuals. That between the dependent infant and their attachment figure has a primary status and a biological function in development.

Attachment behaviour Behaviour activated whenever a baby, young child or adult needs the close physical and emotional proximity of a safe adult.

Attunement The process through which the infant's carer, by mirroring and then leading change in the vitality and affect of the infant, enables the young child to develop regulation of stress, affect and impulse.

Brainstem The most basic structure of the brain, controlling basic life functions such as blood pressure, heart rate and body temperature. Centrally involved in physiological state regulation.

Cortex The cerebral cortex mediates all conscious activity, including planning, language, speech, problem solving. It is also involved in the creation of narrative memory and perception and recognition of environmental stimuli.

Dissociation   A defence against overwhelming stress where the individual cuts themselves off from conscious awareness of their senses, that makes use of the human capacity to split awareness.

EMDR   Eye movement desensitisation and reprocessing is a therapeutic technique that involves using certain patterns of rapid eye movements while holding an image of the trauma and the feelings associated with that image. It seems to work, although explanations for the success remain at the level of hypothesis.

Empathy   The capacity to imaginatively enter into the experiences of another human being.

Hippocampus   A structure of the subcortex shaped like a seahorse. It is part of the limbic system and is importantly involved in emotional regulation, linking words to feelings, learning and memory.

Hyperarousal   A disorder involving persistent deregulated stress.

Hypervigilant   Unable to relax, constantly scanning the environment for threat.

Imaginal flooding   A therapeutic technique that enables the person to revisit the trauma safely in imagination and to discover that they can survive.

Implosion therapy   A version of imaginal flooding in which the person is encouraged to experience that they can survive a level of traumatic re-experiencing they believe will be disintegrative.

Insecure attachment   A pattern of attachment where the infant's need for physical proximity and emotional security is based on insufficient experience of a responsive and attuned caretaker. As a result the infant develops a generalised, internal expectation of an unresponsive and dissonant set of relationships that damages the capacity to appropriately deal with loss and frustration. Insecure attachment is a pattern in which the child's needs for affective attunement, stimulation, stress regulation and impulse regulation are not adequately met by the attachment figure. This results in persistent anxiety for the child.

Limbic system   A group of linked structures in the brain centrally involved in emotion, memory and the processing of complex social and emotional information.

Meta-cognition   Cognition is knowledge, or thinking that involves what we know. Meta-cognition is the structure of knowledge, or thinking that involves pattern-matching. Cognition and meta-cognition are activities of the cerebral cortex.

Midbrain   Those structures in the brain that follow the development of the brainstem and control motor activity, appetite and sleep patterns.

Neuron   A brain cell that receives and transmits information. Neurons form complex networks that are shaped by environmental experience.

Neurophysiology   The science of brain and body.

Non-directive hypnosis   A therapeutic technique following the work of Milton Erickson in particular. The therapist enables the person to enter a deeply relaxed state, and then works through the person's own metaphors for their experience to create alternative possible responses to stimuli, including traumatic stimuli.

Parasympathetic   The sympathetic branch of the nervous system operates when bodily activity increases and energy is being expended; the parasympathetic branch of the nervous system operates when bodily activity is decreasing and energy is being restored. Self-assertive emotions tend to produce sympathetic nervous system activity, self-transcending emotions are more likely to produce a parasympathetic response.

Reintegrative shame   The process through which the carer, by breaking and then re-establishing attunement, enables the young child to develop regulation of the shame affect and of impulse.

Secure attachment   A pattern of attachment where the infant's need for physical proximity and emotional security is based on sufficient experience of a responsive and attuned caretaker. As a result the infant develops a generalised, internal expectation of a responsive and attuned set of relationships that encompasses the capacity to appropriately deal with loss and frustration. Secure attachment is a pattern in which the attachment figure adequately meets the child's needs for affective attunement, stimulation, stress regulation, and impulse regulation.

Self-assertive emotions   Emotional experiences that reinforce the isolation of the individual, such as fear, rage, or distress. The energy accumulated tends to resolve explosively.

Self-transcending emotions   Emotional experiences that reinforce the participation of the individual in a social and ecological network. Compassion, awe and joy are examples. The energy tends to build and then ebb away.

Shame-bind   A pre-verbal pattern induced in the child when the consistent response of the attachment figure to a particular behaviour is contempt (combining the affects of disgust and dissmell). The infant experiences shame linked to the affect, drive or need that motivated the behaviour.

Systematic desensitisation   A therapeutic technique in which people are repeatedly exposed to traumatic imagery while in a state of relaxation.

Temperament   Innate behavioural style, contributing to the development of personality. Temperament characteristics are influenced, but not caused, by caregiving. Three categories describe most, but not all, children: easy, slow to warm up, and difficult.

Time line therapy   A therapeutic technique that may enable people to make different emotional connections to their own history.

Traumatic amnesia   Loss of memory for all or part of the traumatic event.

Traumatic hypermnesia   Inability to forget all or part of the traumatic event, even when engaged with other experience.

Use-dependent   The specific changes in neurons and neural networks that follow activation. These changes, and the neural networks themselves, are altered by repetitive patterned stimulation.

Visual/kinaesthetic dissociation   A therapeutic technique that enables people to make use of their capacity to dissociate images from feelings, which can be useful in reducing hyperarousal when people are being triggered by their own internal images of the trauma.

Vocalise   To communicate with purposeful sounds that are not language.

Index